# Reading

## WORKTEXT

**For use with Second Edition**

MW00767936

## *If Skies Be Blue When the Sun Rides High*

Tell me a story,
If thunder crack,
If rain be falling,
If skies be black.

Tell me a story,
If clouds be few,
If sun be beaming,
If skies be blue.

Tell me a story,
And I'll tell one too—
If skies be cloudy,
If skies be blue.

Tell us a story
When the sun rides low,
Drawing the dark
Over all below.

Tell us a story
When the sun rides high,
Drawing the day
To the top of the sky.

Tell us a story
Of when and of why,
When the sun rides low,
When the sun rides high.

*~Dawn L. Watkins*

BJU PRESS
Greenville, South Carolina

NOTE:
The fact that materials produced by other publishers may be referred to in this volume does not constitute an endorsement of the content or theological position of materials produced by such publishers. Any references and ancillary materials are listed as an aid to the student or teacher and in an attempt to maintain the accepted academic standards of the publishing industry.

**Reading 2 Worktext**
**Second Edition**

Produced in cooperation with the Bob Jones University School of Education and Bob Jones Elementary School.



**Photo Credits:**
PhotoDisc/Getty Images 113 (all)


Greenville, South Carolina 29614


Printed in the United States of America


ISBN 978-1-57924-174-2

15 14 13 12 11 10

# Directions Don't Bug Me

Name ______________________________

**Draw It**

Finish the picture.

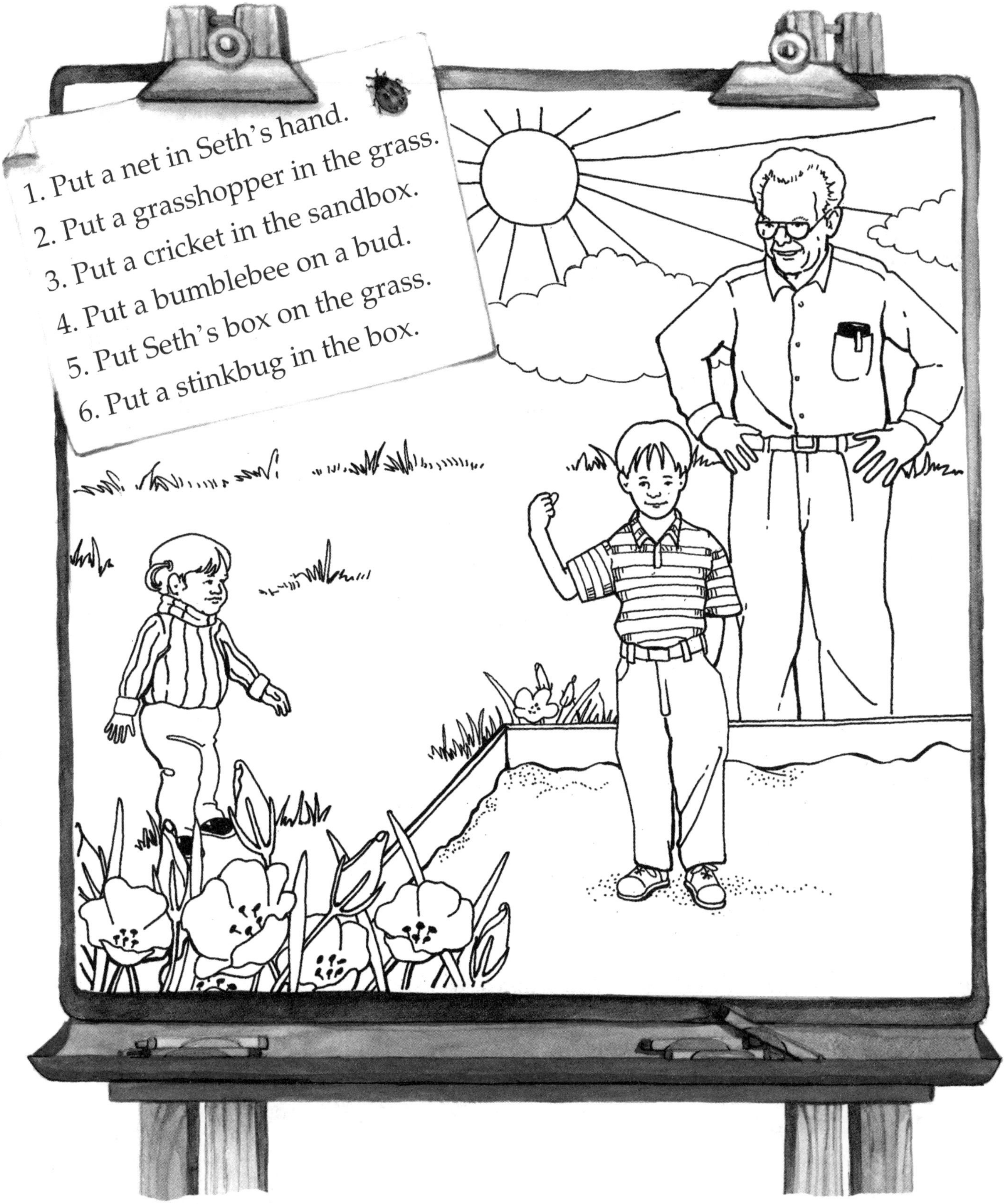

1. Put a net in Seth's hand.
2. Put a grasshopper in the grass.
3. Put a cricket in the sandbox.
4. Put a bumblebee on a bud.
5. Put Seth's box on the grass.
6. Put a stinkbug in the box.

# Busy Bugs

## Match Up

Draw lines to match the bugs to the right word.

hot mad dig fed rug

## Which One?

Circle the word that describes each picture. Write the word.

rug bug jug

dam jam ram

net pet jet

big fig pig

nod pod rod

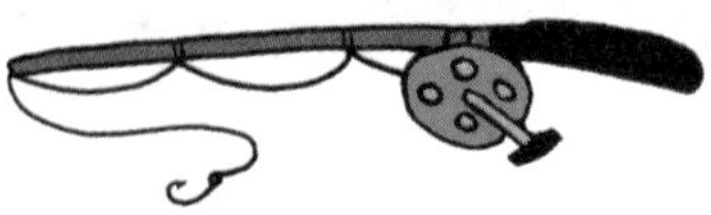

# Bug Talk

Name ______________________

**PSALM 145:16**

*Thou openest thine hand, and satisfiest the desire of every living thing.*

## Who Says?

Write the name of the person who said each sentence.

Seth

Grandad

Jenny

______________ "This one is a dandy."

______________ "Bugs not here."

______________ "The box is not here!"

______________ "Pick happy bug."

______________ "Just don't get it mad."

______________ "I have to get some bugs."

## Get in Line

Draw bugs to put the sentences in order. The first one is done for you.

[ ] Jenny had the box, and the lid was off.

[ ] Seth will get another bug for his project.

[] Seth put his bugs in a box.

[ ] Jenny held up the stinkbug in her hand.

# Family Quilt

## Choose One

Hear the word-family words.
Circle the letters that begin the name of each picture.

| | |
|---|---|
| chum | chip |
| drum | ship |
| plum | trip |
| strum | whip |

| | | |
|---|---|---|
| pr<br>sp<br>pl<br>cl  | sh<br>th<br>tr<br>st  | br<br>bl<br>fr<br>tr  |
| th<br>wh<br>sh<br>ch  | sl<br>sh<br>st<br>tr  | ch<br>sh<br>cr<br>cl  |

## Choose Again

Hear the word-family words.
Circle the letters that end the name of each picture.

| | |
|---|---|
| bent | catch |
| tent | match |
| went | patch |
| spent | scratch |

| | | |
|---|---|---|
|  sk<br>st<br>sp<br>sh |  nt<br>nd<br>ng<br>st | 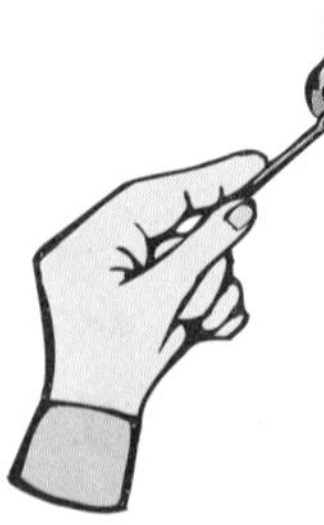 th<br>tch<br>sh<br>nk |
|  ng<br>nt<br>nk<br>st |  sp<br>nt<br>nd<br>mp |  sh<br>ch<br>st<br>th |

# Up a Tree for Lunch

Name

## Write About It

You are having lunch in a tree house.
Write three or four sentences about what you would eat.

## Draw It

Draw and color your lunch here.

# Squirrel Tales

## ▶ Which One?

Circle the word that tells what each squirrel did.

| buzzed | flagged | batted |
| licked | dented | rocked |
| trotted | fished | wagged |

## ▶ Sentence Sense

Fill in the circle beside the missing word.

"Is it chilly?" _____ Randy.

○ dropped    ○ planted

○ asked    ○ fitted

The boys_____ at the squirrel.

○ ended    ○ grinned

○ printed    ○ shifted

Ben _____ the nest to Mom.

○ handed    ○ chopped

○ rubbed    ○ cashed

The squirrel _____ the nut.

○ wagged    ○ backed

○ asked    ○ dropped

**Reading 2A: "Sticky Fingers,"** pp. 8-11, Lesson 4
Phonics: reading one- and two-syllable words ending in -*ed*

# It's Lost!

Name ______________________________

**LUKE 6:37**
*Forgive, and ye shall be forgiven.*

## Which One?

Fill in the circle to mark the best answer.

1 What did Mom get from Granny?

○ Mom got a pin.

○ Mom got a scarf.

○ Mom got a mask.

2 Who had Mom's scarf?

○ Ben had Mom's scarf.

○ Dad had Mom's scarf.

○ Randy had Mom's scarf.

3 Where did Randy put the scarf to dry?

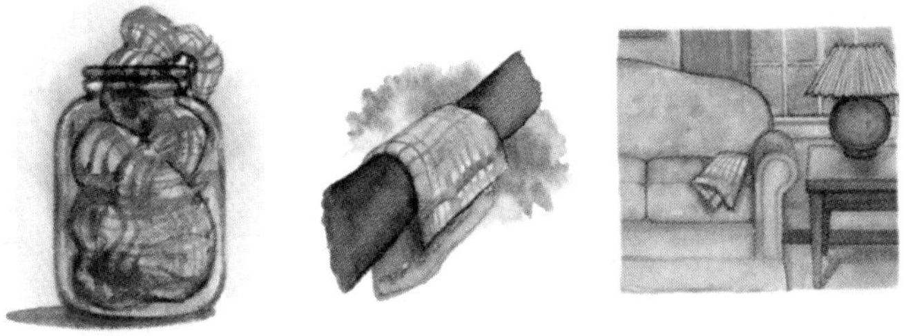

○ He put it on a branch.

○ He put it in a bottle.

○ He put it in the house.

4 What did Randy ask Mom?

○ "Will you help me hunt?"

○ "Will you forgive me?"

○ "Will you get the jelly?"

# Which Nut?

## Match the Sounds

Color the nuts to match the vowel sounds on the squirrels.

# Who and When

Name ______________________________

### Who Says?

Circle faces to tell who is speaking.

| | Mom | Dad | Randy | Ben |
|---|---|---|---|---|
| "You're in for it! Mom will be upset!" |  | | | |
| "That's Mom's scarf!" |  | | | |
| "Have you seen my new scarf?" |  | | | |
| "I think a squirrel built its nest with the scarf." |  | | | |
| "Will you forgive me?" |  | | | |
| "Then I was not the real robber. The squirrel was playing too." |  | | | |

### Get in Line

Number the events in story order.

| | |
|---|---|
| Randy asked Mom to forgive him. ___ | Ben and Randy found a nest and Mom's scarf. ___ |
| Randy dripped jelly on the robber mask. ___ | Randy put the dishcloth on a branch to dry. ___ |

# Two Silly Bulls

## Count It

Read the words and count the number of syllables in each word.

rab • bit

ban • ner

dig • ger

pep • per

Sun • day

cob • web

hub • cap

pig • pen

## Mark the Spot

Color the vowels red. Put a big dot between the syllables.

b a s k e t    c h i p m u n k

c o n t e s t

w h i s p e r    b a t t e r

# Do You Hear What I Hear?

Name ______________________________

## Listen

Draw a line to match the word that sounds like the sound made by the object it names.

crackle

snap

sizzle

tick

swish

pop

## What Is It?

Circle the word that makes you hear a hummingbird.

*Can you catch that buzz?*
*That puff that can fly?*
*Do you know what it was?*
*Did you see it go by?*

## Draw and Write

On other paper, draw more pictures and write sentences for these words: *meow, clip-clop, swoosh.*

# Rags and Jingle Need Help

## Feed Rags

Draw opened lids on the cans with open syllables. The first one is done for you.

go    lap    sat

cup    so    me    my    cry

## Feed Jingle

Find more words with open syllables. Draw opened lids on them.

fid•dle    ta•ble    sa•ble    nib•ble

bot•tle    ti•tle    rid•dle

la•dle

cat•tle

# Tuna Task

▶ **Which Ones?**

Put an **X** on every tuna can that tells who.

| | Rags | Jingle | Uncle Mack | Clem |
|---|---|---|---|---|
| 1. Who wanted tuna for lunch? | TUNA | TUNA | TUNA | TUNA |
| 2. Who fell off the deck? | TUNA | TUNA | TUNA | TUNA |
| 3. Who got crabgrass rash? | TUNA | TUNA | TUNA | TUNA |
| 4. Who is afraid of rats? | TUNA | TUNA | TUNA | TUNA |
| 5. Rags and Jingle ran into _____. | TUNA | TUNA | TUNA | TUNA |
| 6. Who had a tuna can? | TUNA | TUNA | TUNA | TUNA |
| 7. Who thumped Clem on the nose? | TUNA | TUNA | TUNA | TUNA |
| 8. Who had tuna for lunch? | TUNA | TUNA | TUNA | TUNA |

**Reading 2A: "The Tuna Tangle,"** pp. 24-27, Lesson 9
Comprehension: recalling facts and details about character actions

# Long and Short

## Sort Them

Give out the tuna cans. Draw a line to Miss Long if the first syllable of the word has a long vowel. Draw a line to Mr. and Mrs. Short if the first syllable has a short vowel.

## Sentence Sense

Use words from Miss Long's tuna cans to complete the sentences.

Toby has a ____________ bed.

The baby has a ____________ hand.

The ____________ pig slept in the mud.

The ____________ had on a pink dress.

# Title Talk

Name ____________________

## Choose the Best

Read the stories. Circle the best title for each story.

A title of a story is a name that tells about the whole story.

**Jimmy Paddles**
**Fish for Dinner**
**Jimmy's Fish to Remember**

"I want to remember this day," Jimmy said. "I want to remember the big fish I helped to catch."

"Come with me, Jimmy," said Dad. "I will think of something we can do that will help you remember."

Jimmy went with Dad to the dock. Dad lifted a paddle off the rack. "I will do a sketch of our big fish on this paddle. Will that help you remember?" Dad asked.

"Yes, it will," Jimmy said, grinning.

---

**Brad Catches the Bus**
**A Nest in a Cap**
**Brad's Pet Chipmunk**

As Brad jumped on the bus, a chipmunk got on too. The chipmunk was little and quick. No one was looking when the chipmunk dashed to the back of the bus. No one was looking when it jumped into a cap.

Brad went to the back of the bus. "Come sit here," Jeff said to Brad.

Jeff picked up his cap and lunch box so that Brad could sit by him.

"Chip, chip," went the chipmunk. Jeff jumped!

"This is my cap—not your nest!" he said.

# Vowel Condos

### Make a Word

Add Marker *e* to make long vowel words.

can

cub

can____

cub____

### Which Ones?

Color the door *red* if the condo has a long vowel word.

| | | |
|---|---|---|
| fire<br>301 | pin<br>302 | lip<br>303 |
| rope<br>201 | game<br>202 | late<br>203 |
| cake<br>101 | mat<br>102 | made<br>103 |

# How Do You Feel, Tessa?

Name ______________________

## Choose the Best

Circle the right word.

Cassy went to jump rope. Kent went to ride his bike. Tessa sat on the steps.

Tessa felt ______.

excited sad

Tessa skated past Apartment 48. A man lifted a bike from the van. "It's a bike just like mine!" said Tessa.

Tessa felt ______.

excited unhappy

Cassy has a friend in Apartment 28. Kent has a friend in Apartment 32. Tessa said, "I don't have a friend here."

Tessa felt ______.

sad silly

The lady looked up. Tessa said, "I am Tessa Stevens. I am seven. Do you have someone my age?"

Tessa felt ______.

shy friendly

Mother tells Tessa that the Blakes are moving into Apartment 48. Mother thinks there may be someone Tessa's age.

Tessa felt ______.

angry happy

Mrs. Blake said, "Come back and visit us."
"I will," said Tessa.

Tessa felt ______.

happy silly

# Moving Day

Miss Long is enjoying her in-line skates. Miss Silent and Marker *e* have come along too.

fade

fail

## ▸ Choose Two

Read the words in each in-line skate. Circle the two long vowel words in each.

| | | |
|---|---|---|
| tail<br>trick<br>tame | meat<br>make<br>mat | tip<br>tape<br>team |
| sock<br>sail<br>seal | patch<br>peak<br>pile | weep<br>wipe<br>whip |
| leak<br>lake<br>lick | bike<br>boat<br>bunk | kick<br>keep<br>kite |

# Skating Friends

Name ____________________

PROVERBS 17:17
*A friend loveth at all times.*

## Which One?

Fill in the dot next to the right answer.

1. Where did Tessa live?
   - ○ on a farm ○ in a house ○ in an apartment
2. What did Tessa want?
   - ○ a bike ○ a friend ○ a pair of skates
3. What did Tessa see at Apartment 48?
   - ○ a bike ○ a scarf ○ a robber
4. What did Tessa tell her mother about Simone?
   - ○ Simone is happy. ○ Simone is sad. ○ Simone is shy.
5. What did Tessa's mother tell her to do?
   - ○ speak to Simone ○ take Simone a doll ○ ask Simone for a bike
6. Where did Tessa want Simone to go with her?
   - ○ to a picnic ○ to the dentist ○ to Sunday school
7. What did Tessa help Simone do?
   - ○ jump rope ○ skate ○ ride a bike

## What Do You Think?

On other paper tell why you think Simone changed her mind about Sunday school.

# Hopping and Hoping

"__________ before two"

tapping

"__________ before one"

taping

## ▸Paint It

Color the skates *blue* if the word has a short vowel sound.
Color the skates *green* if the word has a long vowel sound.

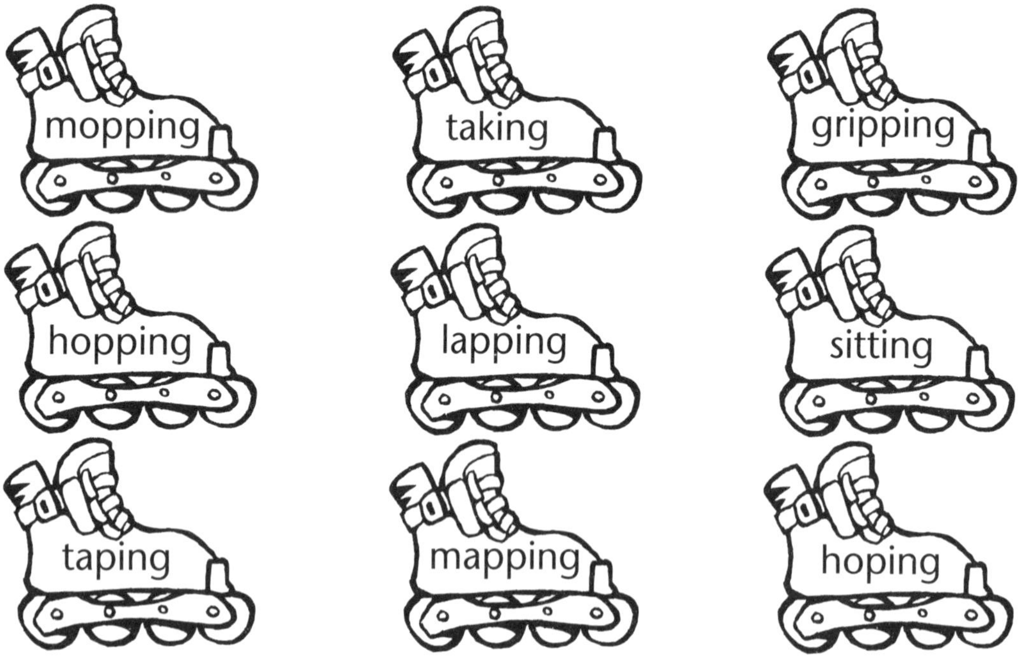


## ▸Sentence Sense

Circle the right answer.

1. Kent was (ridding, riding) his bike.
2. Tessa was (sitting, siting) on the steps.
3. Cassy and her friend were (skipping, skiping) rope.
4. Tessa was happy about (makking, making) a new friend.

# Finding Main Street

Name ______________________

## Finding Main Street

Put an ***X*** by the main idea.

Becky helped Dad clean the house. She made the beds while Dad scrubbed the dishes. Next she wiped the table. Then Becky made a card for Mom and put it on the clean table. At last it was time to go get Mom and Becky's baby sister.

_____ Becky is a good helper.

_____ Becky likes to make beds.

_____ Dad can clean.

Jean had a party in March. She asked many of her friends to come. They liked playing games. Jean liked opening her gifts. Jean and her friends liked eating the cake too.

_____ Friends like to play games.

_____ Jean has a party.

_____ Cake is good to eat.



Dan and Dad went to get a pet. Dan saw lots of pets. There were fluffy cats. There were little fish and big fish. They saw creeping crabs and singing birds. A yapping puppy licked Dan's hand. This was the pet Dan wanted!

_____ Fluffy cats make good pets.

_____ Little fish like to swim.

_____ Dan looks for a pet.

# Thorns and Horns

## Choose One

Fill in the circle next to the word that names the picture.

| | | |
|---|---|---|
| 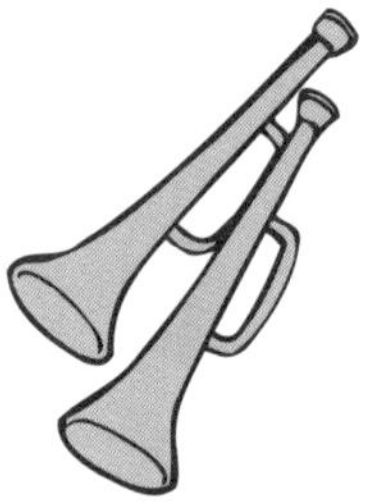 ○ corks ○ horns ○ thorns |  ○ porch ○ storm ○ scorch |  ○ corn ○ cork ○ cord |
| ○ cores ○ thorns ○ shore  |  ○ horn ○ sport ○ fort |  ○ core ○ sore ○ stork |

## Choose Six

Write the words with /or/ as in  .

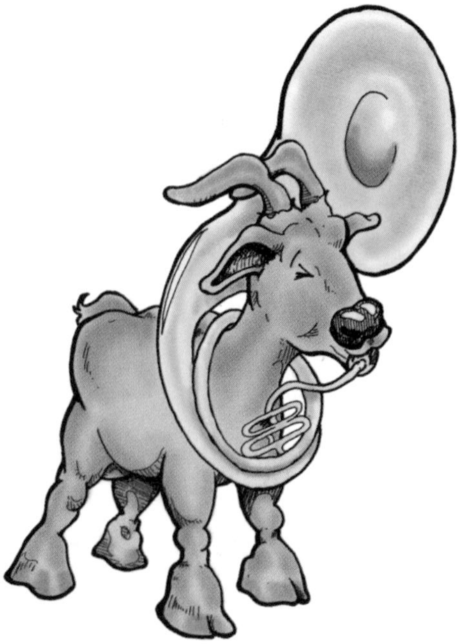

# Story "Scents"

Name ______________________

### Which One?

Circle the title that best tells about each set of words.

| |
|---|
| **This Is My Farm** |
| **Hens in the Haystack** |

barn
haystack
horse
hens
ducks

| |
|---|
| **Missing Pets** |
| **Bugs! Bugs!** |

ladybug
cricket
cockroach
bumblebee
ant

### Get in Line

Put the pictures in story order.

# With Harp and Horn

### ▸ Fall In

Write the names under the sounds.

| ar | | | or |
|---|---|---|---|
| | harp<br> | barn<br> | |
| | corn<br> | horn<br> | |
| | fork<br> | car<br> | |

### ▸ Which One?

Circle the words that match each picture.

| | | | |
|---|---|---|---|
|  | a big barn<br>a barnyard<br>a bragging bug |  | a marking pen<br>a barking puppy<br>a broken pipe |
|  | a missing penny<br>a park bench<br>a parking spot |  | a shabby car<br>a sharp cry<br>a shopping cart |
|  | a green garden<br>a glowing star<br>a gray guilt |  | a gas grill<br>a charming lady<br>a lively kitten |

# Boastful Bug

Name ______________________________

**PROVERBS 16:18**
*Pride goeth before destruction, and an haughty spirit before a fall.*

## ▸ Mark It Off

Put an ***X*** on the one in each row that does not fit.

## ▸ Which One?

Circle the best answer.

1. Little Bug popped a button off his (shoe, coat).
2. The (duck, frog) liked fat bugs best.
3. A (cat, breeze) saved Little Bug from the duck.
4. Little Bug was nearly eaten by the duck, for he was not (brave, quick).
5. Little Bug could tell he was not (brave, clever) when the crow's shadow fell over him.
6. The (crow, frog) could not see well.
7. The frog tried to get Little Bug with his (tongue, leg).
8. Little Bug went back to his (home, school).

# Bossy R

## Make a Word

Put the letters at the top of the row in the spaces to make words. Read the words.

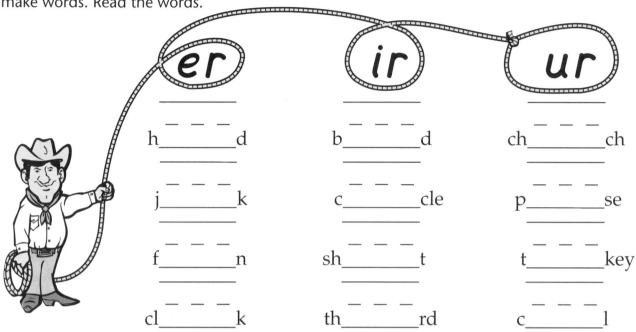

| er | ir | ur |
|---|---|---|
| h______d | b______d | ch______ch |
| j______k | c______cle | p______se |
| f______n | sh______t | t______key |
| cl______k | th______rd | c______l |

## Sentence Sense

Put a word from the word bank in each space.

| Word Bank |
|---|
| church |
| bird |
| fern |
| dirt |
| turkey |
| her |

1. We went to __________ on Sunday.
2. Bert likes to play in the __________.
3. The __________ is living in a nest.
4. Mom pressed __________ skirt.
5. My plant is a __________.
6. We will be eating __________ for dinner.

# God's Servants Serve Others

Name

> GALATIANS 5:13
> *By love serve one another.*

## Write About It

Write two or three sentences that tell you how you can help someone.

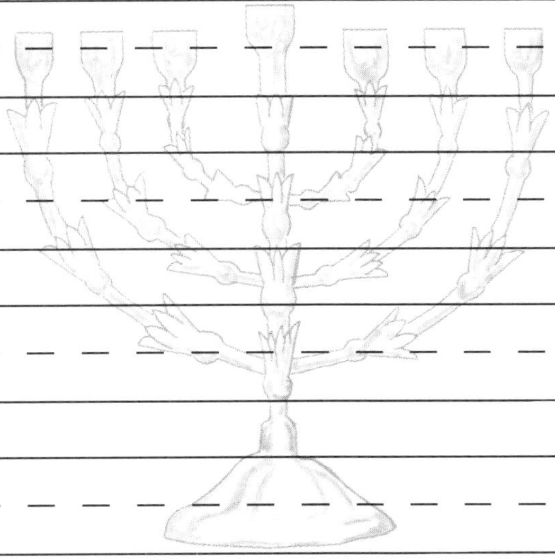

## Draw It

Draw and color a picture to illustrate your story.

# Pass the Potatoes, Please!

## Which One?

Say the name of the picture. Color the potato that has the same beginning blend.

| | | |
|---|---|---|
|  |  |  |
| pl fl bl | gl sl pl | bl cl sl |
|  |  |  |
| pl fl sl | pl bl sl | fl cl bl |

## Make a Word

Choose a blend from a potato to end each word.

1. Mother asked Bobby to he____ pick up the blocks.
2. The glasses are on the top she____.
3. I cut myse____ when I fell off the swing.
4. The dog gave a ye____ when Tim stepped on its tail.
5. Do not drink all your milk in one gu____.

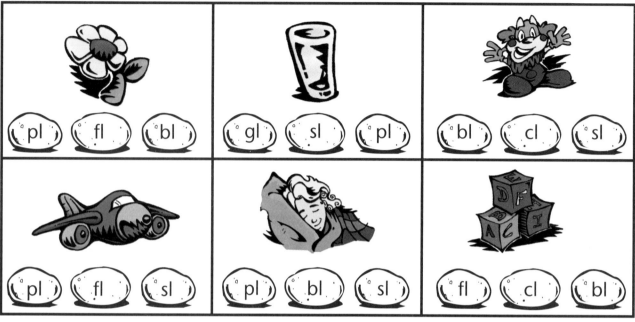

# Samuel! Samuel!

Name ______________________

### Is It True?

Fill in the circle beside *True* or *False*.

1. Eli punished his sons.

   ○ True

   ○ False

2. Eli's sons lived in the tabernacle.

   ○ True

   ○ False

3. Samuel wanted to serve God.

   ○ True

   ○ False

4. Samuel heard someone speak to him.

   ○ True

   ○ False

5. Samuel got up to see who said his name.

   ○ True

   ○ False

6. Eli said he spoke to Samuel.

   ○ True

   ○ False

7. Eli sent Samuel back to bed.

   ○ True

   ○ False

8. When Samuel went back to bed, he rested well.

   ○ True

   ○ False

# Blending Blends

**Choose One**
Write a blend in each blank to complete the words.

____ush

____ay

____ain

____og

____y

____um

____in

____ess

**Choose Again**
Write a blend from the box to make a word. Read the sentence to see if it fits.

| |
|---|
| gr |
| cr |
| dr |
| fr |
| pr |
| br |
| tr |

1. My ____iend has a red bike.
2. Mrs. Pratt ____ives us to school.
3. Bill's little sister has a ____oken leg.
4. Our cat was stuck in a ____ee.
5. David showed Dad the ____ade on his spelling test.

# Here I Am!

Name ______________________

## Picture This

Put an ***X*** beside the sentence that fits the picture.

| | |
|---|---|
| Samuel ran to Eli. | 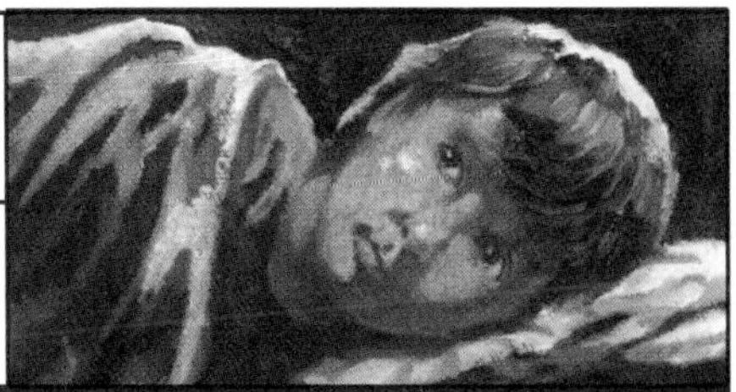 |
| Samuel heard someone speak to him. | |
| Eli blinked and looked at Samuel. |  |
| Samuel went back to bed. | |
| Samuel sat up and stretched. |  |
| Samuel had to tell Eli what God had said. | |
| Samuel lit the lamps. |  |
| Samuel rubbed the brass cups with a rag. | |



## Which One?

Fill in the circle beside the right answer.

1. Samuel's mother went with him to the ______.
   - ○ tabernacle
   - ○ school
   - ○ doctor

2. God was not happy with ______.
   - ○ Samuel's mother
   - ○ Eli's sons
   - ○ Samuel

3. Samuel's mother went to visit him in the ______.
   - ○ summer
   - ○ winter
   - ○ spring

4. God wanted to speak to ______.
   - ○ Samuel
   - ○ Samuel's mother
   - ○ Eli

# Stars Skate

## ▸ Which One?

Draw a circle around the right word.

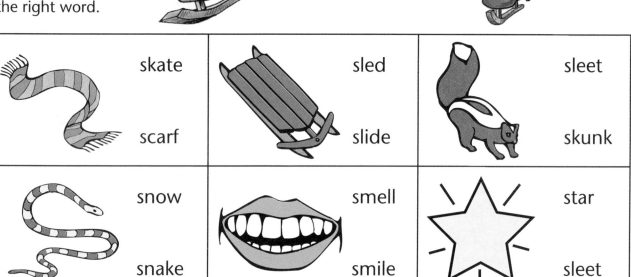

| | | | | | |
|---|---|---|---|---|---|
| 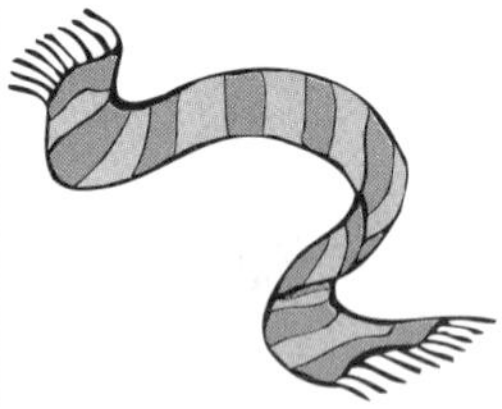 | skate<br>scarf |  | sled<br>slide |  | sleet<br>skunk |
|  | snow<br>snake | 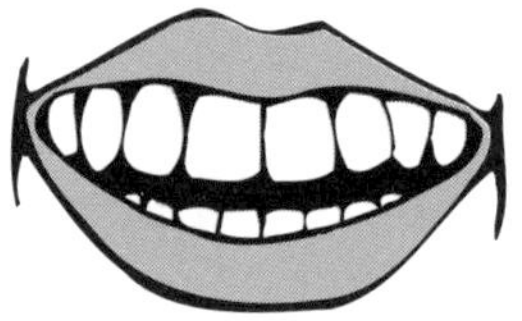 | smell<br>smile |  | star<br>sleet |

## ▸ Make a Word

Complete each word by writing one of the blends in the blank.

| sn sm sk | sc sl st | st sk |
|---|---|---|
| ___all | ___iff | de___ |
| ___ow | ___ide | fa___ |
| ___unk | ___eet | la___ |
| ___oke | ___arf | li___ |

# Missing Persons

Name ______________________

### Who Did It?

Write a name in each space.

Father

Anne

Billy Sunday

1. ______________________ liked to hear Billy Sunday preach.

2. ______________________ ran like the wind when he played baseball.

3. ______________________ and ______________________ saw the church where Billy Sunday trusted Christ.

4. ______________________ stayed to listen to music.

5. ______________________ became a Christian at a tent meeting.

6. ______________________ was a baseball player who became a preacher.

7. ______________________ gave Anne a hug.

8. ______________________ hummed a tune they had sung at the tent meeting.

# Baseball Crawl

## Mark It

Underline the letters ***au*** and ***aw*** on each baseball. Read the words.

## Which One?

Write one of the baseball words in each blank.

1. The ____________ hid in the grass.

2. One little pig made a home of ____________.

3. ____________ became a servant of Christ.

4. Ann ____________ the church where Billy Sunday trusted Christ.

5. The big dog licked its ____________.

6. Samuel woke ____________ someone said his name.

# Billy Sunday, How Did You Feel?

Name ____________________

## Face It

Circle the picture that shows how Billy Sunday felt.

> **PHILIPPIANS 1:6**
>
> *Being confident of this very thing, that he which hath begun a good work in you will perform it until the day of Jesus Christ.*

1. Billy could not miss the ball. If he missed the ball, his team would lose the game.

worried

cheerful

2. The batter hit that ball with a crack! This was not the time to miss.

laughing

concerned

3. The ball hit Billy's mitt and did not fall out even when Billy tripped.

angry

amazed

5. Every person clapped his hands when the team won.

happy

sad

# Oscar

### Choose One
Write the best word.

/ô/ in *lost*
/ô/ in *ball*

1. When Joshua woke up, he ________ his dog, Oscar.  — called / flossed

2. Joshua wanted to play ________ with Oscar.  — cause / ball

3. He looked for Oscar ________ day.  — all / long

4. "You have a phone ________," said his mother.  — call / boss

5. It was Farmer John. He found Oscar sleeping in his ________.  — loft / lawn

6. Joshua smiled. His little dog was not ________.  — fall / lost

# In God's Will

Name ______________________________

**COLOSSIANS 1:9**

*We . . . do not cease to pray for you, and to desire that ye might be filled with the knowledge of his will.*

## Which One?

Fill in the circle next to what each one said.

1. 

○ "I will quit playing baseball if my team will let me go."

○ "God had a plan for Mr. Sunday."

○ "God heard him, and He heard me too."

---

2. 

○ "I cannot leave if they will not let me."

○ "God's plan for Mr. Sunday was for him to be a preacher."

○ "God has a plan for your life, Anne."

---

3. 

○ "We heard Mr. Sunday preach today in the tent meeting."

○ "I cannot leave if they will not let me."

○ "You said you would play."

---

4. 

○ "We heard Mr. Sunday preach today in the tent meeting."

○ "God still wanted Mr. Sunday to be a preacher."

○ "God has a plan for your life, Anne."

---

5. 

○ "Papa saw him play one time."

○ "God had a plan for Mr. Sunday, Anne."

○ "God has a plan for your life, Anne."

# Cooking with Book and Spoon

## Sentence Sense

Write the correct word.

1. The ______________ will read from his cookbook.

   cook / hook

2. He chopped up a turnip.

   A turnip is a ______________.

   toot / root

3. He dropped a mixer, which made a loud ______________.

   boom / zoom

4. He cleaned up the mess. He did a ______________ job.

   good / hood

## Mark It Out

Read the words. Put an ***X*** on the word that does not have the same vowel sound as the other two.

| | | | |
|---|---|---|---|
| 1. | book | moon | wood |
| 2. | boom | food | good |
| 3. | look | room | root |
| 4. | spoon | hood | zoom |

# Same Starting Sounds

Name ______________________________

Poets like the sounds of words. Sometimes they put words close together that have the same starting sounds.

## Which Letter?

Read the poem. Underline three words that have the same starting sound in each line. Write that letter on the line. The first one is done for you.

### Bees

*Sometimes skimming by sunflowers,* ___S___

*Sometimes humming over high hay,* ______

*Bees buzz by, tending their nectar;* ______

*They stop sometimes but never stay.* ______

## Your Turn

Add words that start with the sounds of the other words.

1. Time to take ______________ teacups to Tilly.

2. My mother made me many ______________.

3. Fred found Fran's ______________ flag.

# Toothless

### Which One?

Circle the best answer.

1. An animal in the zoo is a _____.

   baboon    balloon    bedroom

2. String is kept on a _____.

   stool    spool    school

3. The one who brushes a horse is a _____.

   broom    grass    groom

4. You learn to study at a _____.

   school    pool    tool

5. A plant in the woods is a _____.

   raccoon    toothbrush    toadstool

### Which Tooth?

Write one of the circled words under the correct tooth.

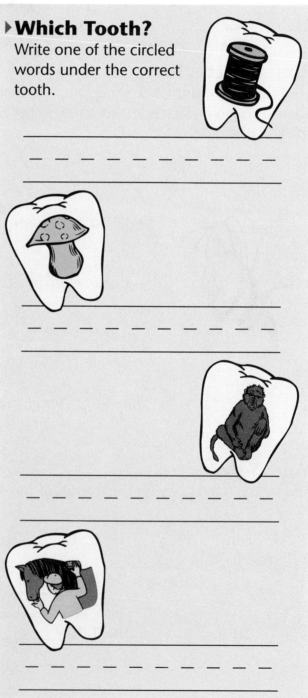

_______________

_______________

_______________

_______________

# Tell Me a Tale, and I'll Tell a Tale

______________________________
Name

Folktales began in times past when there were no books. Someone made up a tale and told it to someone who told it to someone and so on. All the parts of the tale were not the same in the telling, but it was still the same tale. People sometimes wrote folktales so that they would not forget. Sometimes they sang them. All lands have folktales. There are many kinds of folktales.

A. Some have kings and queens.

B. Some have animals that say and do things like people.

C. Some tell of everyday life.

D. Some folktales answer "why."

## Think About It

Read the folktale descriptions above.
Write the letter of the kind of folktale in the blank.

______ 1. A little kitten has lost its mother. It asks a goose, a dog, and a goat if they have seen her.

______ 2. A tale tells why the bunny has a little tail.

______ 3. A great king looks for someone who always tells the truth.

______ 4. A little girl keeps house for her mother and father. She must do many new jobs in a little time.

# Bob's Summer Day

## Choose One

Write the correct word.

1. Bob has a ________________ on his broken foot.

splint
stripe

2. He cannot ________________ his itching foot.

string
scratch

3. His friends are ________________ in the pool next door.

splashing
scraping

4. Bob wants to ________________ and run.

stretch
scrub

5. Mother makes some ________________ ice cream for Bob.

splinter
strawberry

6. Bob is so happy that he wants to ________________.

splat
scream

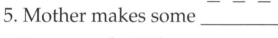

# Folktale Fun

Name ______________________________

## Choose One

Fill in the circle next to the right one.

"To Market" is a folktale that tells

- ○ about a king and queen.
- ○ about animals that say and do things like people.
- ○ about everyday life.
- ○ about "why."

In a folktale, someone has to find an answer of some kind.

What answer did Fritz find?

- ○ Fritz kills the goose. Then he sells the fox and eats the corn.
- ○ Fritz sets the fox free. He takes the goose back to the market.
- ○ Fritz takes the corn and the fox to the other side of the river. Then he goes back for the goose.
- ○ Fritz feeds the corn to the goose and feeds the goose to the fox. He sits down and weeps.

## Read and Do

### The  and the 

A  went to sleep under a . A  walked into the 's . The  woke up. "Don't eat me!" said the . "Someday I will help you." The  said, " You are too little," but he let the  go free. Soon the lion got into a trap. He called for help. The  came and bit the . The  said, "I am sorry for what I said, little . You are not too little to help."

Circle *True* or *False*.

1. This folktale is about animals that say and do things like people.

   True False

2. The  had to find a way to tie up the 

   True False

3. The  had to find a way to cut the .

   True False

# The March Family

/ch/

## Which One?

Look at the March family. Fill in the circle beside the right word.

1. Susie March likes to help her mother bake a ______ of cookies.

○ catch

○ batch

2. On Sunday the March family goes to ______.

○ church

○ chimney

3. Don and Carl March play ______.

○ catch

○ hopscotch

4. Did Susie get a bug bite? Her arm is starting to ______.

○ itch

○ scratch

## Choose One

Fill in the right word.

matches stitches fetches

1. Fido, the Marches' dog, ____________ the newspaper every day.

2. Mrs. March makes ____________ in the torn shirt.

3. Mr. March needed two ____________ to light the fire.

# Do You Remember?

Name ______________________

HEBREWS 13:5
*I will never leave thee.*

## ▸Compare

Draw a line to the right land.

| |
|---|
| 1. A king rules here. |
| 2. People are free to serve God here. |
| 3. The Allertons and the Mullinses go to live here. |
| 4. God's people cannot stay here and obey God. |
| 5. There are Indians here. |
| 6. The Allertons and Mullinses left friends here. |

## ▸Compare Again

Write ***R*** if the sentence tells about *Remember.*
Write ***J*** if the sentence tells about *Joseph.*

| | |
|---|---|
| 1. I am excited about the trip. ______ | 3. I am excited about meeting new people. ______ |
| 2. I wish I could stay. ______ | 4. I fear the Indians. ______ |

# Turtle Serves First

## ▶ Which One?

Fill in the circle beside the best word.

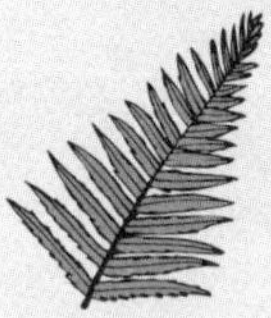

|  |  |  |  |
|---|---|---|---|
| ○ fern<br>○ first<br>○ turn | ○ burn<br>○ herd<br>○ bird | ○ purse<br>○ serve<br>○ shirt | ○ nurse<br>○ stir<br>○ nerve |
| ○ churn<br>○ chirp<br>○ clerk | ○ fur<br>○ thirst<br>○ turtle | ○ first<br>○ burst<br>○ verb | ○ skirt<br>○ first<br>○ alert |

## ▶ Sentence Sense

Write a word from the word bank in the blank.

| | |
|---|---|
| servant | 1. The _____ ate all the seed. |
| jerk | 2. Mom put the keys in her _____. |
| birds | 3. The van stopped with a _____. |
| fern | 4. Samuel was a _____ of God. |
| purse | 5. Granny put the _____ in a pot with some dirt. |

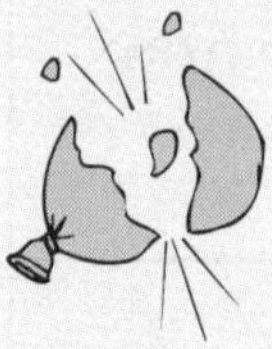

# Map Madness

Name ____________________

## Read a Map

Use the map key to answer the questions below.

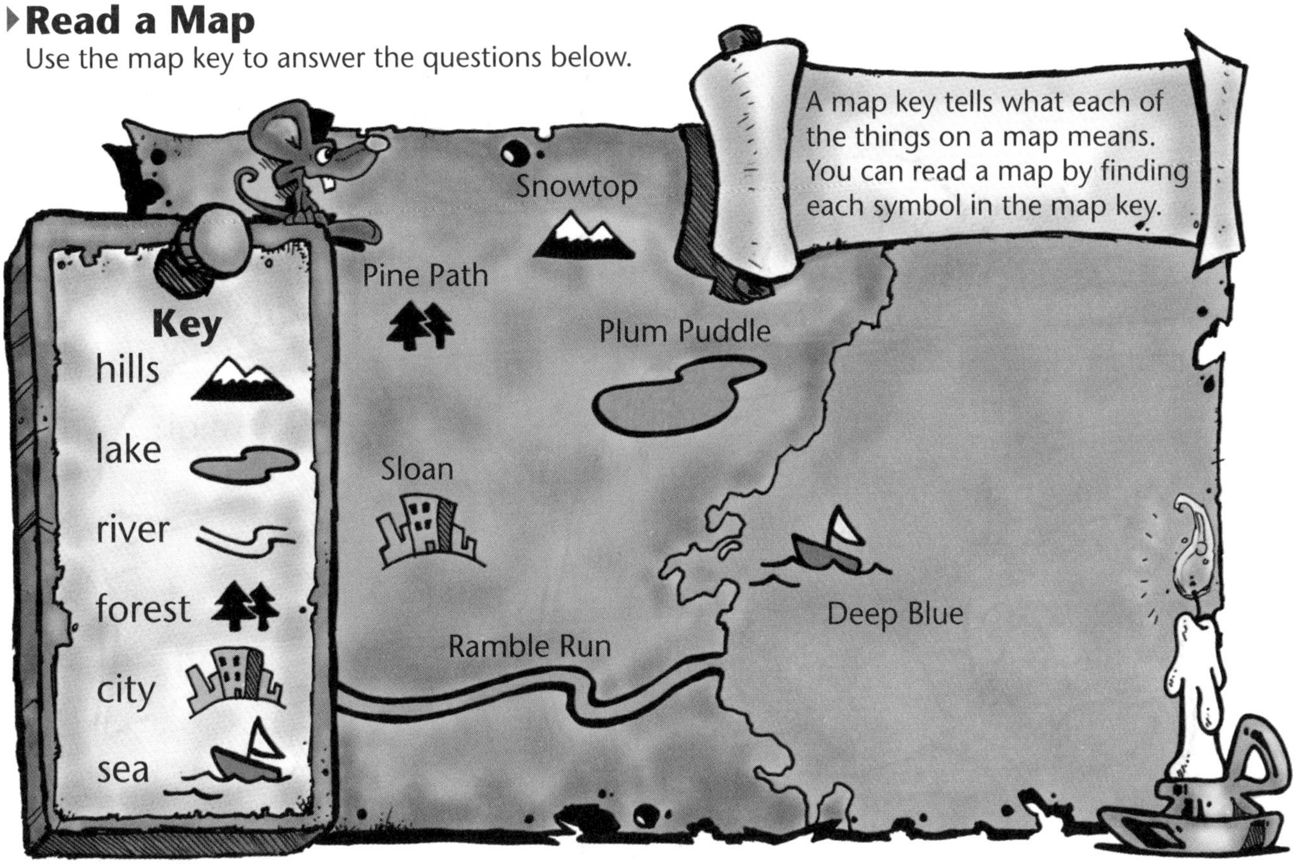


1. What is the name of the city?

2. Where would you go to paddle down a river?

3. Where would you go camping in the forest?

4. Where could you go rowing on a lake?

5. Where could you find seashells?

6. Where could you go hiking in the hills?

# Quiet as a Mouse

/ī/

## Paint It

Color each mouse with *igh.*

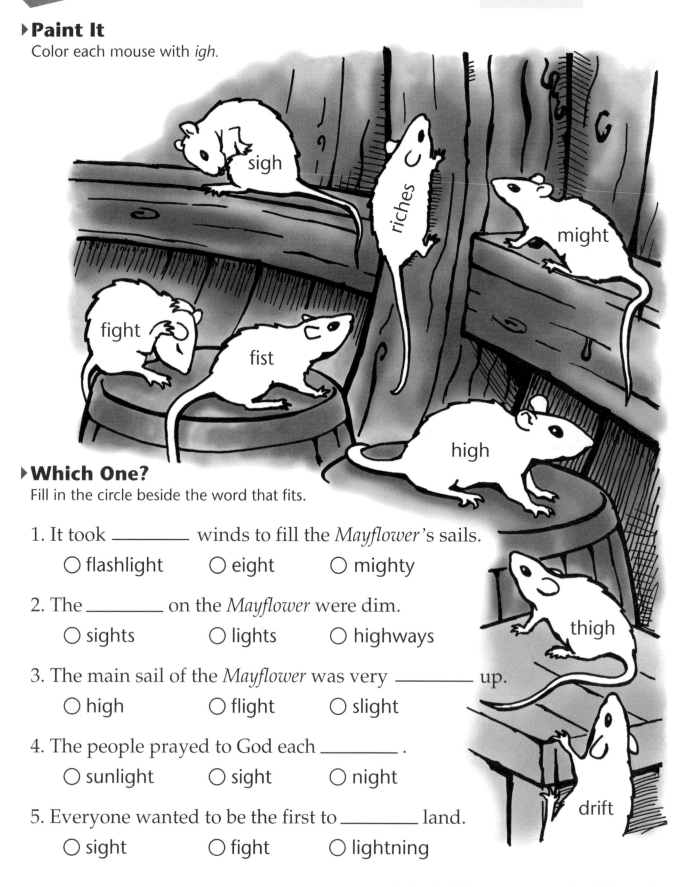

## Which One?

Fill in the circle beside the word that fits.

1. It took ________ winds to fill the *Mayflower*'s sails.
   ○ flashlight ○ eight ○ mighty

2. The ________ on the *Mayflower* were dim.
   ○ sights ○ lights ○ highways

3. The main sail of the *Mayflower* was very ________ up.
   ○ high ○ flight ○ slight

4. The people prayed to God each ________ .
   ○ sunlight ○ sight ○ night

5. Everyone wanted to be the first to ________ land.
   ○ sight ○ fight ○ lightning

# Curtain Time!

Name ______________________

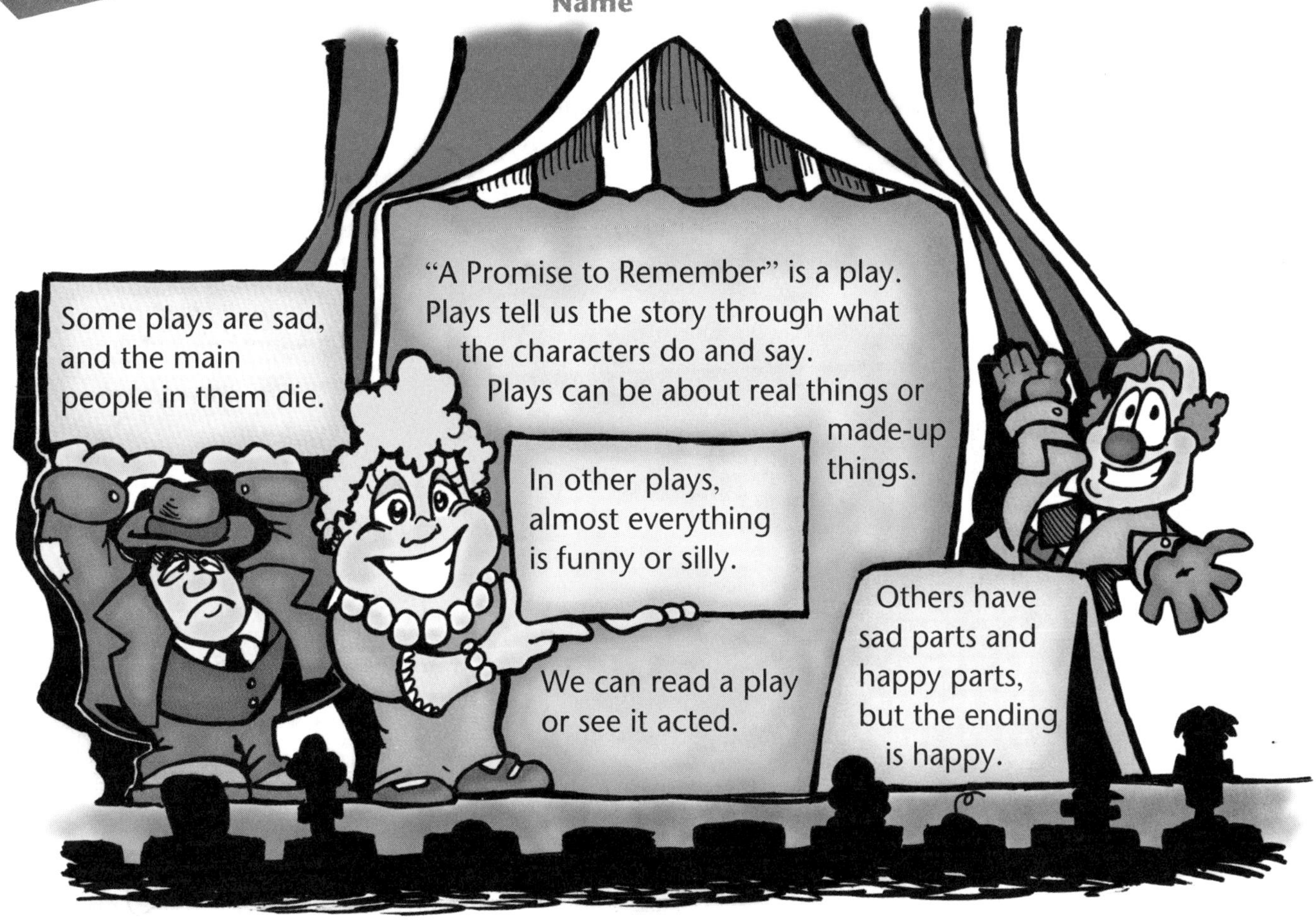

"A Promise to Remember" is a play.
Plays tell us the story through what the characters do and say.
Plays can be about real things or made-up things.
Some plays are sad, and the main people in them die.
In other plays, almost everything is funny or silly.
We can read a play or see it acted.
Others have sad parts and happy parts, but the ending is happy.


## Tell About It

Write about a play you have seen.

## Sail Away

### Mark the Spot

Divide each word by putting a dot between the syllables.

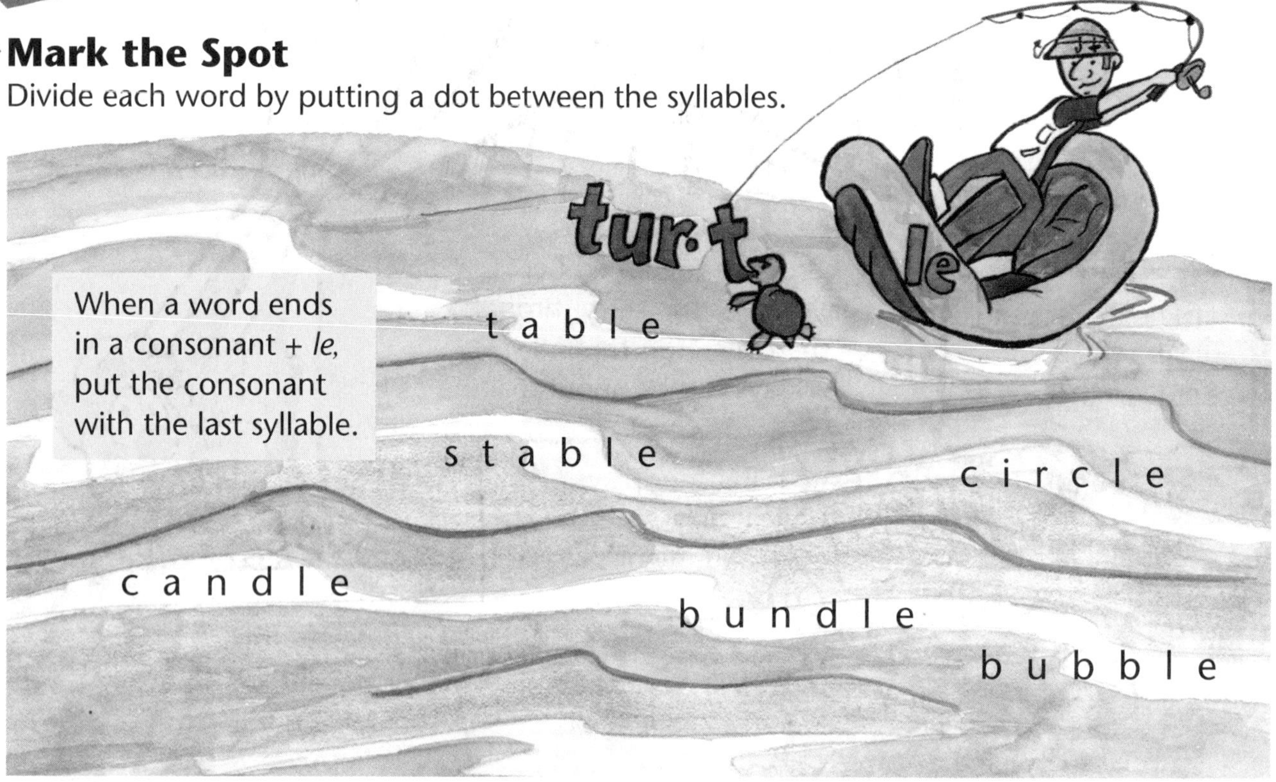


### Which One?

Circle the word that matches.

| | | | | | |
|---|---|---|---|---|---|
|  | apple<br>ankle<br>babble |  | bottle<br>beetle<br>feeble |  | grumble<br>kettle<br>trickle |
|  | juggle<br>people<br>puzzle |  | tackle<br>juggle<br>jungle | 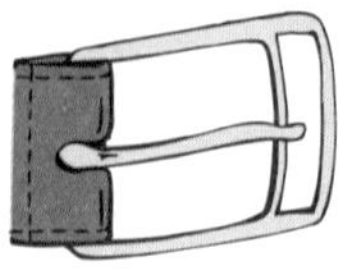 | buckle<br>rattle<br>bumble |
|  | riddle<br>saddle<br>sniffle |  | eagle<br>beagle<br>jungle | 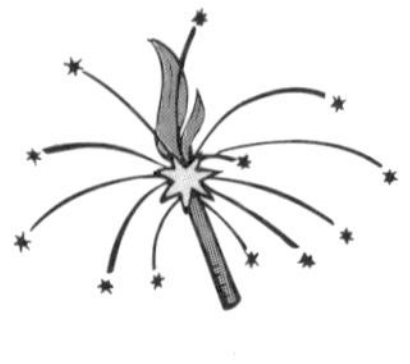 | simple<br>sparkle<br>sprinkle |

# A Puzzle to Remember

Name ______________________________

## Work the Puzzle

Use the words in the list to fill in the puzzle.

**Across**

2. what Mr. Allerton said they must not bring with them
4. Remember had a fear of these.
6. Remember's friend
8. the family who traveled with the Allertons
9. the name of the ship

**Down**

1. the One who would look after the Allertons and the Mullinses
3. the name of the Allertons' daughter
5. where the Allertons and the Mullinses were going
7. the one who mocked the families

Mullins
fear
sailor
Remember
America
Joseph
Indians
God
*Mayflower*

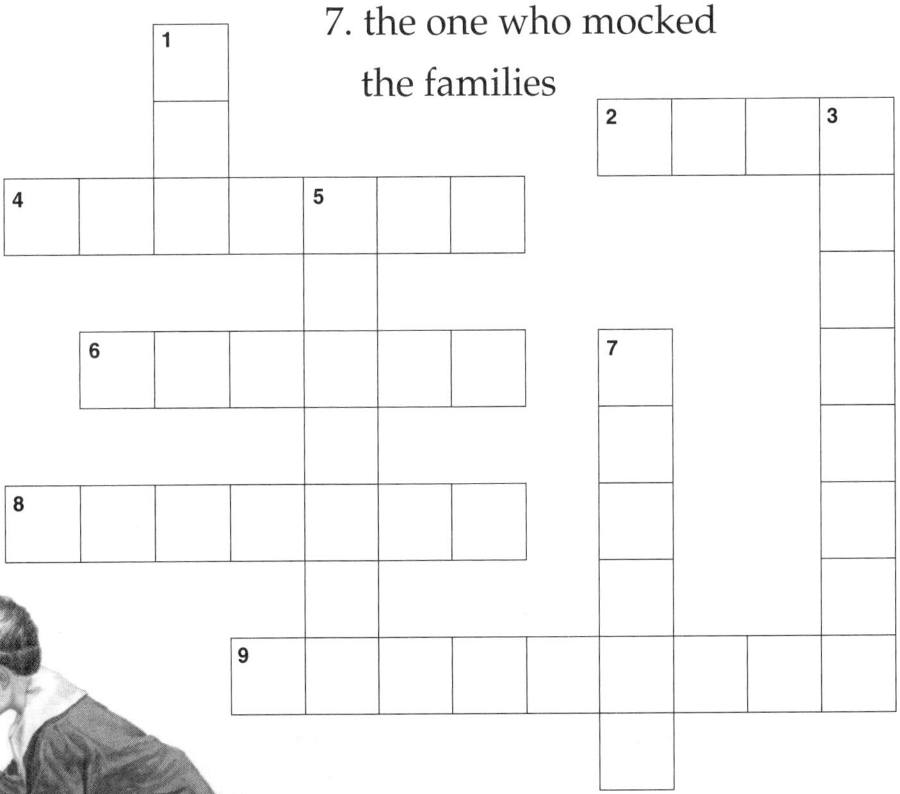


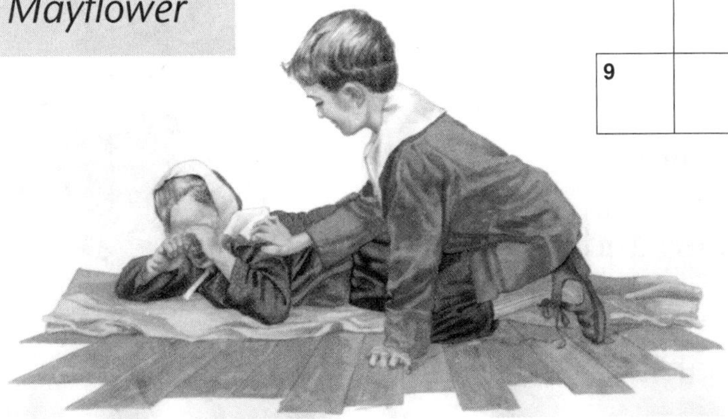

# Knight Knifes Knots

## Which One?

Fill in the circle beside the word that fits the sentence.

1. The ______ rode up to the castle.
   ○ knight ○ knife
2. He wanted to give the king's ______ a comb.
   ○ naughty ○ daughter
3. The knight ______ on the door.
   ○ knocked ○ knob
4. His ______ made a TAP-TAP-TAP.
   ○ knuckles ○ knee
5. No one stirred, so he turned the ______ and went in.
   ○ knife ○ knob
6. There sat the king's daughter with her ______ on her lap.
   ○ knocking ○ knitting
7. She was tangled in the ______ the yarn had made.
   ○ knots ○ knife
8. Her pet ______ sat sadly by.
   ○ limb ○ lamb
9. The knight ______ down and cut the knots.
   ○ knelt ○ knob
10. The king's daughter gave him a pot of ______ gold.
    ○ bright ○ might
11. The knight, the king's daughter, and the ______ were happy ever after.
    ○ climb ○ lamb





**Reading 2A: "A Promise to Remember,"** pp. 74-88, Lesson 32
Phonics: applying silent consonant letter generalizations: *igh*, /ī/; *kn*, /n/; *mb*, /m/

# It's Raining Cats and Dogs

Name

## What Does It Mean?

We say many things that cannot be taken just as we say them. Choose a statement from the box to tell the real meaning of the words under the pictures.

| |
|---|
| I am very hungry. |
| Are you teasing me? |
| I will not do more than this. |

That is where I draw the line.

Are you pulling my leg?

I could eat a horse.

# Sore Turtles March

## Fill It In

Put a word from the box in each sentence.

| | | |
|---|---|---|
| star | turn | skirt |
| verse | curb | shore |

1. Philip can say his Bible ______________.

2. Mr. Barber is parking his car by the ______________.

3. The crab is digging in the sand on the ______________.

4. We looked for the first ______________ in the dark sky.

## Which One?

Circle the *r*-influenced vowels heard in each picture.

| | | | | | | | |
|---|---|---|---|---|---|---|---|
|  | or<br>ar<br>ir |  | ur<br>or<br>ar |  | ar<br>or<br>er |  | or<br>ar<br>ur |
|  | or<br>ur<br>ar | 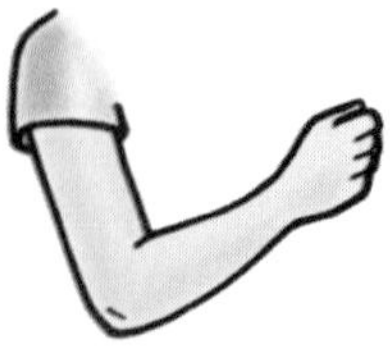 | ur<br>or<br>ar |  | or<br>er<br>ar |  | ar<br>or<br>ir |
|  | ar<br>or<br>ur |  | ar<br>ir<br>or |  | ur<br>ar<br>or |  | or<br>ar<br>er |

# Are You Speaking to Me?

Name ______________________

Sometimes the author has a character from the story speak to the reader; that's you.

## Pick the Speaker

Refer to the story "Philip and His Farm" to find out whom Philip is speaking to. If Philip is speaking to you, the reader, circle the child reading a book. If Philip is speaking to a character in the story, circle the picture of the character.

Oh, my name is Philip.
Did I tell you that yet?
(Page 90)

"My friend has a fish,
and it stinks." (Page 94)

Soon Crabcake left, but I
was sad only because I
didn't have a pet anymore.
(Page 93)

## Write About It

Pretend that you are Philip. Tell a reader why you cannot have a furry pet.

# An Elephant on the Telephone

/f/

## ▸Match Them Up

Read each sentence and draw a line to the right elephant.

The elephant is talking
on the telephone.

Ralph took a photograph
of the elephant.

The elephant got
a tennis trophy.

Will you teach phonics
to the elephant?

# Meanings You Can Hear

Name ____________________

crash!

buzzzzz!

rattle!

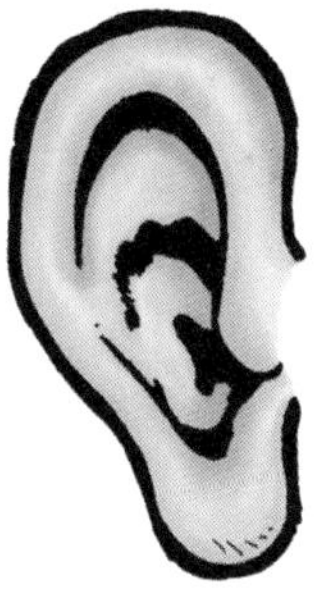

Sometimes writers use sound effect words to help us hear the action. The words may be spelled correctly, or some letters may be drawn out.

## Label It

Label the picture below by putting these words on it.

| | | |
|---|---|---|
| swish | snap | bleat |
| hiss | roar | munch, crunch |

# Stray Words

## Which One?

A few word families do not follow the rules. Read the word families on each lamb. Write the word that is described.

| | | | |
|---|---|---|---|
| bolt<br>colt<br>jolt | a bump or crash | grind<br>kind<br>mind | to rub and crush |
| child<br>mild<br>wild | a little boy or girl | fold<br>gold<br>hold | to clasp in your hand |
| mold<br>sold<br>told | what old food has on it | mind<br>find<br>kind | what you use to think |

## Ring It

Circle the picture that matches the sentence.

1. This sheep is safe in the fold.

2. The gold pin looked like a little colt.

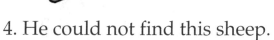

3. This wild dog could hurt sheep.

4. He could not find this sheep.

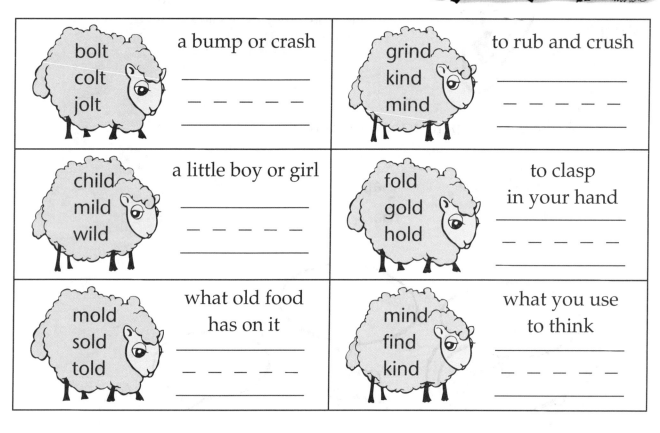

# If I Were a Shepherd

Name

## Write It

Write a story about being a shepherd and looking for your stray lamb.

## Draw It

Finish a picture to go with your story. Draw a shepherd and his lamb.

# Proud Clowns

## Let's Sort

Write each word under the picture that has the same vowel sound.

pound trot boat shop blow cow tone rock shout

## Match Up

Circle the words that have the same vowel sound as the word *out*. Draw a line to the matching picture.

a sparkling crown

a cheering crowd

a drowsy kitten

a funny clown

a hunting hound

a bowing man

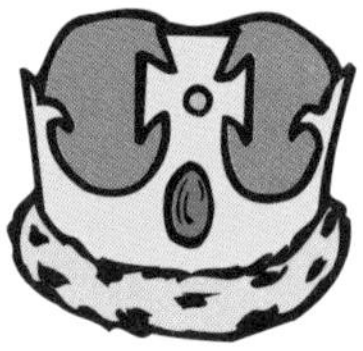

# Do You Know?

Name ______________________

**JOHN 10:14**
*I am the good shepherd, and know my sheep.*

## Which One?

Circle *True* or *False* for each sentence.

True False 1. The shepherd tried to keep his flock from harm.

True False 2. A mother sheep and her babies were lost from the flock.

True False 3. The shepherd heard faint cries from far away.

True False 4. Snow began to fall as the shepherd looked for the lamb.

True False 5. The shepherd had one hundred sheep in his flock.

## Let's Sort

Write each word in the correct box.

| | | | |
|---|---|---|---|
| butterfly | penguin | beaver | crow |
| tadpole | robin | bee | whale |

| Animals That Fly | Animals That Swim |
|---|---|
| | |
| | |
| | |
| | |

# Boys Enjoy Noise

## /oi/

### Fill It In

Write a word from the box in each sentence.

| boil | enjoy | spoil | voice |
|---|---|---|---|

1. The milk will ________ if it is left sitting on the table.
2. Did you ________ your trip to the zoo?
3. He yelled with a loud ________.
4. The water will ________ when it gets very hot.

### Which One?

Circle the word that describes each picture.

| | | | |
|---|---|---|---|
|  | coin<br>cane<br>cone | 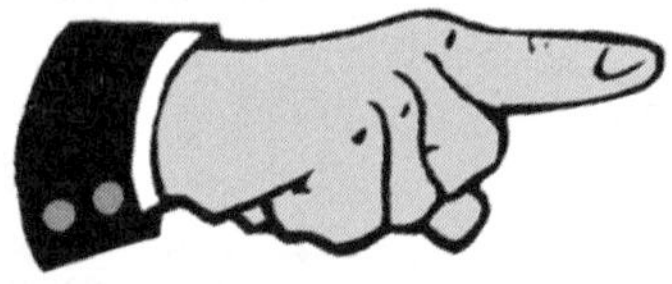 | paint<br>point<br>pail |
|  | all<br>ail<br>oil |  | bay<br>boy<br>bone |
|  | toy<br>top<br>tray |  | noisy<br>tinfoil<br>cowboy |

# The Good Shepherd

Name ______________________________

> **JOHN 10:14**
> *I am the good shepherd, and know my sheep, and am known of mine.*

## ▸Which One?

Fill in the circle beside the best answer.

1. Why did the little lamb stray from the flock?
   - ○ He wanted to be alone.
   - ○ He wanted to eat more grass.
   - ○ He did not like the shepherd.

2. Why did the shepherd look for the lost lamb?
   - ○ He wanted to sell the lamb.
   - ○ He wanted his friends to think he was brave.
   - ○ He cared about the little lamb.

## ▸Get in Line

Number the sentences in story order.

_____ The shepherd lowered his staff and lifted the lamb.

_____ The shepherd left the fold to look for the lamb.

__1__ The sheep trotted past the shepherd into the fold.

_____ The kind shepherd cleaned the bleeding cuts.

_____ The shepherd and his friends met to give thanks and praise.

_____ The shepherd looked down the side of a steep cliff.

# Round Clown Coin

## Paint It

Color the  brown if it has a word with the sound of *oi* as in *coin*.

## Draw It

Circle the correct answer. Draw a picture to go with your answer.

It is something a king has.

crown shout

It is something very tall.

ground tower

It is a kind of hunting dog.

house hound

It is something that floats in the sky.

brown cloud

# Tale Titles

Name ______________________

### Choose One
Read the story. Circle the best title.

"I'm going to box," said Joey Kangaroo. Joey walked until he found a shrub. Pow! He hit the shrub with his fist. Crack! The branches broke, and Joey tumbled into the shrub.

"Ouch!" he cried. "I've got a thorn in my paw! Maybe I'll box with something that has no thorns!"

Joey Lives by a Shrub

Joey Goes Boxing

Joey Goes for a Walk

### Write It
Write the story title from above next to the picture which best illustrates it.

______________________

______________________

______________________

# Footstool Fun

## Same Letters—Two Sounds

Draw a line from the word to the picture.

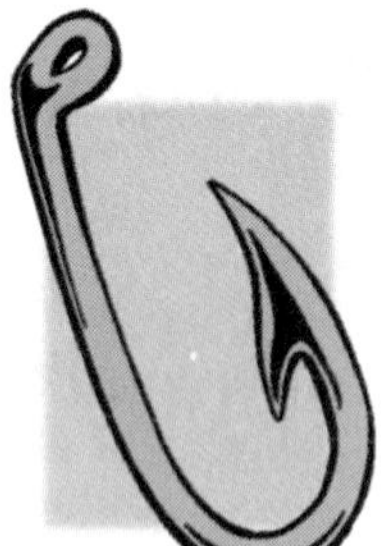

hook
book
took
look
shook

stool
fool
spool
tool
pool

## Fill It In

Write a word from the box in each sentence.

| | | | |
|---|---|---|---|
| room | brook | book | foot |

1. I would not like the kangaroo to kick me with his ______________.

2. Are there fish in the ______________?

3. Dan read a ______________ about Australia.

4. Pick up all the toys in your ______________.

# Zoo Clues

______________________________
Name

## Choose One

Read each clue and decide whether it tells about a *kangaroo* or a *koala*. Write the letter beside it.

_____ 1. I can kill a man or animal with my strong back legs.

_____ 2. I like to box and play tag.

_____ 3. I have very sharp claws.

_____ 4. I stay in my mother's pouch for 25 weeks.

_____ 5. I can grow to be seven feet tall.

_____ 6. I ride on my mother's back.

_____ 7. My tail can be three feet long.

_____ 8. I stay in the trees most of my life.

_____ 9. My name means "no drink."

_____ 10. I can sleep on a branch without falling.

A. kangaroo

B. koala

## Write One

Write the correct word in the blank.

Australia eucalyptus

Where do kangaroos live?

______________________________

What do koalas eat?

______________________________

# New Pool

## Choose One

Circle the word in each box that tells about the picture.

| | | |
|---|---|---|
|  flew<br>brew<br>drew | 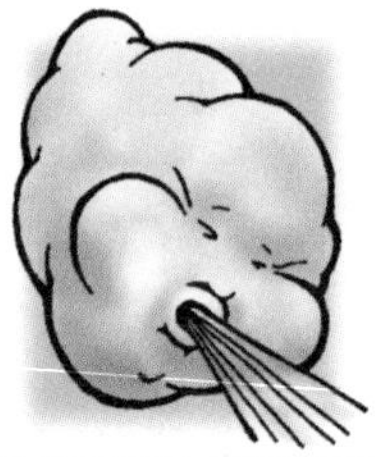 new<br>blew<br>crew |  jewelry<br>stew<br>threw |
|  kangaroos<br>balloons<br>baboons |  afternoon<br>poodle<br>raccoon |  chew<br>grew<br>news |

## Choose Again

Fill in the space beside the word that best fits each sentence.

1. Mother packed some ________ in Drew's knapsack.
   ○ food ○ mood

2. She told the children to eat lunch at ________ .
   ○ moon ○ noon

3. The children ________ what was for lunch.
   ○ knew ○ flew

4. Drew found ________ in his box for the dog biscuits.
   ○ room ○ broom

5. Drew ________ one dog biscuit to Scout.
   ○ stew ○ threw

6. Scout began to ________ the biscuit.
   ○ crew ○ chew

7. Drew wanted to find some ________ treasures.
   ○ flew ○ new

# Is That a Fact?

Name ______________________

## You Decide

Circle ***yes*** if the sentence tells a fact about kangaroos.
Circle ***no*** if it is something that the writer made up.

| | | |
|---|---|---|
| 1. Kangaroos have very strong legs. | yes | no |
| 2. Kangaroos can jump very far. | yes | no |
| 3. Kangaroos can tell jokes like people can. | yes | no |
| 4. Kangaroos keep their little ones in a pouch. | yes | no |
| 5. Kangaroos bake muffins. | yes | no |
| 6. Kangaroos sleep in beds and sit in chairs. | yes | no |
| 7. Kangaroos can grow to be seven feet tall. | yes | no |
| 8. Kangaroos pack boxed lunches. | yes | no |

# Triple Scoops

/ōō/

## What Flavor?

Color each scoop that has a word that rhymes with the picture.

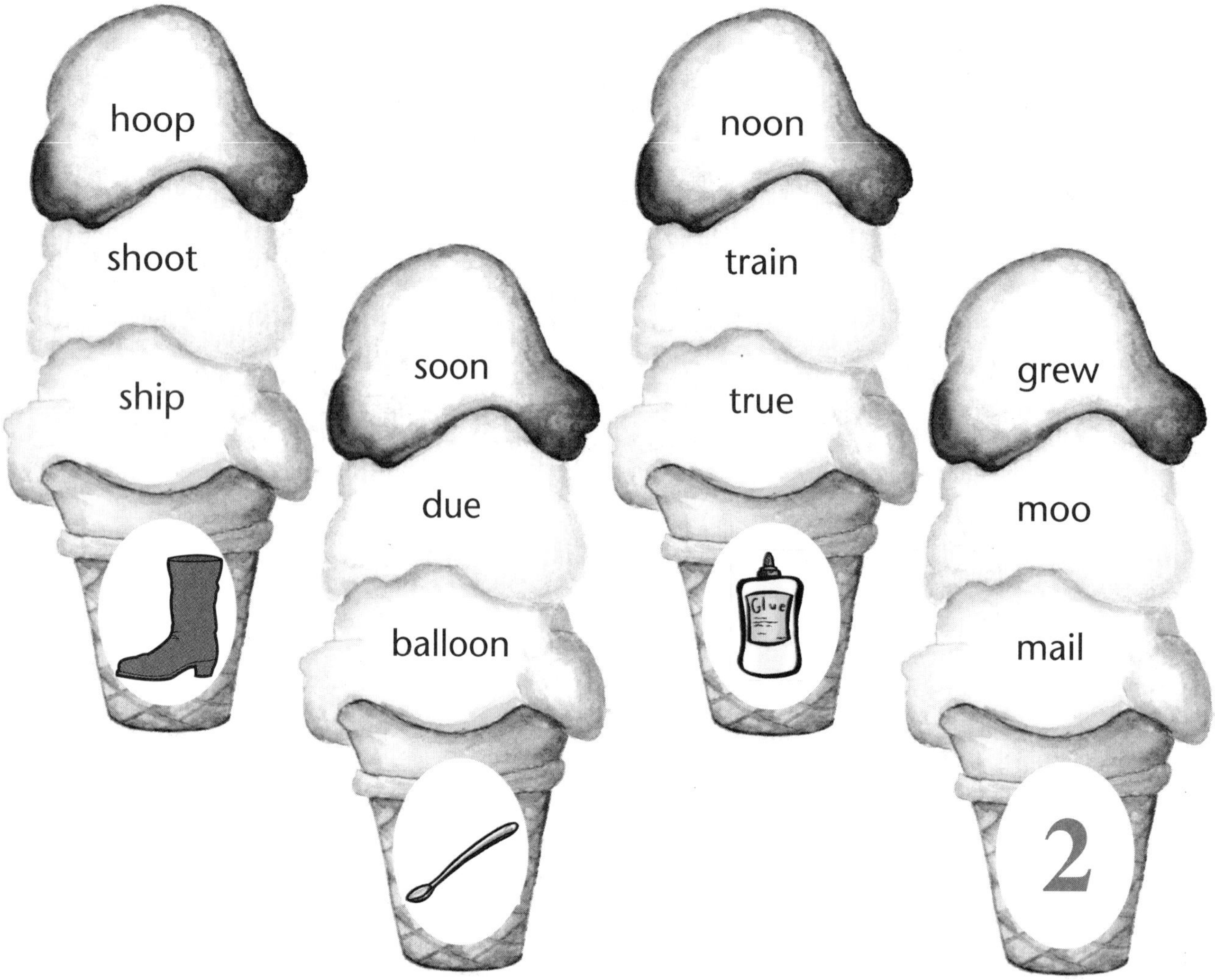


## Fill It In

Fill in the space beside the word that best fits the sentence.

1. Kate asked for two ________ of ice cream.

   ○ scales ○ scoops ○ scores

2. Kit wanted to get some ice cream ________ .

   ○ tea ○ too ○ tie

3. Kit dropped ice cream on the ________ chair.

   ○ bell ○ blow ○ blue

**Reading 2A: "Kate Kangaroo,"** pp. 117-20, Lesson 43
Phonics: using letter-sound association: *oo*, /ōō/ as in *cool*; *ue*, /ōō/ as in *blue*; and *ew*, /ōō/ as in *few*

# Lazy Kate

Name ____________________

## Choose One

Fill in the circle beside the word that best fits the sentence.

| | | |
|---|---|---|
| 1. Kate Kangaroo likes to ________. | ○ sleep | ○ eat |
| 2. Kate's house had a ________ roof. | ○ dirt | ○ grass |
| 3. Kate and Kit ________ to help. | ○ do not like | ○ like |
| 4. Kate made her bundle for Dad ________ she swam in the pond. | ○ before | ○ after |
| 5. The grasshopper ________ the bundle of grass. | ○ stole | ○ ate |
| 6. Kate ________ want to help fix the roof. | ○ did | ○ did not |
| 7. Kate was ________ as they hopped home to fix the roof. | ○ happy | ○ sad |
| 8. Kate took a nap under a ________. | ○ rock | ○ tree |

# Uncle Short Pays a Visit

kiss

## Paint It

Mr. and Mrs. Short have a guest. Uncle Short has come for a visit. Color the kangaroos beside the words that have a short vowel followed by two consonants.

spill  lip  cliff  left 

got  mitt  will  dot 

pick  chess  drip  glass 

## Write It

In each space, write a word from beside a kangaroo that you colored.

1. The cold wind gave me a ______________.

2. It is fun to catch a ball in a ______________.

3. A windowpane is made of ______________.

4. The ______________ is very steep.





**Reading 2A: "Kate Kangaroo,"** pp. 121-24, Lesson 44
Phonics: identifying short vowel words with closed syllable pattern *VCC*

# Kangaroo Feelings

Name ______________________________

### Choose One

Fill in the circle beside the word that shows how the kangaroo felt.

1. When Kate could not find the bundle of grass, how did she feel?

   ○ angry ○ sad ○ happy

2. When Dad, Kit, and Kate hopped home to fix the roof, how did Kate feel?

   ○ lonely ○ excited ○ happy

3. When Kate did not bring the tar, how did Dad feel?

   ○ sad ○ happy ○ excited

4. When Kate saw all the work not finished, how did she feel?

   ○ tired ○ sad ○ angry

### Choose Again

Circle *True* or *False.*

| | | |
|---|---|---|
| 1. Kate cut a bundle of grass. | True | False |
| 2. Kate brought the tar to Dad. | True | False |
| 3. The rain came into Kate's room. | True | False |
| 4. Dad put tar on Kate's roof. | True | False |

# Rule Breakers

A few word families break the closed syllable rule. These words have long vowels!

### Which Word?

Read the word family on the kangaroo. Write the best word in each sentence.

hold
gold
mold

The ______________ grew on the stale food.

The ring was made of ______________.

child
mild
wild

The ______________ horse kicked the man.

The summer wind was soft and ______________.

find
kind
grind

God says to be ______________.

Pete cannot ______________ his cap.

colt
bolt
jolt

A baby horse is a ______________.

A lightning ______________ hit the tree.





**Reading 2A: "Kate Kangaroo,"** pp. 125-27, Lesson 45
Phonics: reading long vowels in closed syllables: _old, _olt, _ind, _ild (an exception to the normal *VCC* sound)

# Who Am I?

Name ____________________

## Choose One

Read each clue. Write the correct answer in the blank.

| | |
|---|---|
| Kate | Kit |
| Dad | |

I helped gather bundles of grass and tar the roof. I did not quit.

Who am I?

____________________

I laid a roof on our hut and put tar on all but one room.

Who am I?

____________________

I never finished anything I started. At last, I learned a lesson about finishing the job.

Who am I?

____________________

**ECCLESIASTES 9:10**

*Whatsoever thy hand findeth to do, do it with thy might.*



## Mark It Off

Put a big ***X*** on the jobs that Kate did not do.

# Doggy Divide

**Remember:**
Words with double consonants in the middle are divided between those consonants.

### Write and Do

Find a word to match each clue. Write the word in the space with a dot to divide the syllables.

| daddy | bunny | yellow |
|---|---|---|
| dinner | sudden | |

1. a color ____________
2. quick ____________
3. an animal ____________
4. father ____________
5. a meal ____________

### Mark the Spot

Divide the underlined words into syllables.

1. The baby lay in a c r a d l e.
2. My u n c l e Bob drives a truck.
3. A tiger crept through the j u n g l e.
4. Did you learn your B i b l e verses?
5. The tiny t u r t l e peeked out of its shell.

**Remember:**
When a word ends with a consonant plus ***-le***, the consonant usually goes with the ***-le***.

# When Did It Happen?

Name ____________________

## Order It

Number the events in story order.

___

"Look at that pine tree," Dad said. "Maybe you will see some good friends of mine." They all stopped talking and stood still.

___

___

At home Mark went right to work. He cut out two holes in the sides of a milk carton. Dad put a wire hook in the feeder.

___

___

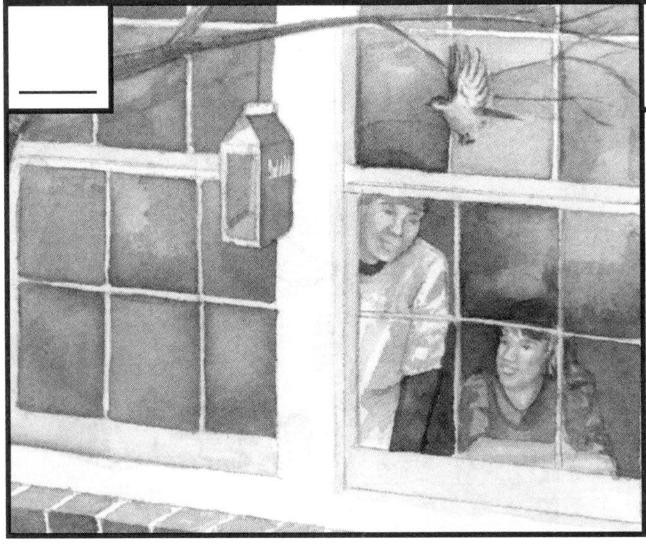

___

They walked by the pine tree where the chickadees were feeding.

"Look how fat they have become!" Mark said.

# Hush! Don't Make a Sound!

## ▸Match Up!

Draw a line from the word to the picture it names.

knife

calf

chalk

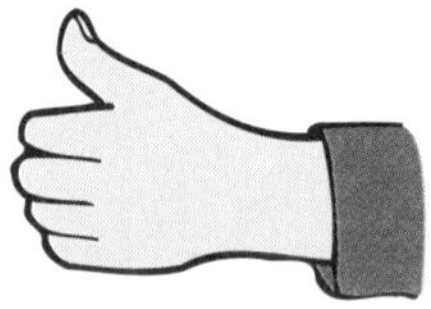

lamb

thumb

## ▸Make a Word

Use the letters in the box to complete the words.

| lk | mb | kn | lf |
|---|---|---|---|

1. *li*______

3. ______*ee*

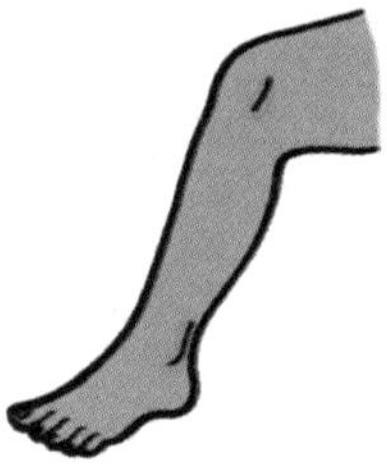

2. *ta*______

4. *ha*______

# See What Happens!

Name ______________________________

## ▸ Choose One

Read what happened first. Fill in the circle beside what it caused to happen.

**This happened . . . . . . . . . . . . so this happened.**

| This happened | so this happened |
|---|---|
| 1. The chickadees ate up all the seeds. | ○ Becky put out seeds every day.<br>○ The chickadees never came back. |
| 2. Mark whistled at a chickadee. | ○ It left.<br>○ It whistled back. |
| 3. Mark and Becky put seeds in their hands. | ○ The chickadees sat in the tree.<br>○ The chickadees took the seeds. |
| 4. A chickadee called to Mark and Becky from a cedar tree. | ○ Becky went to get seed.<br>○ Mark and Becky whistled at the birds. |
| 5. Mother called for the children to come in out of the cold. | ○ Mark and Becky came inside and had hot apple cider.<br>○ Mark and Becky fed the birds. |

# Letter Disguises

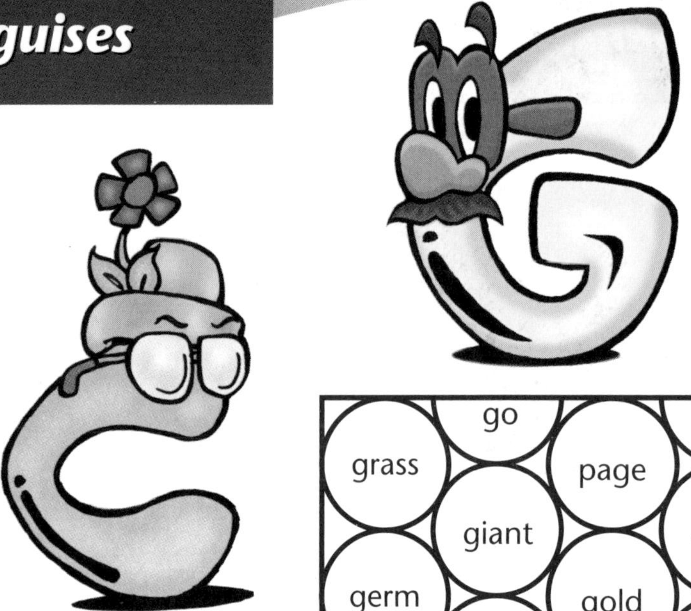

go gave

grass page groan

giant gem game

germ gold gift

gray grab growl

wage ledge gone

goat Roger grow

ginger cage gloss

rage gap greet

## Color It

Color the circle green
if the word has the ***j*** sound
of ***g*** as in ***giraffe***.

## Color Again

Say the name of each picture.
Color it if you hear the ***s*** sound of ***c*** as in ***center***.

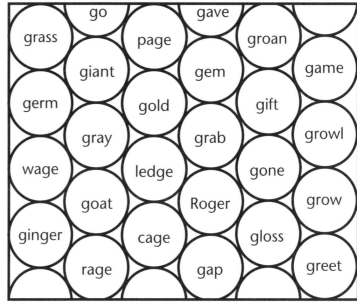

# Yummy for the Tummy

______________________________
Name

## Make It

Color only the things that you would need to make a banana split.

## Get in Line

Number these steps in order as you would do them to make the banana split. The first one is done for you.

_____ Put chocolate sauce on the ice cream.

_____ Put three scoops of ice cream on the banana.

__1__ Ask your mom or dad to cut the banana in half.

_____ Put whipped cream on the chocolate sauce.

_____ Put a cherry on top of the whipped cream.

_____ Put the cut banana in a dish.

_____ Eat the banana split.

# Strange Judge

**Remember:**
These words will have a long vowel before ***-ge*** and a short vowel before ***-dge***.

## ▸Read and Write

Read the word families. Write one of the words to complete the sentence.

| | | |
|---|---|---|
| age, rage, page, wage, cage, stage |  | The ill chickadee was kept in a ________ until it was better. |
| edge, ledge, hedge, wedge |  | The hunters jumped their horses ________ over the ________ of roses. |
| Madge, badge, badger |  | When my class went to see the fire trucks, the fireman gave me a ________. |

## ▸Fill It In

Fill in the circle next to the best answer.

| | |
|---|---|
| 1. Something very big is ___.<br>○ huge ○ page ○ badge | 2. To jump out of the way is to ___.<br>○ ledge ○ dodge ○ pledge |
| 3. A path over a stream is a ___.<br>○ ridge ○ rage ○ bridge | 4. A slice of pie is a ___.<br>○ wage ○ wedge ○ cage |
| 5. One animal is a ___.<br>○ badger ○ edge ○ huge | 6. A play can be done on a ___.<br>○ dodge ○ sledge ○ stage |

# Like a Blanket

Name ______________________________

*"She gazed out the window, thinking that the sky looked like a puffy, gray blanket."*

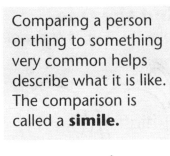

Comparing a person or thing to something very common helps describe what it is like. The comparison is called a **simile.**

## Match It Up

Draw a line to complete each simile.

1. He can swim like a __________ .

2. The cloud looked like a fluffy __________ .

3. Amy can sing like a __________ .

4. The baby crawled as slowly as a __________ .

5. The giant stood as tall as a __________ .

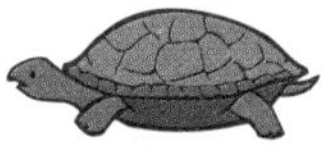

## Which One?

Circle *True* or *False* for each sentence.

| | | |
|---|---|---|
| 1. Mom told Amber to put Buttercup in the barn. | True | False |
| 2. Amber said her glasses fit fine. | True | False |
| 3. Amber took a carrot to Buttercup. | True | False |
| 4. Amber liked the smell of the sweet hay. | True | False |
| 5. Kim called Amber Owl Face. | True | False |
| 6. A tiny mouse made a little cry in the barn. | True | False |

# I Can't Hear You!

## Find the Ones

Color the frames of the glasses that have silent *gh* words.

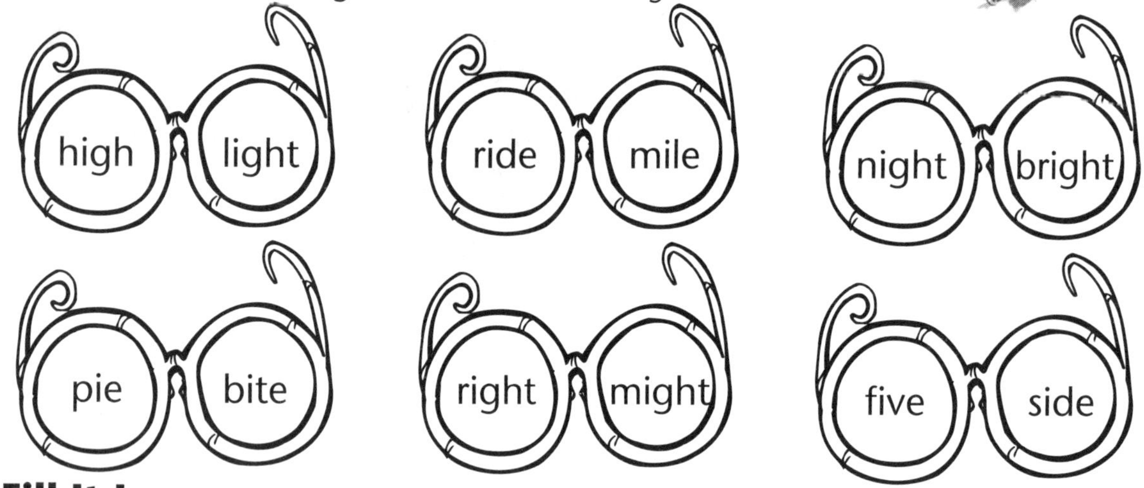


## Fill It In

Write the words from the box in each space.

| | |
|---|---|
| flashlight<br>nightstand | 1. Trisha keeps her ______________ on the ______________. |
| sunlight<br>bright | 2. The ______________ is very ______________ today. |
| night<br>light | 3. God made the moon to give ______________ at ______________. |
| high<br>Almighty | 4. ______________ God rules on ______________. |

# Who Wants to Know?

Name ____________________

**Pick One**
Put an ***X*** in the box under the correct answer.

| | Mom | Amber | Daddy |
|---|---|---|---|
| "What's the matter, Little One?" | | | |
| "Will you let me help you?" | | | |
| "Where did you find it?" | | | |
| "Will he die?" | | | |
| "Would you like to help me, Amber?" | | | |
| "Can I keep him for a pet?" | | | |
| "Do I have an owl face?" | | | |

# The Owls' Ways

## Choose a Word

Read the stories and use one of the highlighted words to answer the question.

Little owls seem to enjoy learning to hunt. They join an older owl and watch for something to catch. Owls do not eat spoiled food. They like to hunt and kill fresh food.

Owls help farmers by catching mice, voles, and rabbits that can destroy gardens.

1. What food do owls not like?

 ______________________

2. What do mice, voles, and rabbits do to gardens?

 ______________________

3. How do little owls seem to feel about learning to hunt?

 They ______________________ it.

Roy was an owl. He was the best hunter in the garden. Every night he went to the garden to hunt.

When he was little, he began picking up anything he saw in the garden soil. Once, he picked up a shiny coin the farmer had dropped. Another time, he swooped down and scooped up a coil of rope.

One night he tried to pick up a kettle of water heating over a small fire the farmer had made in the garden. But Roy missed, and his foot dipped into the boiling water. His foot was all right, but it was red and sore. Roy went home a wiser owl.

1. What did the farmer drop in the garden?

 ______________________

2. Why did water hurt the owl's foot?

 It was ______________________ water.

# Are You Puzzled?

Name ______________________

## ▸ Work It

Work the puzzle. Use the words in the box.

| | | |
|---|---|---|
| dashed | friends | glasses |
| splint | Smarty | snorted |
| apple | stall | gentle |

### *Across*

1. Buttercup ______ as Amber patted her neck.
4. Amber wanted to show the owl to her ______ .
5. Amber was very ______ as she folded the scarf around the owl.
6. Amber found the owl at the back of the ______ .
8. Amber said her ______ pinched her nose.

### *Down*

1. The owl needed a ______ for his broken bones.
2. Amber ______ to the barn.
3. Kim named the owl ______ .
7. Amber took an ______ to Buttercup.

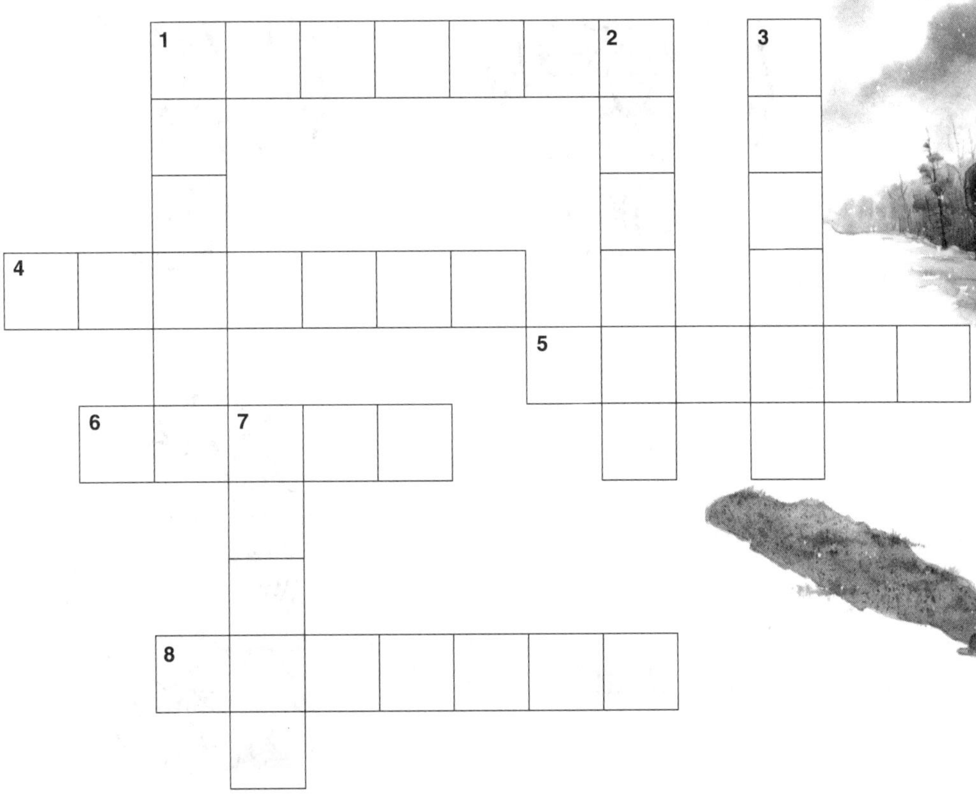

# A Silent Partner

## Draw It

Draw a pair of glasses on each owl that has a silent *l*.

balk

cloud

palm

jolt

walk

slam

## Which One?

Circle the best answer to complete each sentence.

1. Mrs. Smith wrote with blue ( chalk, claws ).
2. The waves of the sea are very ( clam, calm ).
3. The corn grew on the tall ( slide, stalk ).
4. I like to ( tool, talk ) on the phone to Granny.

# Owls

Name ______________________________

## Match Them

Draw lines to match each sentence with the correct picture.

Owls hunt for their food at night.

The great horned owl has long tufts of feathers that look like ears, but they do not hear with them.

One kind of owl, the snowy owl, is pure white with dark flecks.

God has made the owl able to hide in plain sight.

Owls can turn their heads almost all the way around.

# Wrens Wreck Wrestler's Wrist Wrap

The letter ***w*** is silent before the letter ***r***.

## Which One?

Circle the silent ***w*** word on each owl.

## Fill It In

Use a silent ***w*** word from above to complete each sentence.

1. I will ____________ up the shoes and give them to Ben for his birthday.

2. Dad used a ____________ to fix the pipes.

3. Mrs. Gray wants to buy a new pen to ____________ her letters.

4. Ted broke his ____________ when he fell off the ladder.

5. Janene made a pretty ____________ from pine cones.

# Problems! Problems!

Name ______________________________

## Read and Choose

Read each problem. Fill in the circle beside the best choice to solve the problem.

1. Tom knocked a book off of Amber's desk.

   ○ Tom will leave the book on the floor.

   ○ Tom will pick the book up and put it back.

   ○ Tom will sit down and read the book.

2. Three girls want to swing, but there are only two swings on the playground.

   ○ The girls will take turns swinging.

   ○ All three girls will go away and not swing.

   ○ The first two girls who run to the swings will get to swing.

3. Bill broke his arm.

   ○ Ted will play baseball with Bill when his arm is better.

   ○ Ted will help with Bill's lunch tray.

   ○ Ted will wave to Bill each morning.

4. The fireman rang the alarm as Mrs. Dale told the class to quickly get in line.

   ○ Dave was the first to get in line.

   ○ Dave kept reading his book.

   ○ Dave tripped Ed as he got in line.

# The Order of the Day

## Order Them

Color the first letter of each word yellow. Write the words in alphabetical order.

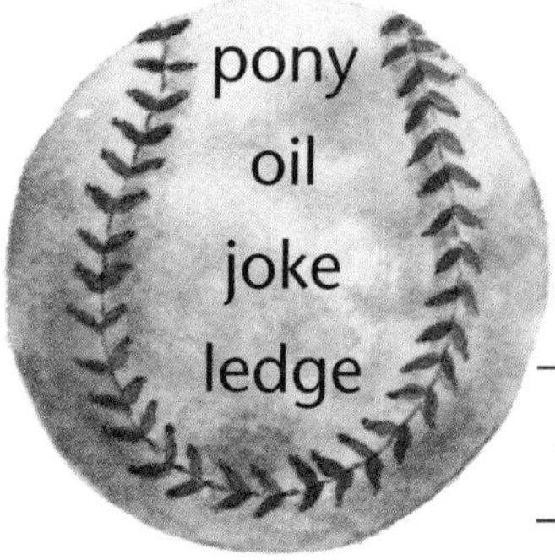

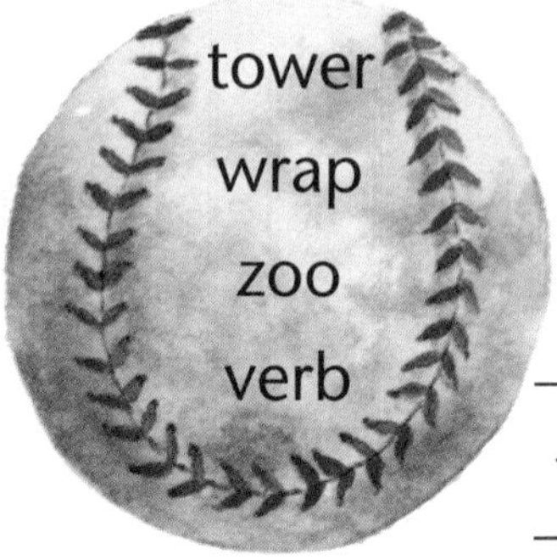

# Batter Up

Name ______________________

### ▸Draw It

Read and follow each direction to finish the picture.

1. Put a baseball mitt on Brad's hand. Make it brown.
2. Draw two trees in the park. Make the leaves green and the trunks brown.
3. Give one of the boys a baseball bat. Make it black.
4. Draw a baseball cap on each boy. Make one blue, one red, and one orange.
5. Draw a baseball in Digger's mouth. Make it brown and white.
6. Draw a baseball mitt for Mike and one for Troy. Make them brown.

# Play Ball!

## Ring It

Circle the words that have a long vowel sound.

## Fill It In

Complete each sentence. Use the words in the box.

| | | | | |
|---|---|---|---|---|
| five | safe | slide | chase | hope |

1. Mike made a long ________________ into third base.

2. The umpire called, "________________!"

3. Andy's team won by ________________ runs.

4. Mike and Brad ________________ to win the next game.

5. Brad let Digger ________________ the balls.

94

**Reading 2A: "Digger Does It,"** pp. 167-69, Lesson 58
Phonics: reading long vowel words with marker *e*

# Who Did It?

Name ______________________________

## ▸ Pick One

Put an ***X*** in the box under the correct answer.

| | | | | |
|---|---|---|---|---|
| 1. Who went to get the phone for Brad? | | | | |
| 2. Who was on a trip? | | | | |
| 3. Who let Brad go to the park? | | | | |
| 4. Who told Digger to get the ball? | | | | |
| 5. Who met Troy and Mike at the park? | | | | |
| 6. Who brought surprises home? | | | | |
| 7. Who said, "Keep your eye on the ball"? | | | | |
| 8. Who had a surprise for Dad? | | | | |

# Mice Cage

gate
cake
prince
circle
age
goat
space
gentle
huge

## Find the Ones

Write the words in the cage that have the soft *g* as in *cage*.

______ ______ ______

Write the words in the cage that have the soft *c* as in *mice.*

______ ______ ______

## Fill It In

Use one of the words you wrote to complete each sentence.

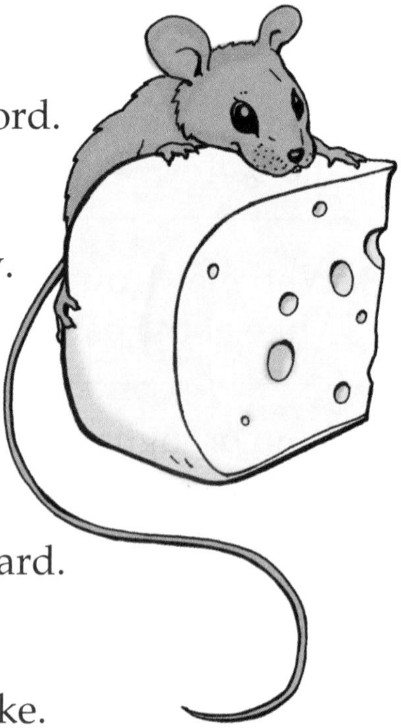

1. Draw a ______ around the right word.
2. Be ______ when you pet the puppy.
3. The ______ wore his crown.
4. Pete has a ______ tree in his back yard.
5. Please leave a ______ in line for Mike.
6. Do you know how to tell the ______ of a tree?

© 1999 BJU Press. Reproduction prohibited.

96

**Reading 2A: "Digger Does It,"** pp. 170-72, Lesson 59
Phonics: reading words with the soft *g* and *c*

# Service Dogs

Name ____________________

## ▸Work It

Use words from the box to complete the crossword puzzle.

***Across***

1. A service dog must be healthy and _____ .
4. Some service dogs use _____ to hold things for their owners.
6. Service dogs can help their owners get out of _____ .
7. A _____ will teach the dog what to do.
8. Service dogs go to _____ for a long time.

***Down***

2. Service dogs are trained to help people with _____ .
3. A service dog has a _____ and a harness.
5. Service dogs are _____ and will not harm you.

| | |
|---|---|
| leash | backpacks |
| wheelchairs | friendly |
| gentle | disabilities |
| school | trainer |

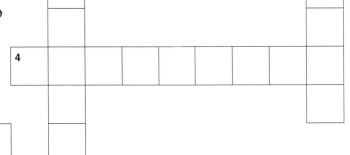

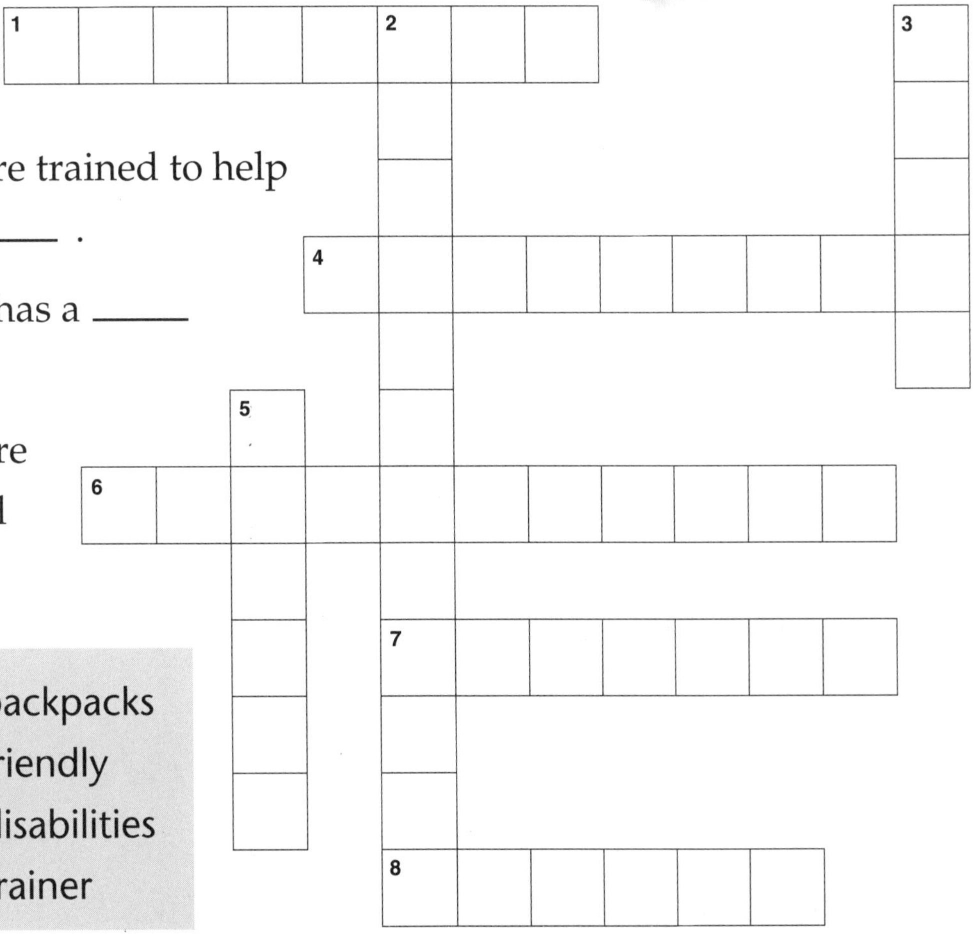

# Claude's Paw

## Find the Ones

Claude is learning to shake, but he does not shake hands. He is using his paw.

On each bone, circle the word that has the same sound as *paw*.

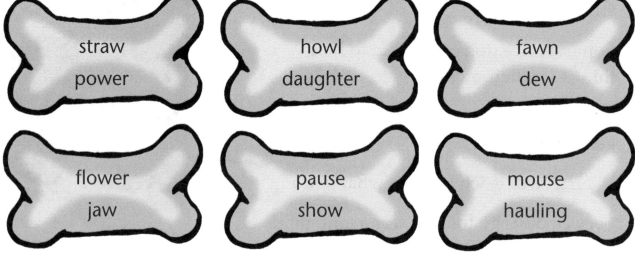

| | | |
|---|---|---|
| straw<br>power | howl<br>daughter | fawn<br>dew |
| flower<br>jaw | pause<br>show | mouse<br>hauling |

## Fill It In

Complete each sentence. Use the words in the box.

| taught | haul | claws | caught | hawk |
|---|---|---|---|---|

1. We saw the ________________ fly to the top of a tree.

2. Paul ________________ his dog to catch a ball.

3. Eric helped Dad ________________ the wood out to the barn.

4. The hawk has sharp ________________ for catching its food.

5. Tom almost ________________ the baseball.

# Tell Me About It

Name ______________________________

## Ring It

Draw a circle around the adjective that tells about each one of these in the story. You may need to look back over the story.

| | | |
|---|---|---|
| 1. Wren's yawn | loud | quiet |
| 2. Crow's feathers | clean | dusty |
| 3. brook | wet | dry |
| 4. wind | warm | cool |
| 5. branch | high | low |

## Match It Up

Draw a line from the picture to the adjectives that tell about it.

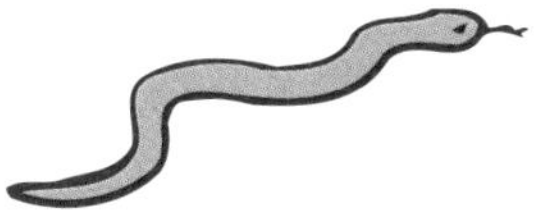

long and slender

warm and golden

soft and furry

wet and cold

fast and shiny

red and sweet

# The Dog and Her Shadow

When ***y*** changes to ***i***, it still says /ē/.
*(happy, happier)*

## Pick One

Write the correct word in the blank.

1. Daisy, the dog, ____________ some meat in her mouth.
carry carried

2. She wanted to cross the river and put her ____________ paws into the water.
furry furriest

3. When Daisy saw her shadow in the water, she felt ____________
greedy greediest
and grabbed for her shadow's meat.

4. Her meat dropped into the water. Daisy ran up and down the shore. Thorns from the ____________ scratched and cut her.
berry berries

5. Daisy ____________, but she could not get her meat back.
hurry hurried
Her greed made her lose everything.

# Surprise!

Name ______________________

## Get in Line

Number these sentences from "Wolf Pack" in story order.

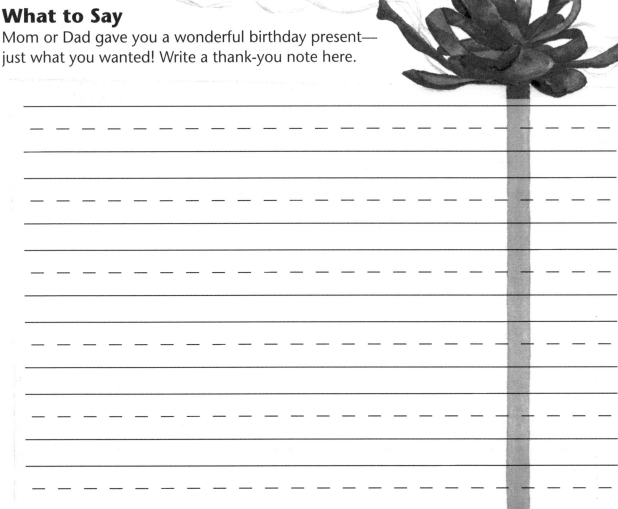

_____ Father read a verse from the Bible.

_____ Mother and Father sang a song to wake her.

_____ She got a cap and sled for her birthday.

_____ The girl was asleep in the kitchen.

_____ She ate her treat of cookies and coffee.

## What to Say

Mom or Dad gave you a wonderful birthday present—just what you wanted! Write a thank-you note here.

# Wrist and Thumb

### Which One?

Fill in the circle beside the word that belongs in each sentence.

Beth _____ a letter to Kim.

- ○ wrote
- ○ wren
- ○ wrist

Mom hung a _____ on the door.

- ○ wrap
- ○ write
- ○ wreath

Tom broke his _____ .

- ○ wrong
- ○ wrist
- ○ wrinkle

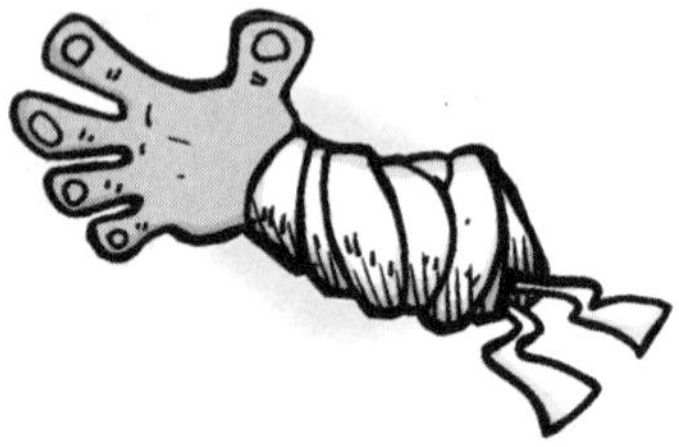

Ned will _____ the gift.

- ○ wring
- ○ wrench
- ○ wrap

### Write One

Add ***wr*** or ***mb*** to make a word to match each picture.

| | |
|---|---|
| _____ite  | co_____  |
| plu_____er  | _____ench  |
| li_____  | _____inkles  |
| _____ing  | la_____  |

# The Rest of the Story

Name ______________________________

## What Next?

Read each story. Fill in the circle beside what happened next.

At Sam's birthday party, the boys played a lot of fun games. Mother called everyone to the table for some cake. Sam blew out all eight candles while the boys sang to him.

- ○ Sam went to sleep.
- ○ Sam opened his birthday gifts.
- ○ Mother made a cake.

Bill and his dad went camping last weekend. They packed their tent, sleeping bags, food, dishes, and a flashlight. After the tent was set up, Bill's dad made a campfire.

- ○ They drove to the campsite.
- ○ They cooked lunch over the campfire.
- ○ They put out the campfire.

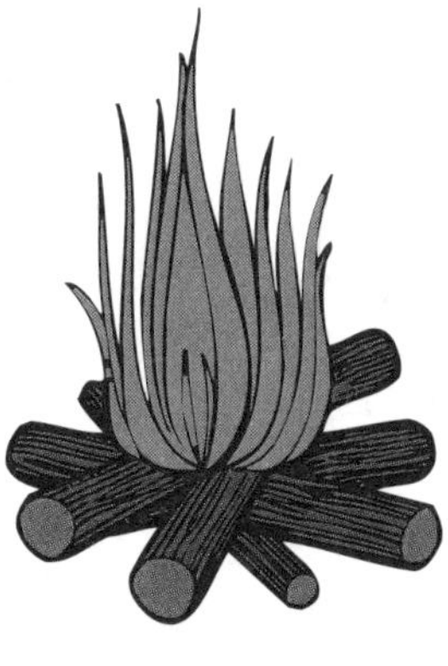

Grace wanted to surprise Mom and Dad Saturday morning. She went to the kitchen and made pancakes. Grace put a plate full of pancakes on a tray. She picked a rose from the garden and put it in a glass of water on the tray.

- ○ Grace ate the pancakes.
- ○ Grace got out some flour and eggs.
- ○ Grace took the tray to Mom and Dad.

# Red Head

Sometimes ***ea*** sounds like short ***e***.

## ▸Listen

Read each sentence. Circle the picture that has the same vowel sound as the word in color.

| | ē | ĕ |
|---|---|---|
| 1. The dog's fleas made him scratch. |  | 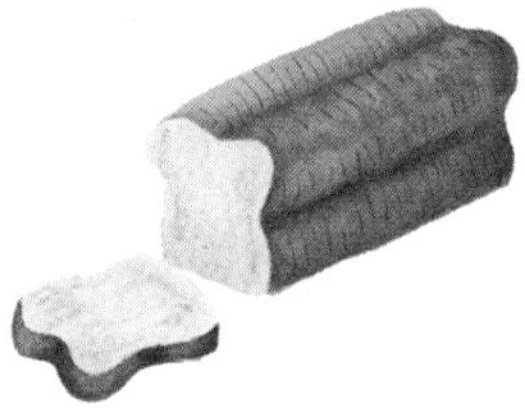 |
| 2. Mother spread jam on our toást. |  |  |
| 3. Are you ready for school? |  | 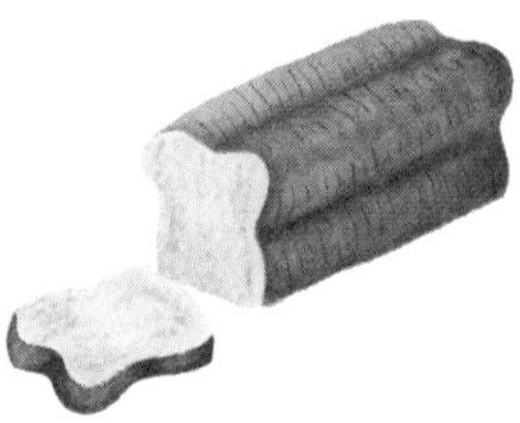 |
| 4. On a chilly day our breath looks like steam. |  | 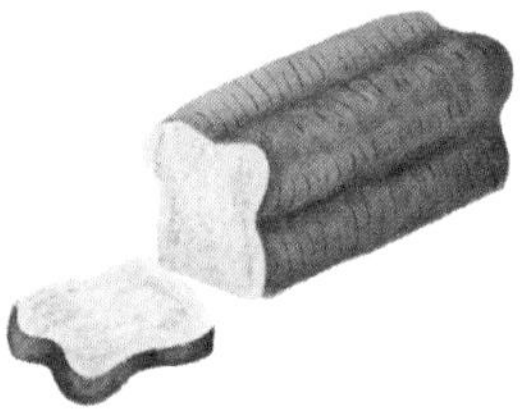 |
| 5. We like to keep our classroom clean. |  | 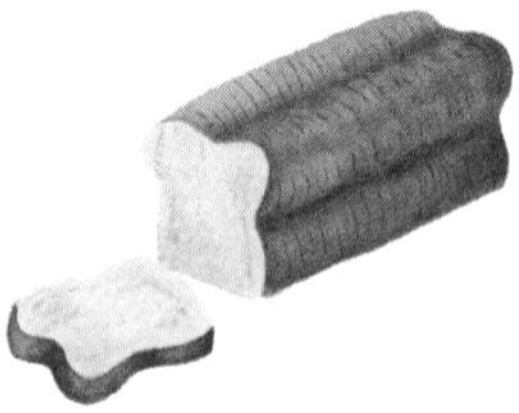 |
| 6. May I please have a cupcake for lunch? |  |  |

# Read and Think

Name ______________________

**Psalm 91:15**

*He shall call upon me, and I will answer him: I will be with him in trouble.*

## Choose One

Fill in the circle beside the answer that best fits the sentence.

1. Lapland's sky does not stay _____ for long in the winter.
   - ○ dark
   - ○ blue
   - ○ light

2. When it is dark, the wolves _____.
   - ○ go to sleep
   - ○ come out for food
   - ○ cut holes in the lake

3. The girl slept in the _____.
   - ○ bedroom
   - ○ kitchen
   - ○ living room

4. The soft present was a bright red _____.
   - ○ stocking cap
   - ○ sled
   - ○ overcoat

5. Father cut holes in the frozen lake _____.
   - ○ to go swimming
   - ○ to get a drink
   - ○ to get water for the animals

6. The verse said _____ would take care of the girl.
   - ○ Mother
   - ○ Father
   - ○ God

## Ring It

Follow the instructions.

| | |
|---|---|
| Circle the things that are used in a kitchen. | 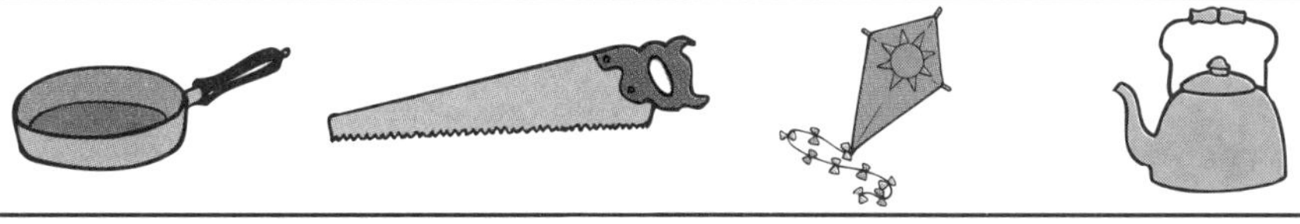 |
| Circle the things that are used at school. |  |
| Circle the animals that are pets. |  |
| Circle the things that make music. |  |

# Contraction Construction

1

has n_t

Take out a letter or letters.

2

has n_t

Put in an ***apostrophe.***

3

hasn't

Put the two words together.

## ▸Make One

Write the contraction of the two words.

was not ____________ are not ____________

could not ____________ have not ____________

would not ____________ is not ____________

does not ____________ did not ____________

## ▸Fill It In

Use a contraction from the box to complete each sentence.

| isn't | doesn't |
|---|---|
| aren't | |

1. A wolf ____________ usually come out in the daytime.

2. A wolf howl ____________ a cheerful sound.

3. Wolves ____________ friendly animals.

# Under and Below

Name ________________________________

## Find the Two

Circle the two synonyms in each set of words.

| | | | |
|---|---|---|---|
| road<br>desk<br>highway | lake<br>farewell<br>goodbye | center<br>middle<br>down | singing<br>tapping<br>hitting |
| tell<br>say<br>run | cold<br>chilly<br>shiny | clean<br>find<br>locate | firmly<br>sadly<br>strongly |

## It's the Same

Circle the synonym for the word in the box.

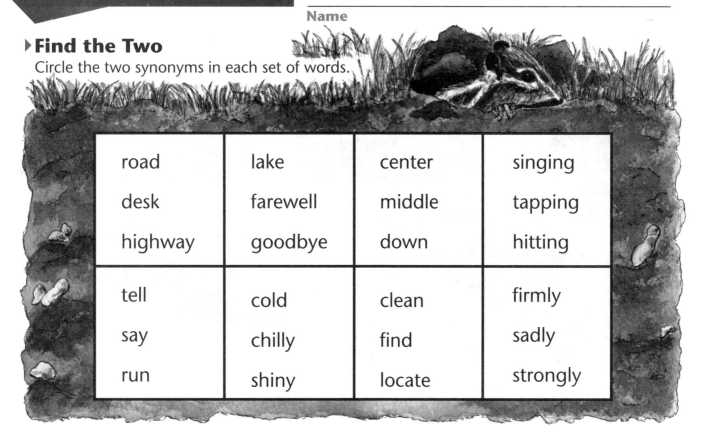

1. The citizens were talking at Glass Pond.

   screaming   speaking   singing

2. Chipmunk spoke quietly to his friends.

   softly   quickly   loudly

3. Chipmunk is bigger than Ant.

   purple   larger   tiny

4. Chipmunk started his trip to find a king.

   finished   wanted   began

# Off to Find a King

### ▸Write It

Follow the path to find a king. Use one word from the *red* box and one word from the *blue* box to make a compound word to match each picture.

| | | |
|---|---|---|
| rain | wind | |
| ant | barn | dog |

| | | |
|---|---|---|
| hill | house | |
| bow | yard | mill |

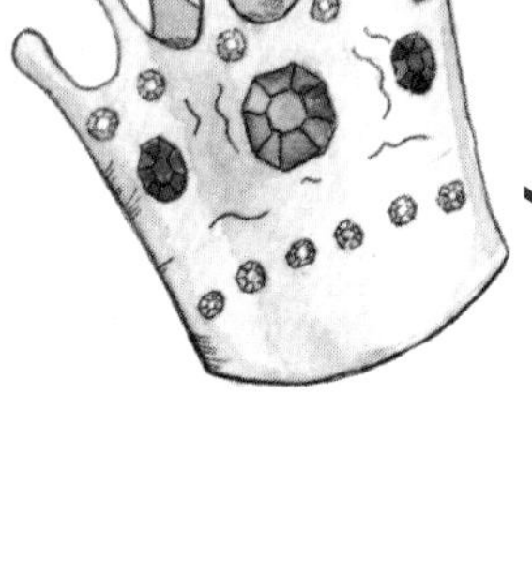

# Name That Animal

Name ____________________

## Which One?

Circle the word that best completes each sentence.

The owl who traveled with Chipmunk was named ( Hiss, Hoot ).

He was named for the ( smell, sound ) he made.

## Match Them Up

Name each animal for the sound he makes.

| Squeak | Purr | Hiss | Quack | Baa-Baa | Moo | Cluck | Grunt |
|---|---|---|---|---|---|---|---|

____________, the duck

____________, the mouse

____________, the hen

____________, the cow

____________, the snake

____________, the cat

____________, the pig

____________, the sheep

## Tell a Tale

Begin a short story using two of these characters' names in an opening sentence. Finish the story on your own paper.

# A Shiny Brass Cobweb

## Paint It

Color each **-y** word and its matching word the same color. Use a different color for each pair of words.

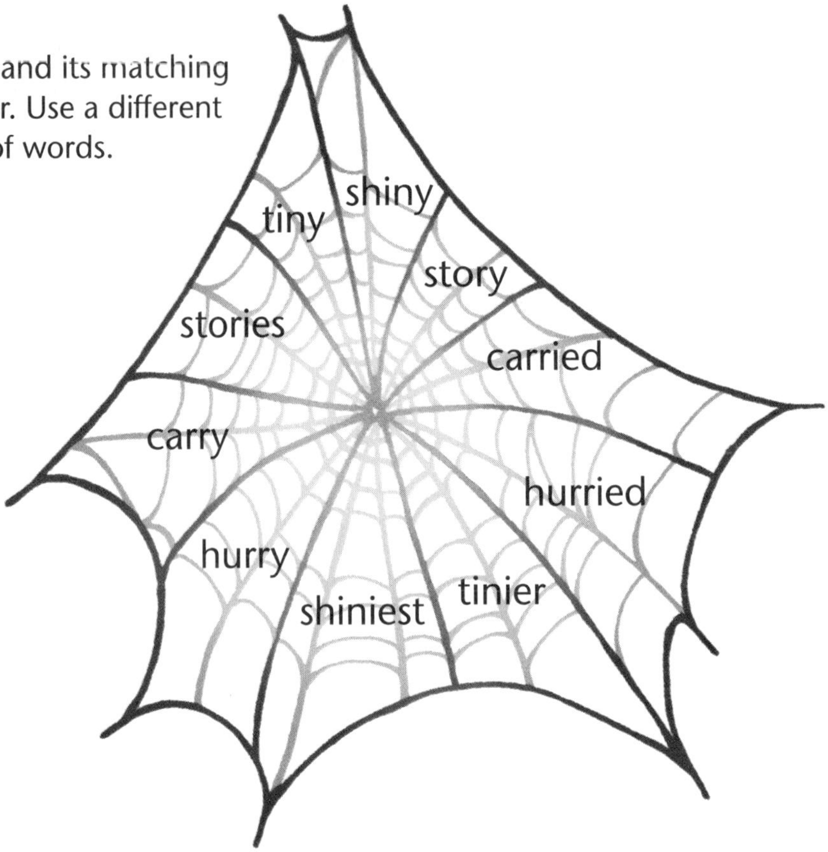


## Fill It In

Read the sentences. Choose a word from the cobweb to complete each sentence.

1. Ant is ____________ than Chipmunk.

2. The gate is a ____________ brass cobweb.

3. Chipmunk ____________ to find a king.

4. Hoot ____________ Chipmunk on his back.

5. Will Chipmunk have many ____________ to tell?

# And Then What Happened?

Name ______________________

## Mark the One

Put an ***X*** beside the sentence in each set that tells what happened first.

____ Raccoons tie up Fox and Chipmunk.

____ Fox grabs some corn.

____ Chipmunk lands on Fox.

____ Fox and Chipmunk find seeds with sharp prickles.

____ Raccoons plant the seeds.

____ Fox tells the Raccoons *not* to plant the seeds.

## Get in Line

Number these sentences ***1-2-3-4-5*** in story order.

____ Fox runs off without Chipmunk.

____ The tree falls over.

____ Raccoons fight each other with swords.

____ Chipmunk runs away.

____ The hills begin growing in the field.

# You're the Apple of My Eye—You Are!

## Write One

Make a contraction from each set of words.

you are ____________________

we are ____________________

they are ____________________

## Use One

Write one of the contractions you made to complete each sentence.

1. "What am I?" asked Snail.

   "____________________ a snail," answered Crab.

2. "What are you?" asked Butterfly.

   "____________________ moths," said the Moths.

3. "Am I green?" asked Grasshopper.

   "Yes, ____________________ green," answered Cricket.

4. "What are you doing?" asked Lamb.

   "____________________ hopping," said the Bunnies.

5. "Are the flowers blooming yet?" asked Bee.

   "Yes, ____________________ blooming," said Hummingbird.

Name ______________________________

## Match Them

Write the number of the title that matches each picture.

1. "Philip and His Farm"
2. "A King for Brass Cobweb"
3. "Kangaroos and Koalas"
4. "Little Lost Lamb"
5. "Kate Kangaroo"
6. "Mice"
7. "Cheerful Chickadees"
8. "Be Wise About Owls"
9. "Owl Face"
10. "The Crow and the Pitcher"
11. "Wolf Pack"
12. "Digger Does It"

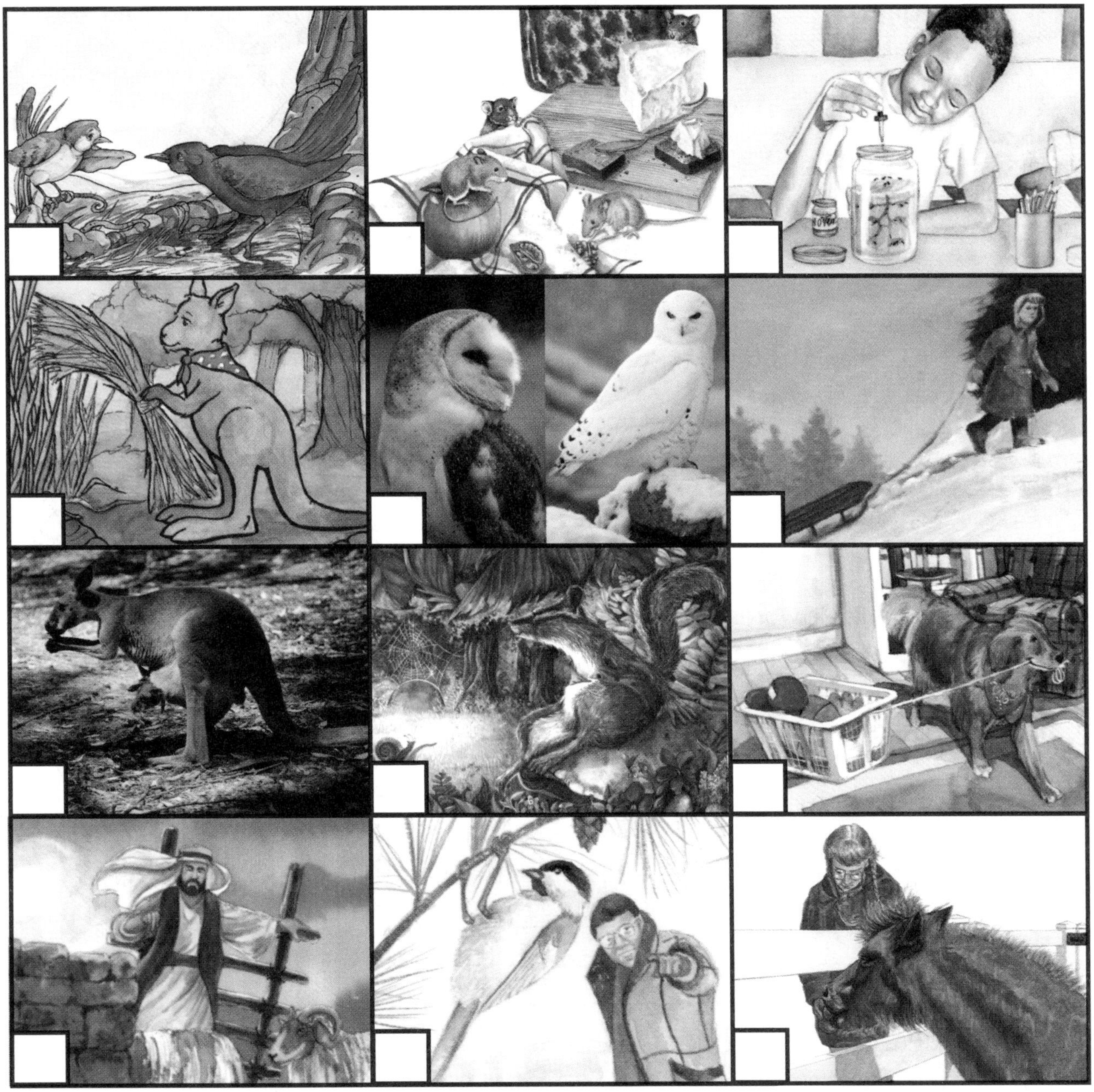

# Countable Syllables

## Count It

Read the word. Write the number of syllables on the leaf.

brave
underground
begins
thanks
slowly

untrue
show
bumblebee
whisper
understood

found
peppermint
carpenter
wise
turtle

## Use It

Use one of the 1-syllable words in this sentence.

1. Turtle was ____________________.

Use one of the 2-syllable words in this sentence.

2. Fox was ____________________.

Use one of the 3-syllable words in this sentence.

3. Chipmunk ____________________ what it meant to be a good, wise, brave king.

# A Character's Character

Name ______________________

## Which One?

Circle the main character of "A King for Brass Cobweb."

## Match Them Up

What did you learn about the other characters? Draw a line from what happened in the story to what it tells about the character.

| | |
|---|---|
| 1. Hoot was afraid of thunder and rain. | • He was not wise. |
| 2. Fox ran away and left Chipmunk with the Raccoons. | • He was not brave. |
| 3. Turtle trusted Snake and his offer to help. | • He was not true. |

## Choose Again

What did you learn about the main character? Circle the word to complete the sentence.

1. Chipmunk agreed to leave Brass Cobweb and search for a king. Chipmunk was _____ .
   unselfish    crabby
2. He kept Turtle from Snake's harm. Chipmunk was _____ .
   sad    true
3. He flew on Hoot's back high up in the sky. Chipmunk was _____ .
   unhappy    brave
4. He didn't trust Fox and his ways. Chipmunk was _____ .
   wise    helpful
5. He kept searching for a king even though he wanted to go home. Chipmunk was _____ .
   rude    faithful
6. He did not know that he would be the king for Brass Cobweb. Chipmunk was _____ .
   humble    sneaky

# Winning Batter

## Color It

Color all the double consonants.

s i t    s i t t i n g

b a t    b a t t e r

## Crown It

Read each sentence. Use the underlined word to make a new word for the blank.

1. Mrs. Short will sit here, and Mr. Short

is ________________ there.

2. Give a bat to

the ________________.

3. If we win the game, Uncle Short will

hit in the ________________ run.

Name ______________________

## Title It

Read the list in each treasure chest.
Write the number of the correct title in the blank.

1. "Cheerful Chickadees"
2. "Philip and His Farm"
3. "Digger Does It"
4. "Wolf Pack"
5. "Owl Face"

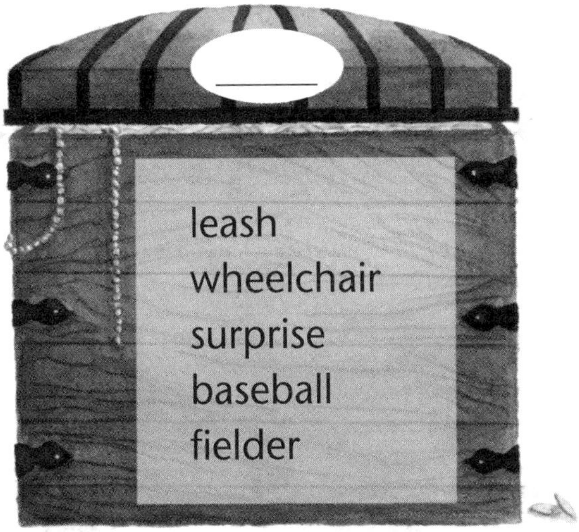


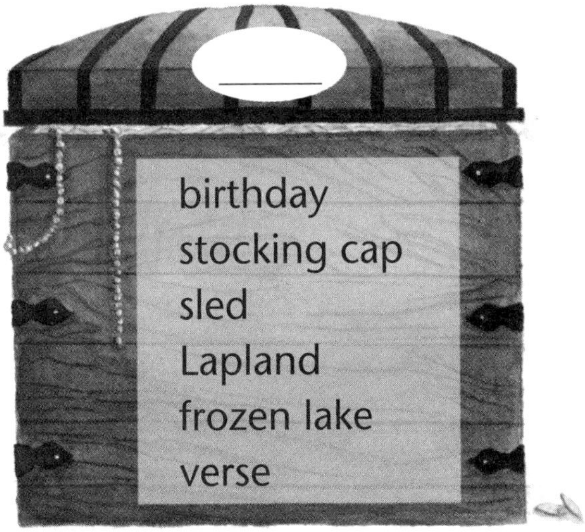


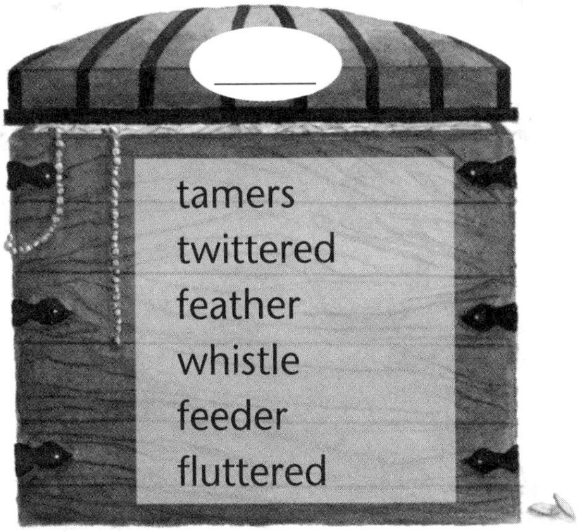


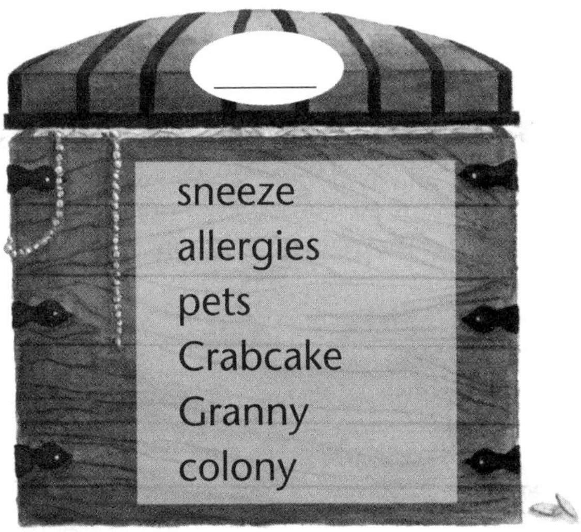


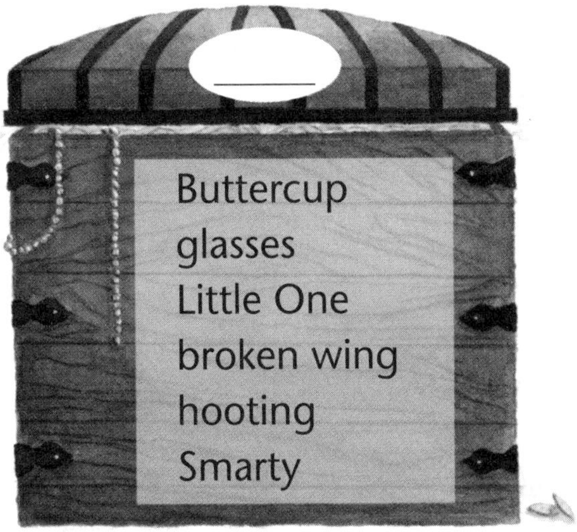

# Old Gold Scroll

## Match Them Up

Write the number of the sentence that matches each picture.

1. The diver found a chest of gold.
2. Are the children very cold?
3. We saw a squirrel scolding a blue jay.
4. The scribe read from his scroll.
5. The car began to roll down the hill.
6. Does everyone pay the toll at the gate?

_____

_____

_____

_____

_____

_____

## Ring It

Draw a circle around the word that best completes each sentence.

1. Mike did not want to race his _____ yet.

   cost    cold    colt

2. Mother _____ Tom to put away his toys.

   toll    told    toad

3. We ate _____ of the cookies while they were hot.

   most    mold    mole

4. The hardware store sells nuts and _____ .

   bonds    bows    bolts

5. He tied his horse to a _____.

   pot    post    pop



**Reading 2A: "Jonathan's Treasure,"** pp. 224-27, Lesson 71
Comprehension: matching related pictures and sentences
Phonics: using letter-sound association: /ō/ in _olt, _ost, _old

# Choices and Cents

Name

Think of a time when you had to choose what to do with your money. What was the choice? How did you spend your money?

## Draw It

Draw a picture of what you bought with your money.

## Tell It

Write a story about what you thought and what you did.

# Wanted— The Vowel Gang

## Write the Ones

Write the missing vowel in each word.

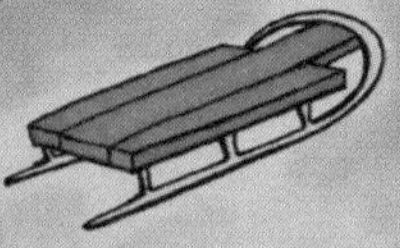

sl_____d

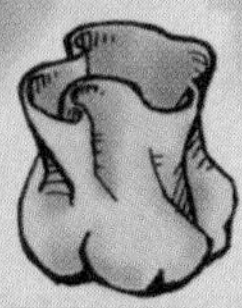

s_____ck

sw_____m

h_____p

j_____mp

sw_____ng

## Use the Ones

Use the words you finished in these sentences.

1. We can __________ down the snowy hill.
2. May I please have a turn on the __________?
3. Ben can __________ like a rabbit.
4. The class put all their trash in a __________.
5. Who will __________ rope with me?
6. Brad likes to __________ in the pool.

# Candy?

Name ______________________________

## Find One

Fill in the circle beside the best word for the sentence.

1. The lady gave Jonathan five ______ .
   - ○ chickens ○ pennies ○ jars
2. Jonathan wanted to buy ______ with his pennies.
   - ○ fish ○ apples ○ candy
3. Jonathan sat on the ______ to think about the candy he would buy.
   - ○ steps ○ ground ○ log
4. Jonathan put his pennies on the ______ by his bed.
   - ○ lamp ○ table ○ rug
5. Mother came to Jonathan's ______ to tuck him in.
   - ○ table ○ barn ○ room
6. Jonathan's ______ was hurting.
   - ○ finger ○ heart ○ leg

## Mark One

Put an ***X*** on the one that does not go with the others in the box.

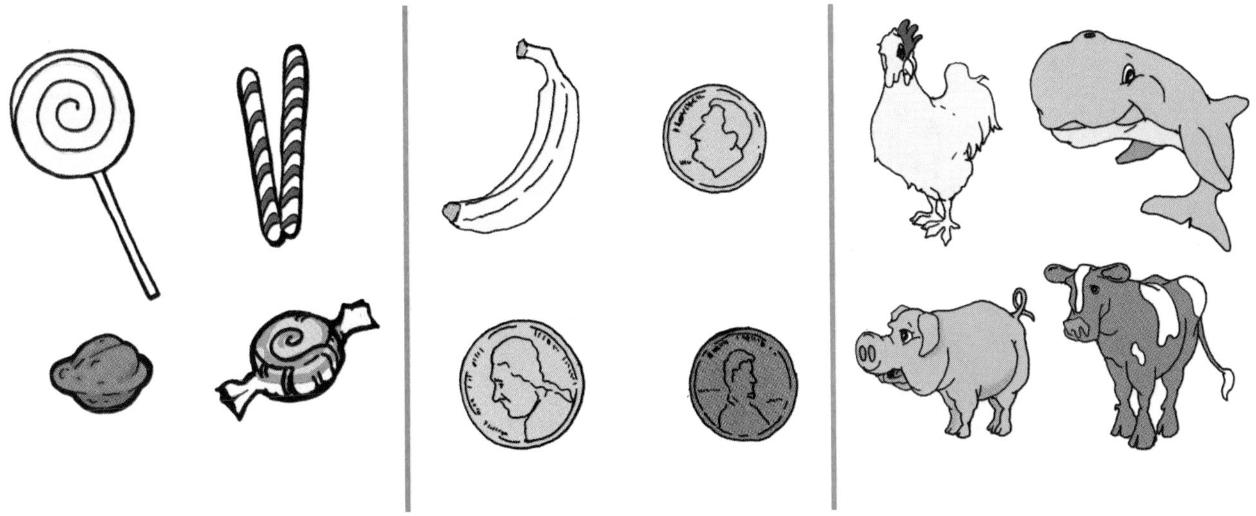

# Go to the Claim Line

## Sort Them

Help Miss Long, Miss Silent, and Marker *e* claim their bags.
Write the words from the tags on the bags to show where they go.

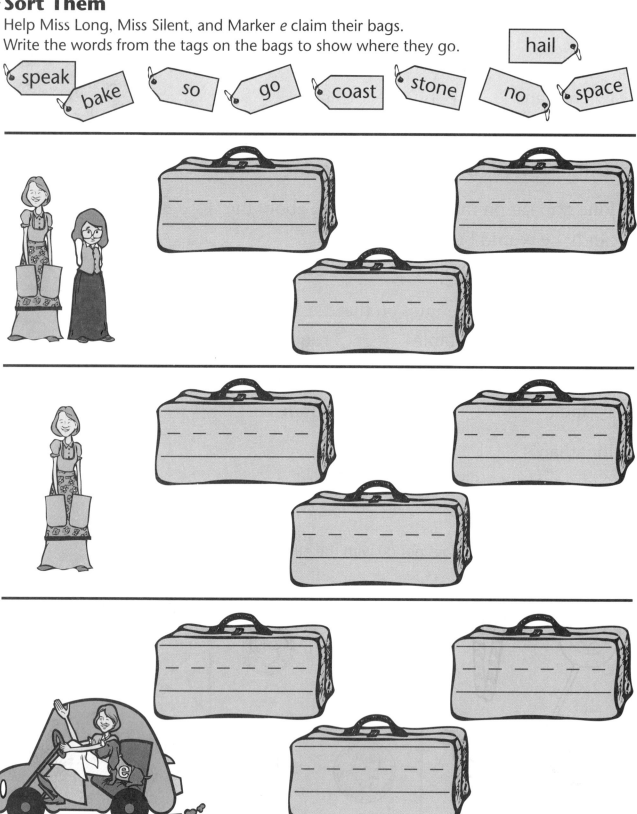

hail

speak   bake   so   go   coast   stone   no   space

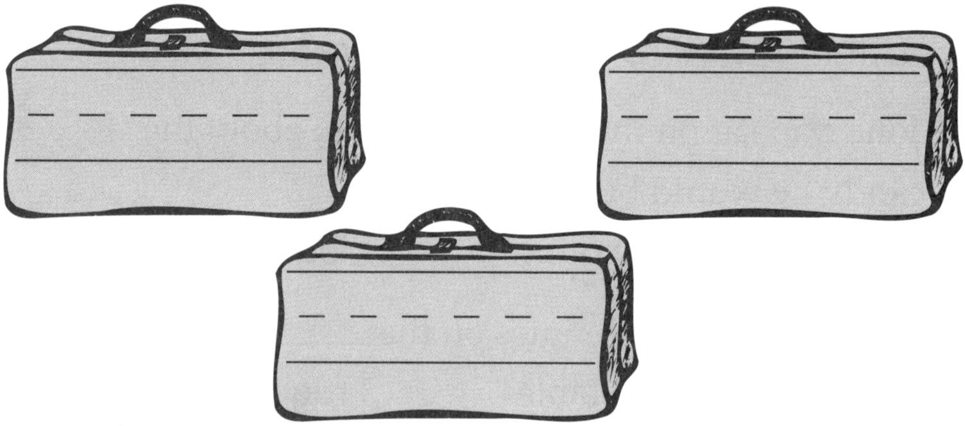

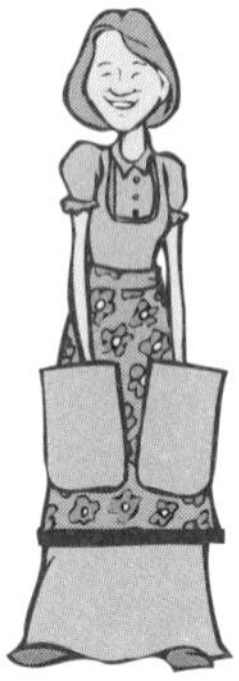

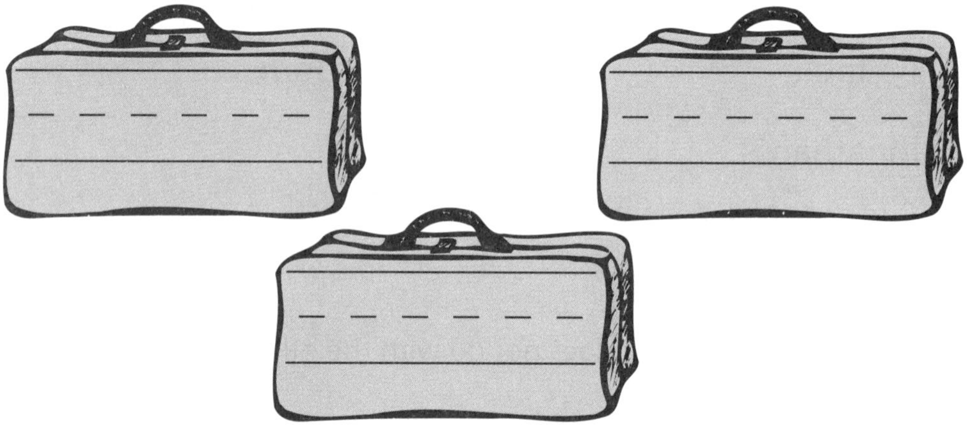

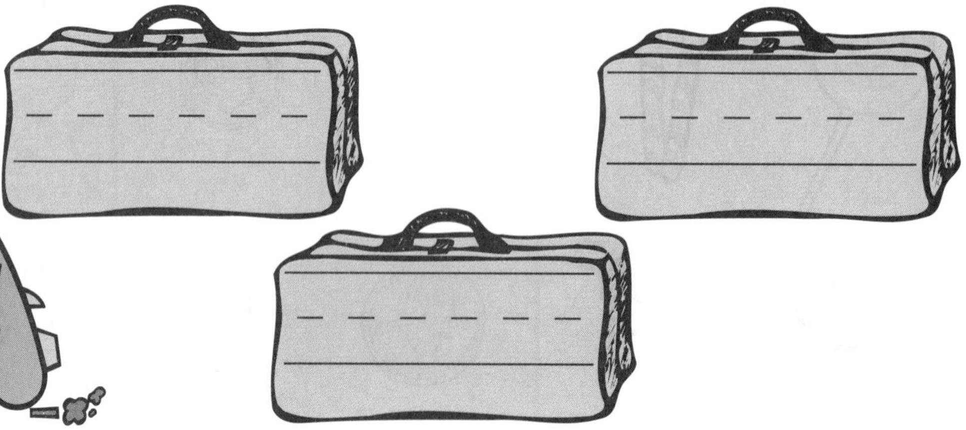

# Who Has It?

Name ______________________

## Answer It

Read each sentence and answer the question.

Dad's farm is in Canada.
Who owns the farm?

The visitor's buggy is black.
What belongs to the visitor?

Jonathan's chickens ate corn.
Who owns the chickens?

Mother sat on Jonathan's bed.
What belongs to Jonathan?

The chicken's house needs cleaning.
Who has a house?

Jonathan's pennies are on the table.
What belongs to Jonathan?

The store's bell rang.
What belongs to the store?

Jonathan's milk pail rattled.
What belongs to Jonathan?

# Turtle and Stork Support Shark's Return

| | | | |
|---|---|---|---|
| fork | purse | horse | fur |
| burn | nurse | yard | shore |
| star | barn | thorn | park |

### Sort Them Out
Write each word under the picture that has the same vowel sound.

### Match Them Up
Draw a line from each sentence to the correct picture.

We went to the park.

Please get a fork.

Amber met the nurse.

Do you see the star?

# Really?

Name ______________________

## Do It

Read and follow the directions.

Can a dog bark?

If a dog can bark,
color the dog *black*.
If a dog cannot bark,
color the dog *brown*.

---

Can a bookcase run?

If a bookcase can run,
put an ***X*** beside the bookcase.
If a bookcase cannot run,
color the bookcase *brown*.

---

Can pencils sing?

If pencils can sing,
color *one* pencil.
If pencils cannot sing,
color *two* pencils.

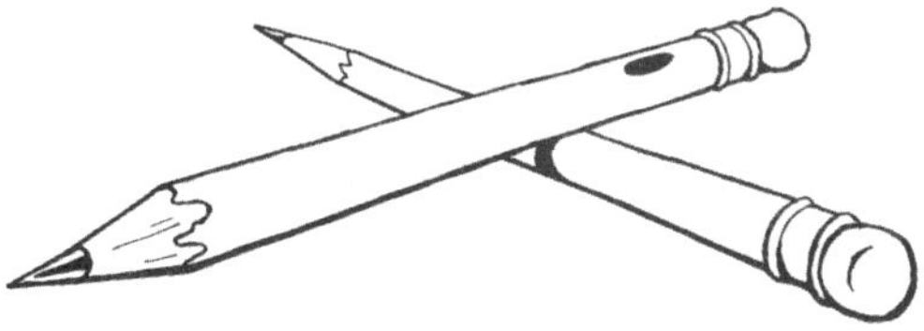

---

Can a ball roll?

If a ball can roll,
color the ball *red* and *yellow*.
If a ball cannot roll,
color the ball *purple* and *green*.

---

Can a clock gallop?

If a clock can gallop,
draw *legs* on the clock.
If a clock cannot gallop,
draw *hands* on the clock.

# Do You Speak Chinese? Yes! I Speak It Very Well.

## Endings

| Read these sentences. | Read these sentences and add the punctuation. |
| --- | --- |
| "The house is on fire!" cried Rosalind. | Where did Jonathan grow up _____ |
| Jonathan Goforth was a missionary to China. | God took care of the Goforths _____ |
| When did Jonathan go to China? | "Jonathan, come quickly _____ " |

## More Endings

Read each sentence. Supply punctuation that tells how you read it.

1. It is very hard to learn Chinese _______
2. Is there an alphabet in Chinese _______
3. There are many kinds of Chinese _______
4. Chinese has about 50,000 characters _______
5. Each character stands for a word or a part of a word _______
6. Do you think you could learn Chinese quickly _______
7. Certainly not _______

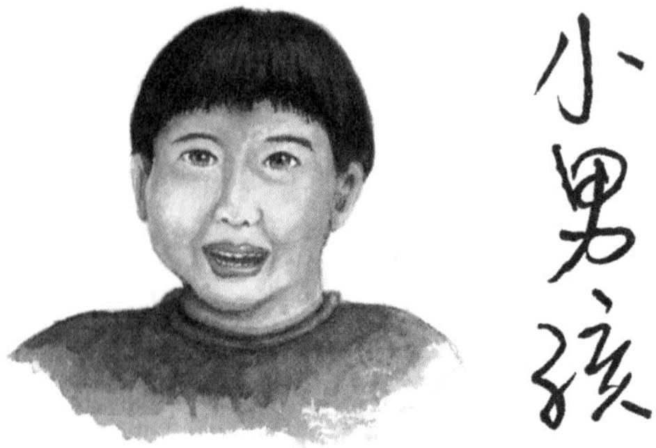

# The Right Choice

Name ____________________

### Read It

Read the story.

Zack Zebra and his cousin Zoe both had homework to do. The day was warm and sunny, and both of the zebras wanted to play. "Let's study later," Zack said.

The zebras left their books and began to play tag. "You're it!" Zack said, tapping Zoe on the foot. Zoe began to chase Zack, then stopped. "Soon it will be dark," she thought, "and I have not done any homework."

"I must go home," she said.

Zack sighed. "You go ahead. I want to play some more."

The next day Zack was very tired. "I stayed up late to do homework," he said. Zoe shook her head.

"I am sorry, Zack. If you had come home with me, we could have worked together. You would not be tired."

Zack nodded sadly. He knew Zoe was right.

### Which One?

Draw a line from the statement to the zebra. If the statement fits both zebras, draw lines to both.

| | |
|---|---|
| wanted to play | stayed up late |
| stopped playing | did homework |
| went home first | was tired |
| played longer | made the right choice |

# Zack Zebra Zoomed and Zipped

## Make Sense of It

Fill in the circle next to the best word choice.

1. Zack Zebra ________ his mother to let him go outside.
   ○ begged ○ bragged
2. Zack sighed when he ________ the water.
   ○ spelled ○ spilled
3. Zack ________ when Captain Stripe told a funny story.
   ○ landed ○ laughed
4. Zack ________ food cooking and asked what was for dinner.
   ○ smelled ○ smiled
5. Zack ________ his friends play a game.
   ○ watched ○ waited

## Fill It In

Write one word from the word box in each sentence.

| | |
|---|---|
| yawned | striped |
| turned | stopped |
| jumped | |

1. Zack ____________ when he heard a noise.
2. Zack ____________ at the edge of the river to drink.
3. The vine called Zack a ____________ horse.
4. The log ____________, showing its teeth.
5. Zack ____________ around quickly.

# Zack Zebra's Journey

Name ____________________

## Follow Along

Captain Stripe sent Zack the Zebra to look for a new watering place. Draw a line to follow the directions Captain Stripe gave him.

1. Go west past the jungle. Do not go through it. There is danger there.
2. At Mumba's Mile, head north toward Wetter Water Crossing.
3. Go over the bridge and turn east.
4. Go past Python Point but keep a sharp lookout! Mona is hiding there!
5. Go to Croc's Creek. Don't go into the water. Croc is lurking!
6. Follow the creek to Lookout Lake where the water is cool and clear.

# Leader Awarded Golden Zebra

## ▸Write a Word

Write the word + *er* or *ed* to make a word to match the picture.

| | | | |
|---|---|---|---|
| 1. wild  |  | 4. catch 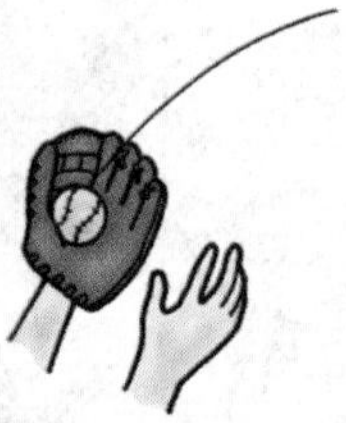 |  |
| 2. end  |  | 5. paint  |  |
| 3. proud  |  | 6. melt  |  |

## ▸Use a Word

Fill in the circle next to the *en* word that fits the sentence.

1. We watched the sky____ into night. ○ lighten ○ darken ○ brighten
2. Dad will ____ the mower blades. ○ soften ○ brighten ○ sharpen
3. Braces are used to ____ teeth. ○ straighten ○ soften ○ sharpen
4. The sailors had to ____ the ship. ○ straighten ○ lighten ○ darken
5. The butter must ____ before we bake cookies. ○ sharpen ○ darken ○ soften

# Critter Chatter

Name ______________________

## Match Them Up

1. Choose the correct ending for each sentence and write the letter in the space.
2. Then draw a line to the one who said it.

a. for new watering places."

b. have used the bridge."

c. about the gold."

d. of Captain Stripe's orders."

e. from hooves walking in it."

f. in this part of the jungle?"

1. "I get so tired ______

2. "What are you doing ______

3. "The water is muddy ______

4. "He's always looking ______

5. "I thought everyone knew ______

6. "Bigger beasts than you ______

# Divide It

## Do Two Things

Draw a dot between the syllables of each word.
Circle the picture that matches the word.

| | |
|---|---|
|  l a d d e r |  k i t t e n |
|  p e n n y |  l e t t e r |
|  r i b b o n | 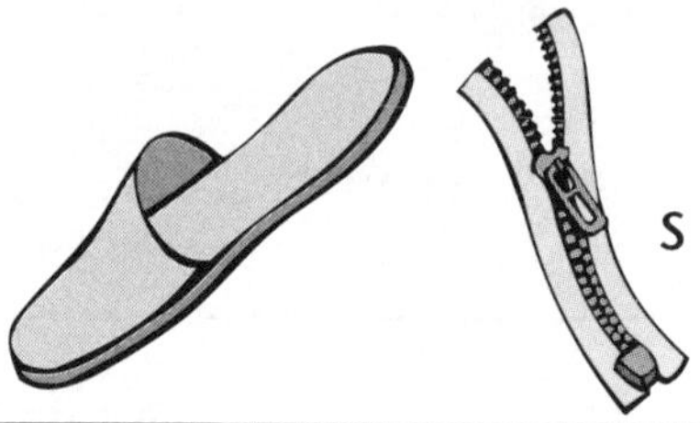 s l i p p e r |

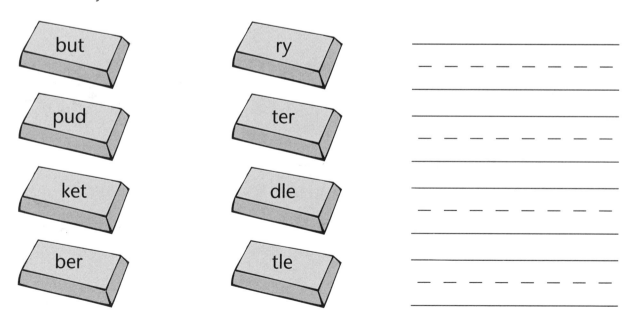

## Do Two More

Match two bars of gold to make a word.
Write the word you made.

| | |
|---|---|
| but | ry |
| pud | ter |
| ket | dle |
| ber | tle |

# Cave Art

Name

## Draw It

Why did Little Fox draw a buffalo? Little Fox had a big wish. What big wish do you have in your heart? Draw a picture of your wish.

## Tell It

Tell about your wish.

# Paw Prints

## Find the Letters

How are the words in each paw *alike*? Read each list and circle the letters that make the vowel sound.

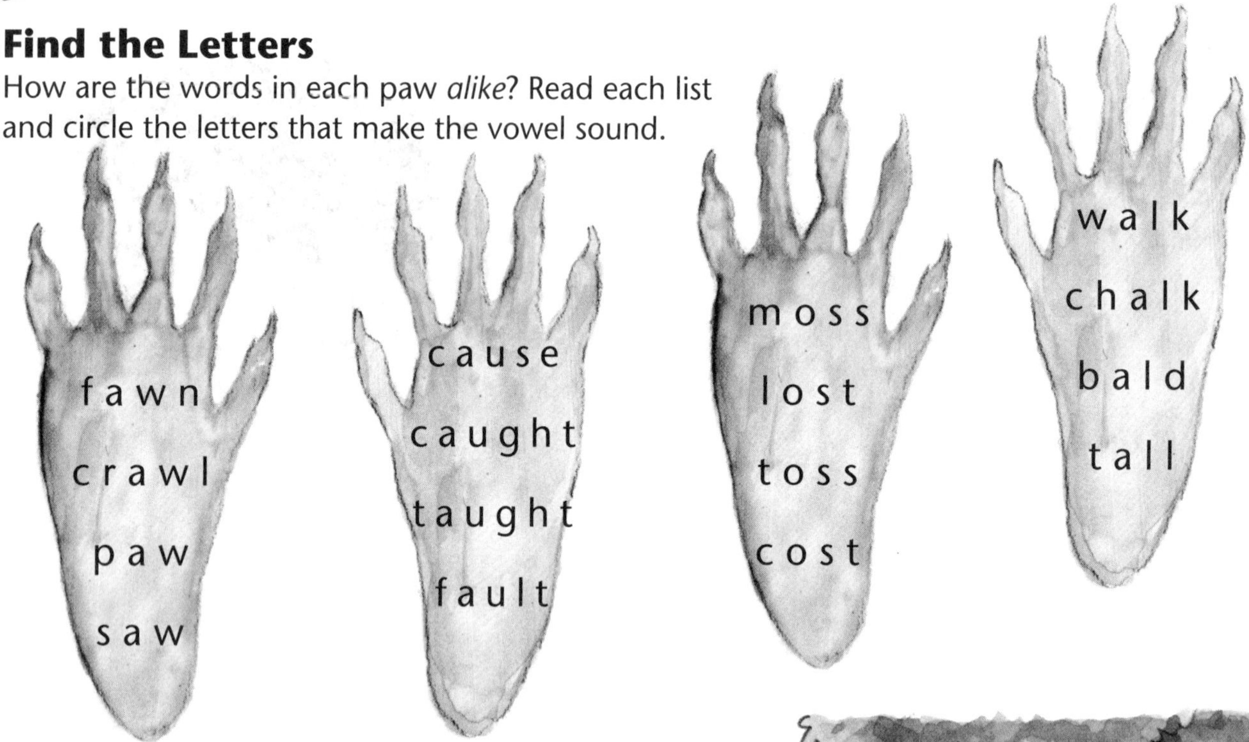


## Use the Words

Use words from the paws to fill in the spaces in these sentences.

**A Dawn Walk**

Early one morning Little Fox took a ________________.

There in the path were fresh ________________ prints.

The prints led him up a bank of slippery ________________.

He had to ________________ under thorny bushes.

The prints stopped by a ________________ tree.

Looking up, Little Fox ________________ a sleeping coon.

**Reading 2A: "The Fire Keeper,"** pp. 257-62, Lesson 80
Phonics: using letter-sound association: /ô/ for *au, aw, o, a(l)*

# Tracking the Story

Name ______________________________

## Match Them

Number the sentences as they happened in "The Fire Keeper." Draw a line from each sentence to the matching picture.

_____ White Cloud smiled at the small boy crouched over the fire.

_____ Little Fox's father looked at the boy's bent head.

_____ Shining Star stumbled past her brother.

_____ Little Fox began to scratch on the wall of the cave with the sharp stone.

_____ The mountain lion landed in the mouth of the cave.

# Flames and Bad Cats

## Do Two Things

1. Read the words in the first list. Color the flame around the marker *e* in each word.

c h a s e
p o k e
w a v e
c h o k e

2. Put "mountain lions" (suffixes) into the words without "fire" (marker *e*).

| | |
|---|---|
| chas ______ | chas ______ |
| pok ______ | pok ______ |
| hop ______ | hop ______ |
| chok ______ | chok ______ |

## Fill It In

Fill in the blanks.

White Cloud said, "Be careful, Little Fox. The smoky fire may make us choke."

She bent over, ______________ from the smoke.

Little Fox said, "I will poke the fire to make the flames burn more brightly."

Little Fox ______________ the fire.

Little Fox pretended to fight a mountain lion. "I will chase the big cat out of the cave!"

Little Fox ______________ the mountain lion away.

Little Fox looked down the trail. "I hope Shining Star comes back soon."

Little Fox is ______________ Shining Star is on her way home.

# Glorious Star—Glorious King

Name ______________________

## Which One?

Circle ***T*** if the sentence is true or ***F*** if the sentence is false.

T F 1. The wise men saw three bright stars in the night sky.

T F 2. One wise man had studied the sky for many years.

T F 3. They did not know why the star was in the sky.

T F 4. The wise men needed many camels to carry food and water.

T F 5. The wise men forgot to take a gift to the new King.

T F 6. They knew just what to take to the new King.

T F 7. The wise men had to choose their gifts.

## Fill It In

Complete each sentence. Use the words in the box.

| | | | |
|---|---|---|---|
| enough | precious | special | marvelous |

1. The wise men saw a ______________ star.

2. They wanted to take their most ______________ gifts.

3. They were going to see a very ______________ King.

4. The servants packed ______________ food and blankets for the trip.

# Starry Sky

## Paint the Sky

Color the star that shows the sound that *y* makes in each word.

| | | | | | |
|---|---|---|---|---|---|
| butterfly | i | e | try | i | e |
| spry | i | e | daisy | i | e |
| sticky | i | e | sleepy | i | e |
| shy | i | e | rusty | i | e |

## Fill It In

Use the words in the box to complete each sentence.

daisy    dry    try    empty    penny    butterfly

1. Ben caught a ____________ in his net.

2. Gail picked a pretty ____________ for her mother.

3. Is the paint on the porch ____________ yet?

4. The students will ____________ to do their best work.

5. Kerry looked and looked for the lost ____________.

6. Brad brought in the ____________ trash cans.

# Dinner Time

Name ______________________________

## Read and Think

Read the story.

A hungry goat saw some sweet grass at the top of a cliff. Since he was a goat, he easily climbed up the rocks. Soon he was munching the grass.

A wolf was hungry too. He saw the goat and licked his lips. But he could not climb up the rocks. So he thought of a plan. He called, "Friend goat, you will get dizzy so high up on the cliff. Come down." But the goat just kept on munching grass.

The wolf called, "Friend goat, the grass is sweeter down here. It would make a better dinner."

Then the goat said, "I think you are not as interested in finding a dinner for me as you are in having me for dinner." And he went back to munching his grass at the top of the cliff.

## Who?

Circle the word or words that answer the question.

| | | |
|---|---|---|
| Who was hungry? | goat | wolf |
| Who could not climb the rocks? | goat | wolf |
| Who ate grass? | goat | wolf |
| Who climbed to the top of the cliff? | goat | wolf |
| Who licked his lips? | goat | wolf |

# One Hump or Two?

## Count Them

Read the words. If the word has one syllable, draw one hump on the camel. If the word has two syllables, draw two humps on the camel.

country

honey

young

from

won

person

trouble
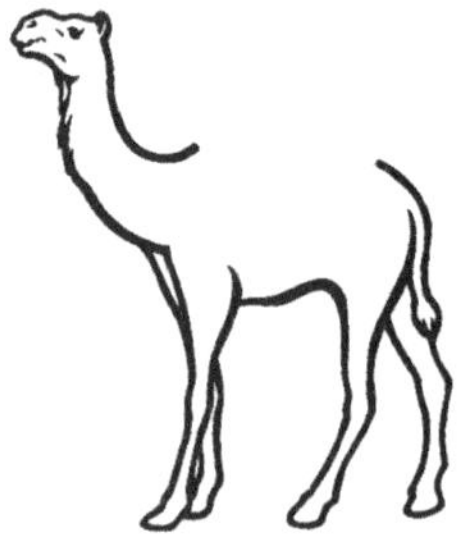

nothing

## Read and Think

A camel's hump does not hold water. It is a huge lump of fat. When the camel goes without eating, the hump shrinks. What do you think happens when the camel eats again?

# Journey

Name

**Matthew 2:2**

*Where is he that is born King of the Jews? for we have seen his star in the east, and are come to worship him.*

## ▸ Write It

A journey now is not like the journey the wise men made to see the special King. Tell about a journey you have made. Where did you go? Who went with you? What did you see?

## ▸ Draw It

Pack up the van with things you would need for a long journey.

# Making New Words

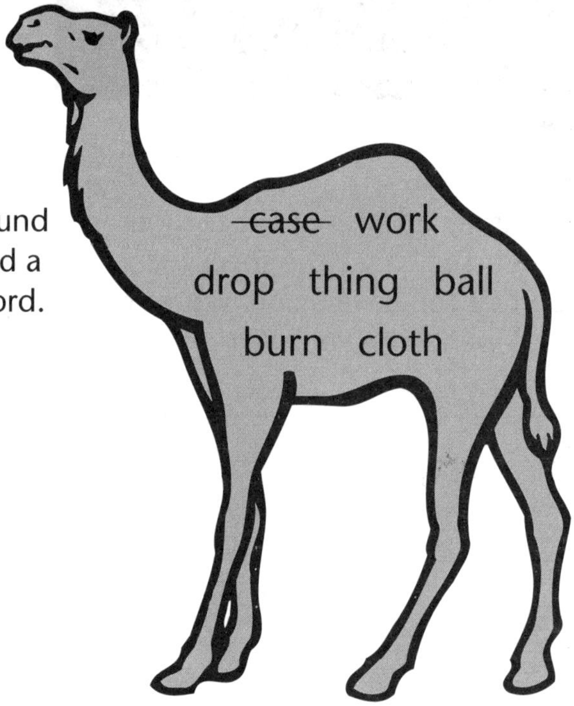

## Divide and Combine

Place a dot between the two words in each compound word. Use the first word of the compound word and a word from the camel to make a new compound word.

b o o k•m a r k

h o m e s i c k

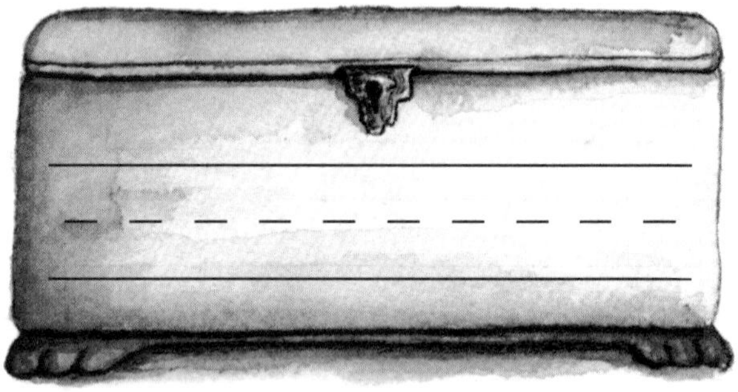

s o m e o n e

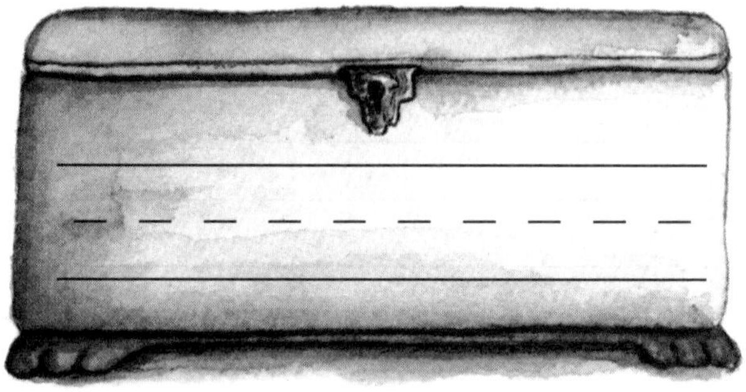

s u n b e a m

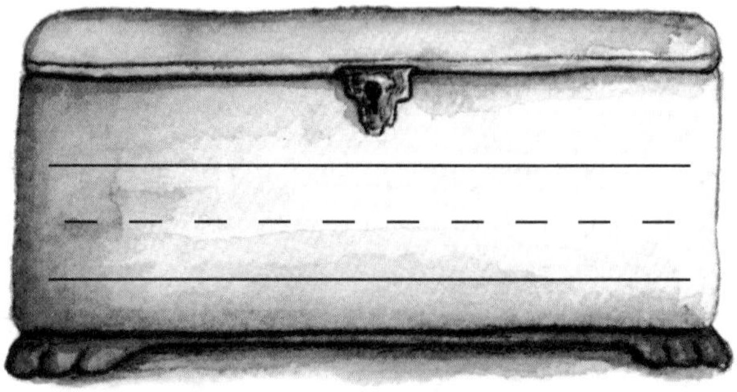

w a s h t u b

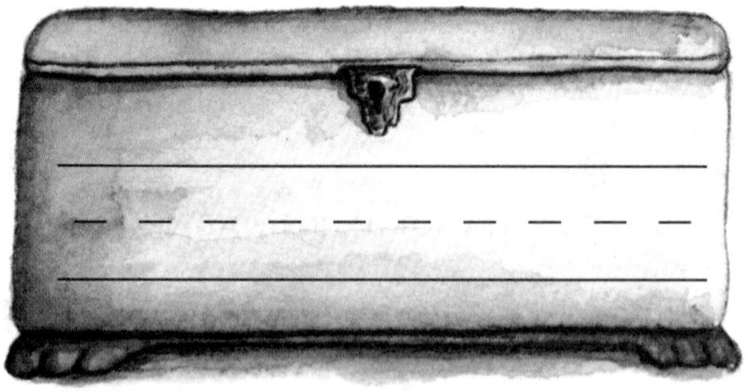

r a i n c o a t

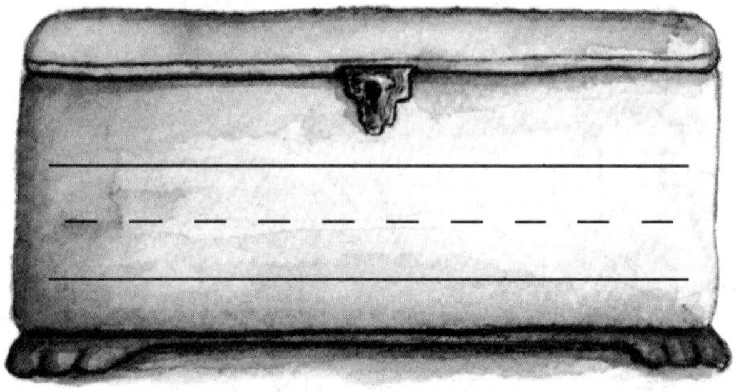

s n o w s u i t

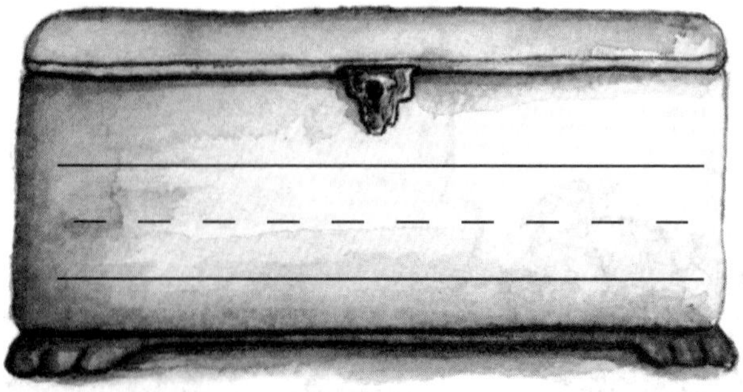

**Reading 2A: "Gifts from the Wise Men,"** pp. 276-78, Lesson 85
Word work: dividing compound words into syllables
Comprehension: combining base words to form a compound word

142

# A King in Bethlehem Town

Name ______________________

> **MATTHEW 2:1b**
> *Behold, there came wise men from the east.*

## Find the One

Circle the best word to finish each sentence.

1. The wise men saw a glorious ______.
   ○ cloud ○ star
2. They used ______ to carry their food.
   ○ camels ○ horses
3. One wise man brought a gift of ______.
   ○ silver ○ gold
4. They did not want robbers to steal their ______.
   ○ gifts ○ camels
5. King Herod was ______ to hear about the new King.
   ○ happy ○ angry
6. Herod wanted to ______ the new King.
   ○ kill ○ crown
7. The new King was born in ______.
   ○ Jerusalem ○ Bethlehem

## Get in Line

Number the sentences in the order in which they happened in the story.

______ Silently they placed their gifts before the Child.

______ Herod's scribes gathered to look in the temple scrolls.

______ A wise man stood outside pointing to the sky.

______ The wise men went back home another way.

______ Carefully the servants loaded the gifts onto the camels' backs.



**Reading 2A: "Gifts from the Wise Men,"** pp. 279-82, Lesson 86
Comprehension: recalling facts and details; recalling sequence of events

# The Chief's Shield

## Listen and Write

Use the words from the shield to complete the sentences.

The letters *ie* can make the /ē/ sound as in *chief*.

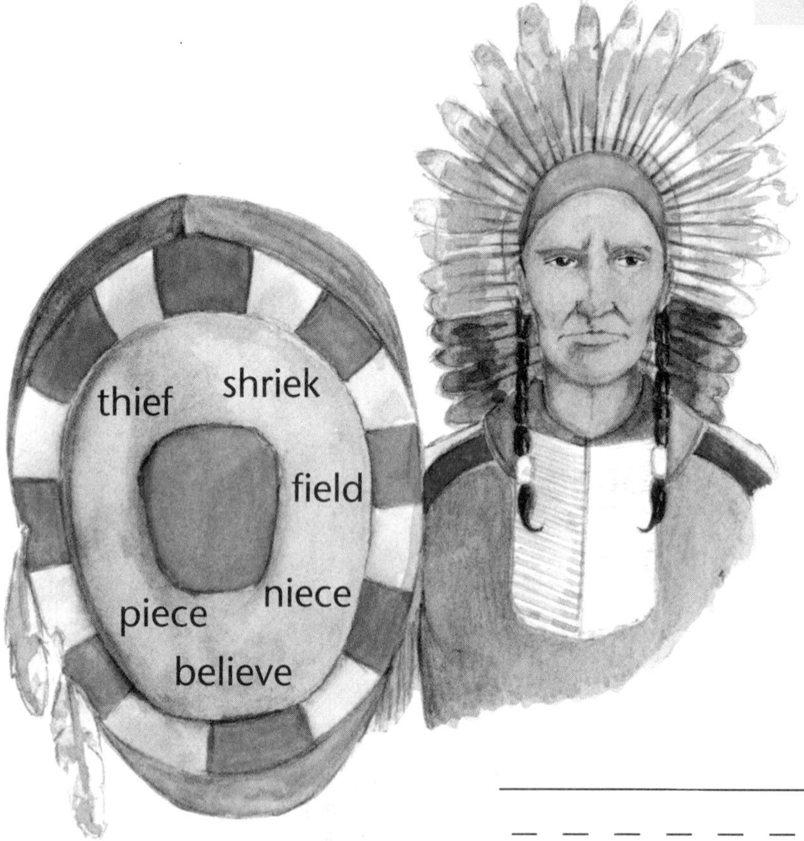


The ch*ie*f painted his sh*ie*ld.

1. The team plays baseball on the ________________ after school.

2. Mother gave us a ________________ of pie after lunch.

3. The ________________ stole the bag of gems from the store.

4. The lady gave her ________________ a precious bracelet.

5. I ________________ that God made me.

6. Mother might ________________ if she sees that snake.

# Gifts from the Heart

Name ______________________________

## Work It

Use the words in the gold bars to fill in the puzzle.

**PHILIPPIANS 2:10**

*That at the name of Jesus every knee should bow, of things in heaven, and things in earth, and things under the earth.*

### *Across*

1. Gold is used to make ______.
4. Gold is a bright yellow______.
5. Myrrh gives off a sweet ______.
6. Jesus is the only true God, and one day everyone will______Him.
8. ______is used to prepare bodies for burial.

### *Down*

2. Gold is found in rocks or______.
3. Myrrh and frankincense are used to make ______.
5. Frankincense is sticky like ______.
7. The finest gift you can give to Jesus is your ______.

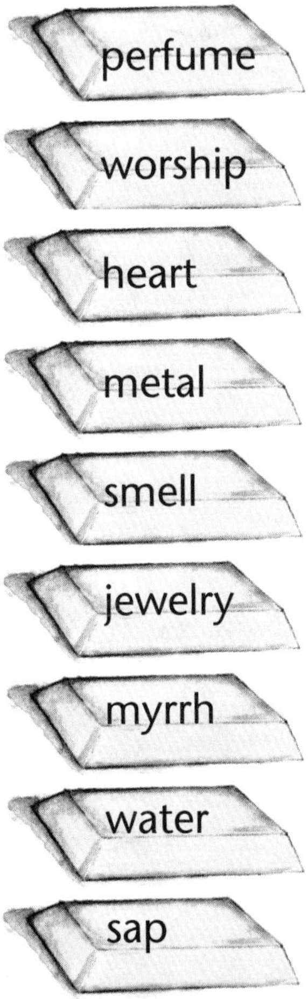


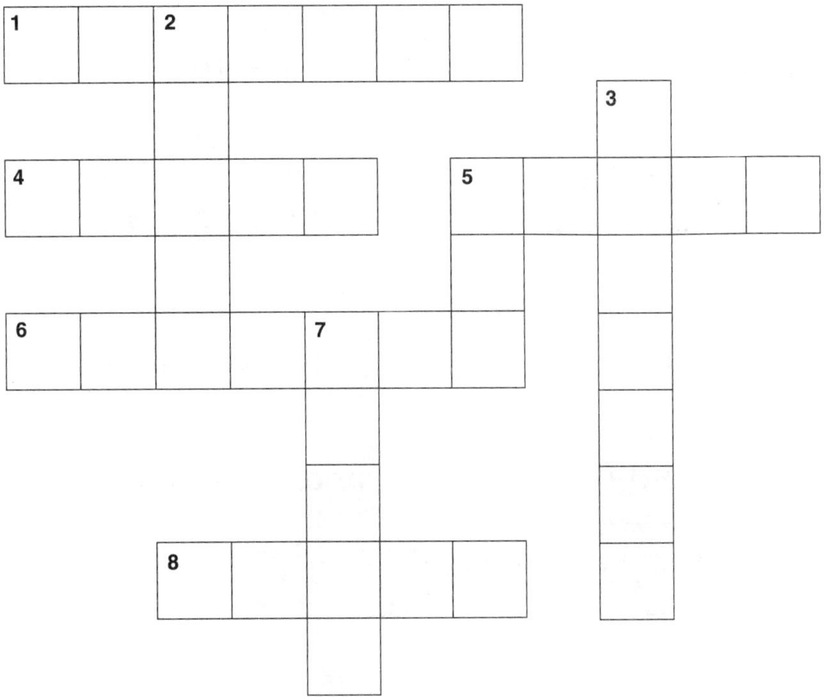

# Wrong Cost

## ▸ Paint the Presents

Color the gift if the word has the same vowel sound as *cost*.

## ▸ Use the Presents

In each space write a word from a gift that you colored.

1. Dad scraped the ____________ off the truck windows.

2. The soft ____________ made green carpet under the trees.

3. Jesus died on the ____________ for our sins.

4. Holly found the mother cat and her kittens in the barn ____________.

5. We woke up when we heard the happy bird's ____________.

# Friends

Name ______________________________

**PROVERBS 18:24**

*A man that hath friends must shew himself friendly: and there is a friend that sticketh closer than a brother.*

## Find All

Fill in the circle next to each sentence that shows Beaver is a true friend.

○ He hummed a happy tune.

○ He asked why Squirrel was sad.

○ He twitched his nose.

○ He went along with Squirrel.

○ He went to visit Squirrel.

○ He pulled Squirrel out of the brook.

○ He looked where he was going.

○ He knocked sharply on the wall.

## Tell All

Write about someone who is a true friend to you. What does this person do to show you that he or she is a true friend? What do you like to do together?

# Cats and Mice

## ▸ Ring It

Circle the cat if the word has a hard *c*.
Circle the mouse if the word has a soft *c*.

coat 

fancy 

race 

except 

price 

count 

cupcake 

excite 

## ▸ Draw It

Draw a picture to go with each sentence.

| | | |
|---|---|---|
| Beaver ate rice for lunch. | The gray squirrel perched on the fence. | Three friends ran a race. |

# A Walk with Beaver

Name ______________________________

## ▸ Read the Map

One day Beaver left his home and took a walk. The map shows the path he took. Each stop is marked with an ***X***. Look at the map to answer the questions.

## ▸ Pick a Place

Fill in the circle beside the answer.

1. Where is Beaver's home?
   - ○ Singing Stream ○ Bubbling Brook ○ Peaceful Pond
2. Where did Beaver stop first after leaving his house?
   - ○ Bubbling Brook ○ Wise Old Owl's tree ○ Squirrel's tree
3. Who lives in a tree next to Bubbling Brook?
   - ○ Beaver ○ Mouse ○ Wise Old Owl
4. Where did Beaver stop after visiting Wise Old Owl?
   - ○ Peaceful Pond ○ Bubbling Brook ○ Singing Stream
5. Whom did Beaver visit last?
   - ○ Squirrel ○ Mouse ○ Wise Old Owl

# A Real Gem

Usually the *g* is soft when it is followed by *e*, *i*, or *y*.

## Paint the Gems

Finish coloring the gems that have the same sound that *g* makes in *gem*.

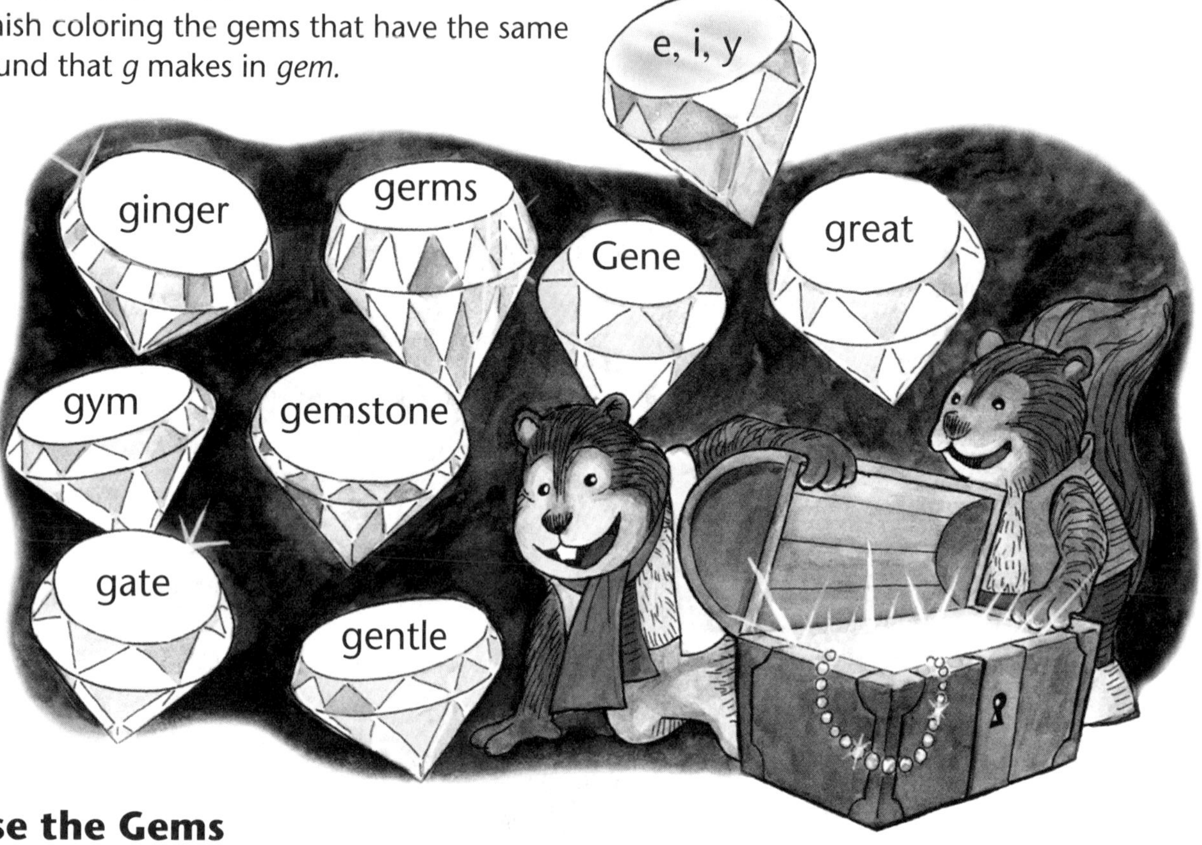


## Use the Gems

Use the words from the gems to complete the sentences.

1. ____________ found a great place for a picnic.

2. Brad wants to buy a shiny ____________ for his brother.

3. You must be very ____________ as you pet the rabbit.

4. Please stay home when you are sick so that you

   won't give your ____________ to a classmate.

# What Are They?

Name ______________________________

## Classify

Write a word from the book in each space.

1. The sun, moon, and stars may be seen in the ________________.

2. A steering wheel, tires, and seats are parts of a ________________.

3. Dolls, games, and stuffed animals are ________________.

4. Pages, titles, and chapters are parts of a ________________.

5. Desks, chalkboards, and books are found in a ________________.

6. Nickels, dimes, and pennies are kinds of ________________.

7. March, May, and June are ________________.

8. A father, a mother, and a sister are members of a ________________.

# Pals and Friends

## Match Them Up

Draw lines between the gems that have synonyms on them.

remain ill unlock toss quick

sick throw stay fast open

## Fill It In

Find a synonym for the underlined word and write it in the space.

glance noise chat happy

1. We heard a loud ______________ that made a <u>sound</u> like a clap of thunder.

2. We had a ______________ about when to <u>talk</u> at school.

3. Brent is <u>glad</u> that the boys are ______________ with the new boat.

4. I will ______________ at the book when we <u>look</u> for something to read.

# Remember This?

Name ____________________

## Match Them Up

Draw a line from the statement to the animal it tells about.
Some of them will tell about both Beaver and Squirrel.

Squirrel

went to visit a sad friend

wanted precious treasure

visited Wise Old Owl

fell into the brook

got his foot stuck

sat by the pond

was the treasure all along

Beaver

## Match Again

Match each title to a treasure found in the story.
Write the number of the title in the blank.

| | | |
|---|---|---|
| 1. "The Fire Keeper" | _____ | a friend |
| 2. "Jonathan's Treasure" | _____ | words of wisdom |
| 3. "Captain Stripe's Gold" | _____ | gold |
| 4. "Gifts from the Wise Men" | _____ | pictures |
| 5. "Squirrel's Treasure" | _____ | pennies |

# Contraction Attraction

PROVERBS 17:17
*A friend loveth at all times.*

## Match Them Up

Draw a line from each scarf to the beaver with the matching contraction.

## Which One?

Draw a circle around the words that mean the same as the contraction in the sentence.

1. I'm going to visit my friend.
   I will   I am   I have

2. She didn't come to school today.
   do not   does not   did not

3. I hope she isn't sick.
   is not   are not   were not

4. We don't want to miss going to the circus.
   does not   did not   do not

5. I haven't seen a circus in two years.
   have not   was not   has not

6. That's why my father is taking us there on Saturday.
   It is   That is   There is

7. I can't wait to see the animals!
   have not   cannot   will not

8. It's more fun than anything I know!
   It is   That is   I will





**Reading 2A: "Squirrel's Treasure,"** pp. 299-302, Lesson 92
Word work: recognizing contractions; matching a contraction with its meaning

# Storm Talk

Name ______________________

**Pick One**

Write the name of the person who said each sentence.

Shanda     Travis     Mama     Daddy     Announcer

1. "Storm's coming! Storm's coming!" ______________

2. "We interrupt this program for the latest news." ______________

3. "Will we have to go to a shelter this time?" ______________

4. "The Lord will take care of us." ______________

5. "Daddy, did you hear the news? A hurricane is coming!" ______________

6. "Tape keeps the glass from flying everywhere if the window cracks." ______________

7. "We have plenty of food." ______________

# Blustery Blends

## Ring It

Draw a circle around the word that has the same beginning blend as the name of the picture.

sling
sweater
special

clock
crust
flower

small
snow
star

please
party
prize

give
glue
gas

spill
shoe
smile

dine
brother
drain

skirt
slide
stamp

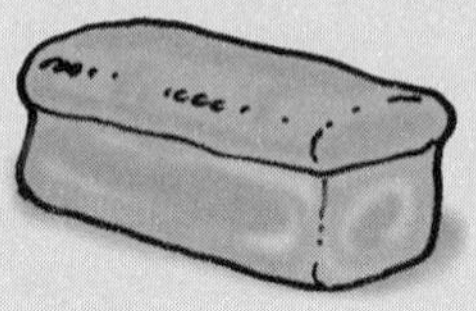

braid
bank
black

## Which One?

Fill in the circle beside the word that best fits the sentence.

1. What is the ________ of the book you're reading?
   ○ twinkle ○ title ○ tune

2. Mom will ________ the stew into our bowls.
   ○ ladle ○ leash ○ loaf

3. Mr. Clark blew the ________ to wake us at camp.
   ○ beagle ○ bookcase ○ bugle

# Reading Between the Lines

Name ____________________

## Read and Think

Sometimes the reader can understand more than what the words of a story say. Read each of these parts of "Hurricane!" and fill in the circle next to the sentence that tells what you know is true without seeing it in writing.

1. "You and Shanda run upstairs and get dressed," said Mama. "We will eat early this morning since Travis is so hungry."

- ○ The children wanted to go out and play.
- ○ Shanda was not hungry.
- ○ The children were still in their night clothing.

2. While everyone was eating, the lights flickered and went out. Daddy turned up the radio. "The hurricane is moving up the coast," said the announcer.

- ○ Daddy did not like to hear about the storm.
- ○ The radio did not need power as the lights did.
- ○ The radio announcer did not like storms.

3. Suddenly they heard a crash! Shanda clutched her mother. Travis sat up. "What was that?" he asked.

- ○ Shanda and Travis were frightened.
- ○ Travis thought Shanda was a baby.
- ○ Mama did not want Shanda to be frightened.

4. Daddy's voice sounded loud and strong when he spoke. "Let's pray again and ask God to give us courage."

- ○ Daddy was angry because the lights were off.
- ○ Daddy trusted God to take care of them.
- ○ Daddy did not feel like singing.

# *Full of Thanks*

What does it mean to be thank*ful?*
It means to be full of thanks.

## Make a Word

Write the correct word.

Full of ____________ = hopeful

Full of ____________ = playful

Full of ____________ = truthful

Full of ____________ = helpful

Full of joy = ____________

Full of care = ____________

Full of pain = ____________

Full of faith = ____________

## Use a Word

Choose a *-ful* word from above to complete each sentence.

1. Travis and Shanda wanted to be ____________, so they put the chairs away.

2. The Parkers are ____________ members of their church.

3. Grandmother is always happy and ____________.

4. We had to be ____________ not to brush against the stove burner.

# Hurricane Happenings

Name ______________________________

### Read and Think

Circle the candle under ***T*** if the sentence is true or ***F*** if the sentence is false.

> PSALM 107:29
> *He maketh the storm a calm, so that the waves thereof are still.*

| T | F | |
|---|---|---|
| | | 1. Travis helped tape the windows. |
| | | 2. Daddy told the story about David and the giant. |
| | | 3. Mama did not want to go outside after the storm. |
| | | 4. Shanda climbed on a fallen tree. |
| | | 5. Shanda and Travis had to go to a storm shelter. |
| | | 6. Daddy said that storms help us trust God. |

### Think and Match

Write the number of the word in the box beside the correct picture.

☐ 

1. jellyfish
2. shells
3. radio
4. lawn chair
5. sleeping bag

☐ 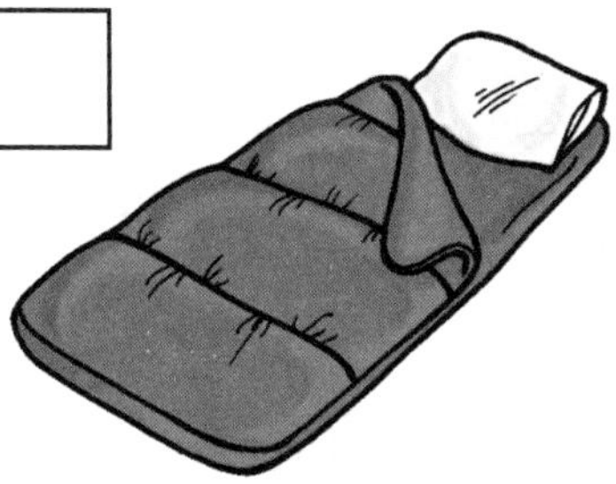

☐ 

☐ 

☐ 

# Shiny Shells

When adding a *y* to the end of some words, drop the marker *e* but keep Miss Long's vowel sound in the first syllable.

### Think About It

/ē/

flake
shake

flak•y
shak•y

### Make a Word

Choose a word from one of the shells, drop the silent ***e***, and add ***y*** to make a word to fit each sentence.

1. We will look for a ________________ spot to eat our lunch.

2. The baby has ________________ pink cheeks.

3. Tommy has six ________________ pennies.

4. The seeds did not grow in the ________________ soil.

5. Mom put a pretty, ________________ cloth on the table.

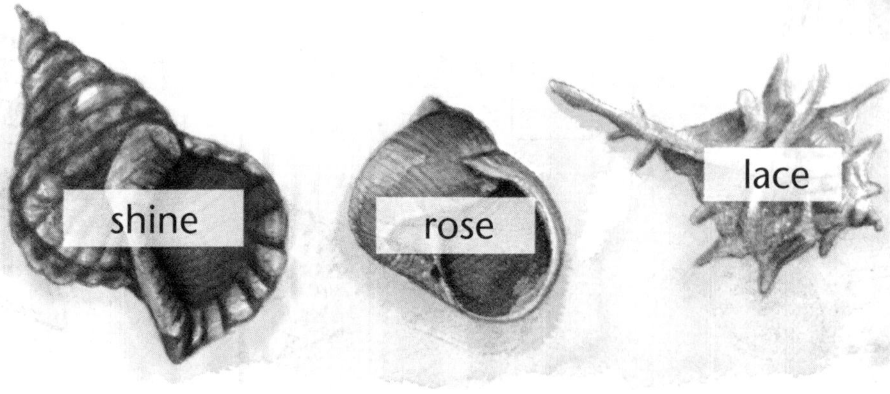

# Zane's Island

Name ______________________________

## Read

Zane sat looking out over the blue waters around the island. Everywhere he looked, he saw beautiful birds and shells. He smelled sweet flower smells. These things did not make him happy. He wanted to see houses and cars and people. He wanted to hear voices.

Zane looked down at his bare feet. His shoes and socks were too small, but the island was warm and he didn't need them. He had outgrown his shirt and cut off his pants to make shorts.

Many of the island trees had tasty fruit. It was easy to catch all the fish he wanted. Zane sighed and thought of his mother's cooking.

## Think

Circle *yes* or *no* for each sentence.

| | | |
|---|---|---|
| 1. Zane is alone on the island. | yes | no |
| 2. Zane has been on the island only a few days. | yes | no |
| 3. Zane doesn't like any food besides fruit and fish. | yes | no |
| 4. There are no houses on the island. | yes | no |
| 5. Zane would like to leave the island. | yes | no |

## Think and Write

Write about how you think Zane will get off the island.
Use your own paper. Attach it to this sheet.

# Bear Fear

## Choose One

Circle the picture that has the same vowel sound as the underlined word.

1. The little boy wanted to wear his new coat. 

2. We could not hear the school bell ringing. 

3. Brenda turned seven years old last Saturday. 

4. The thorn made a big tear in Becky's dress. 

5. We could see tiny fish in the clear water. 

6. Mother gave each of us a big ripe pear. 

## Match One

Draw lines to match each word to the correct picture.

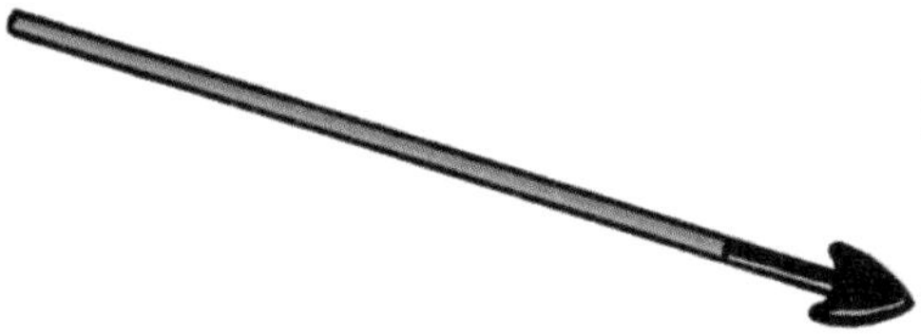

spear

tears

bear

beard

# The Same and Not the Same

Name ____________________

## Match Up!

Draw a line from each sentence to show if it tells about the ship or the canoe. If it tells about both, draw lines to both.

It can carry many people and things.

It can be used for racing.

It can carry just a few people.

It cannot go on small streams.

It takes people places.

It travels on water.

It is moved with paddles.

It is run by a motor.

## Sentence Sense

Match the two parts of each sentence by writing the letter in the space beside the first part.

| | |
|---|---|
| 1. Bert blew out the candles ____ | a. with his name on the cover. |
| 2. Mother cut a slice of cake ____ | b. on his birthday cake. |
| 3. Father thanked the Lord ____ | c. with a sail. |
| 4. Bert's brother gave him a boat ____ | d. for each of us to eat. |
| 5. His parents gave him a Bible ____ | e. for the food. |
| 6. Bert had waited for a new Bible ____ | f. for more than a year. |

# Contraction Treasures

## Find One

Circle the contraction in each sentence. Fill in the circle next to the words that mean the same as the contraction you circled.

1. "I can't wait to ride."

   ○ cannot ○ could not ○ can to

2. "I don't want to ride them."

   ○ did not ○ do not ○ does not

3. Uncle Vance said there wasn't much to tell.

   ○ were not ○ will not ○ was not

4. "Isn't there treasure in that story?"

   ○ it is ○ is not ○ was not

5. Lena won't make her horse trot.

   ○ will not ○ were not ○ was not

6. Marcus and Lena haven't found any treasure yet.

   ○ has not ○ here is ○ have not

## Write the Ones

Write the words for each contraction in the space.

______________________

______________________

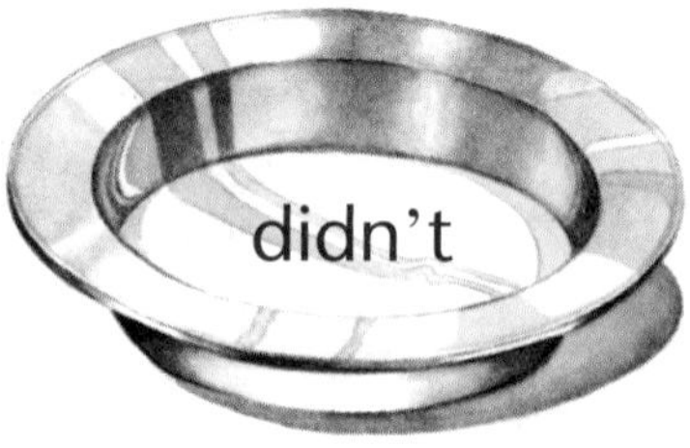


______________________

## Use One

Write a sentence using one of the contractions.

______________________________________________

______________________________________________

# Digging for Words

Name ______________________

## Work It

Use the words in the word bank to fill in the puzzle.

### Across

3. Gussy said Able could be _____ .
4. Able hid the _____ .
6. Lena asked if the _____ had been put in yet.
7. Marcus and Lena were excited about hearing of a _____ .

### Down

1. Marcus read the _____.
2. Marcus and Lena spent their summer on an _____ .
4. The ruins of the _____ were a mile away.
5. They used a _____ to dig for the treasure.

church
island
mystery
candlesticks
trusted
spade
floor
gravestones

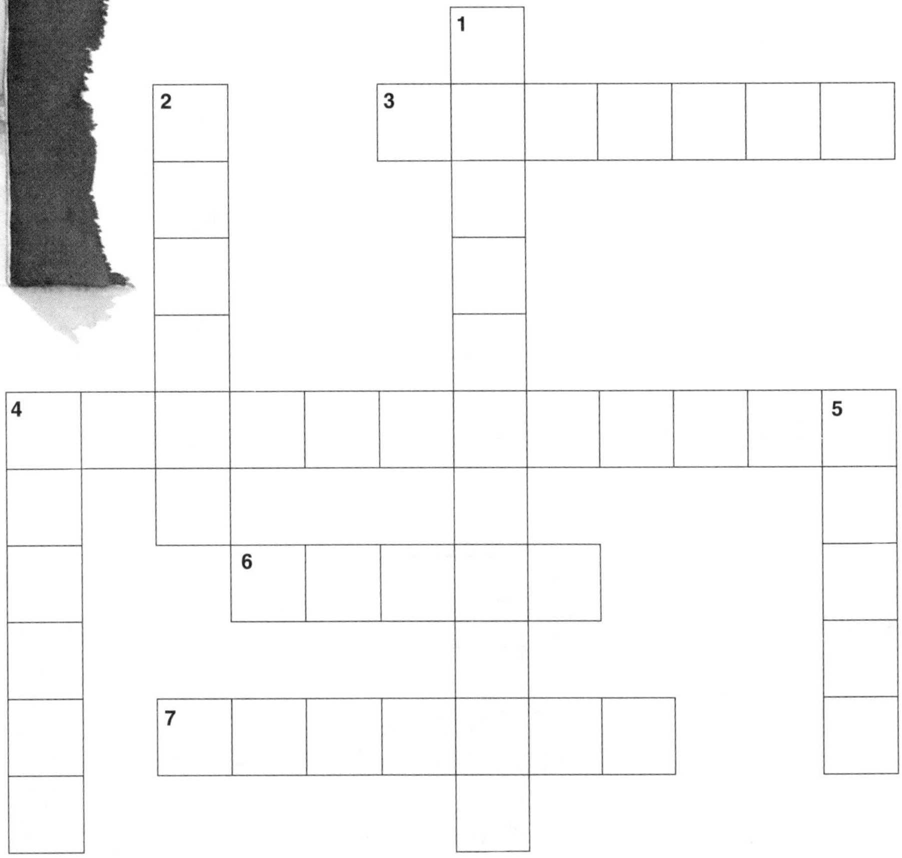

# Finding Treasure

## Find the Two

Circle the two words that are antonyms in each chest.

## Fill It In

Complete each sentence by writing a synonym for the word above the space. Use the words in the box.

| | | | |
|---|---|---|---|
| street | tale | hunting | quickly |

story

1. Aunt Fran said there was treasure in that ____________.

looking

2. Marcus and Lena were ____________ for the church treasure.

road

3. They ran across the ____________ and into the church.

fast

4. Marcus told Lena she would have to go ____________.

166

**Reading 2B: "Sea Island Mystery,"** pp. 25-29, Lesson 99
Word work: recognizing antonyms; using synonyms correctly in sentences

# Home Sweet Home

Name ______________________________

PSALM 69:34
*Let the heaven and earth praise him, the seas, and every thing that moveth therein.*

## Sort Them Out

Not all of these animals are at home in the tide pool. Put an ***X*** on the ones that do not belong. Color the ones that do belong.

## Which One?

Fill in the circle beside the best answer.

1. Animals in a tide pool get food from the _____.
   - ○ sea
   - ○ land

2. A clam has _____ .
   - ○ a closed shell
   - ○ no shell

3. Clams eat _____ .
   - ○ fish
   - ○ plants

4. The _____ uses spikes to stop its enemies.
   - ○ sea urchin
   - ○ starfish

5. Sometimes a sea anemone looks like an _____ .
   - ○ apple
   - ○ orange

6. Sometimes the sea anemone looks like a _____ .
   - ○ flower
   - ○ tree

7. The starfish has _____ arms.
   - ○ four
   - ○ five

8. The _____ has a hard shell.
   - ○ sea urchin
   - ○ crab

# Guess the Guest

## Add a Color

Color each clam with a word that has the same hard *g* sound and lazy *u* as the word *guest*.

guest

## Add a Word

Use a word from the colored clams to complete each sentence.

1. Mr. West wanted to hire a man to ____________ the jewels.

2. Dad asked the scout to ____________ us through the woods.

# Crusty Complained

Name ____________________

## Write One

Write a word from one of the gulls in each sentence.

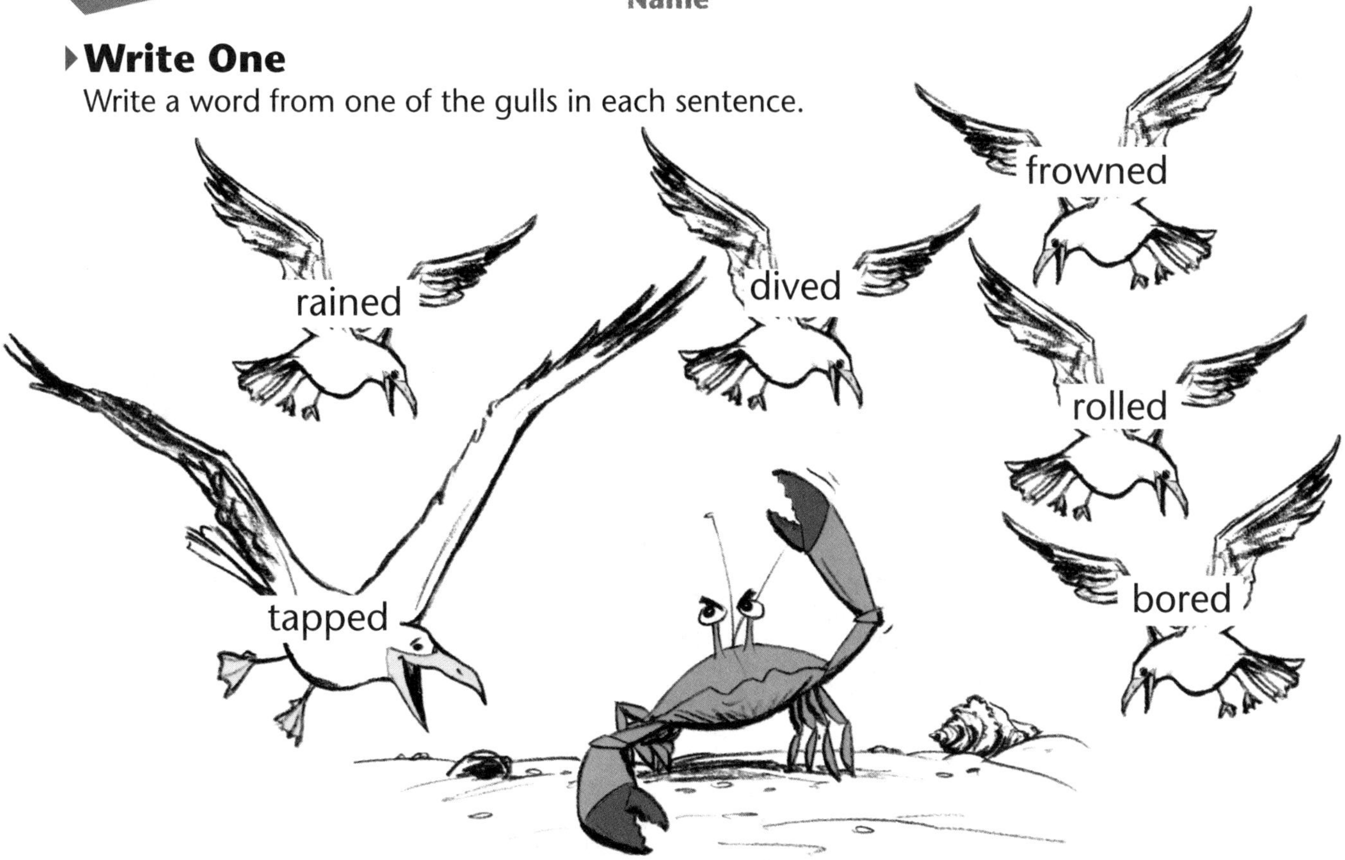


1. Crusty was never happy when it ____________.

2. Crusty is ____________ with his home by the sea.

3. The tide ____________ Crusty away from his home.

4. The gulls ____________ at Crusty's shell.

5. Flea ____________ his feet when he met Crusty.

6. Crusty was being cranky when he ____________ at Flea.

## Sort Them Out

Write each word under the picture with the same vowel sound.

| | | | |
|---|---|---|---|
| horse | yarn | barber | snore |
| shark | thorn | shore | garden |

## Ring It

Circle the word that tells about the picture.

card
cord
word

corn
barn
cord

hard
horn
harp

far
pork
fork

torch
porch
march

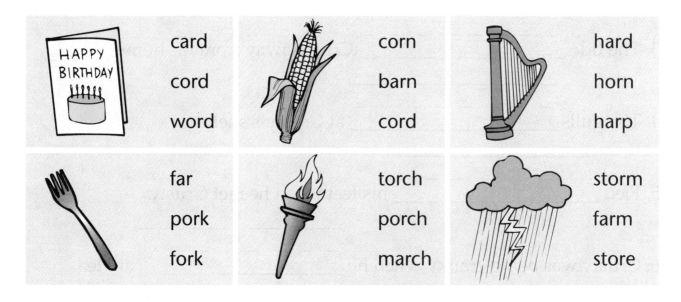

storm
farm
store

# The Huzbumbley Crew

Name ______________________

## Get in Line
Number the sentences in story order.

_____ Crusty left his home by the sea.

_____ Crusty thought Beetle's song was a trick.

_____ The gulls swooped at Crusty.

_____ Flutterby asked to come along on Crusty's adventure.

_____ Flea said he would show Crusty around.

## What Was It?
Write the words that make these contractions.

doesn't → 1. ______________________

he's → 2. ______________________

can't → 3. ______________________

it's → 4. ______________________

## Use One
Write one of the contractions in each sentence.

1. Flea said, "______________________ the way we like it."

2. Crusty ______________________ want to stop.

3. Crusty ______________________ bow.

4. I think ______________________ cranky.

# Alert Bird Saves Turtle

## Circle the One

Circle the word that matches the picture.

ship
shirt
shine

plunge
purple
purse

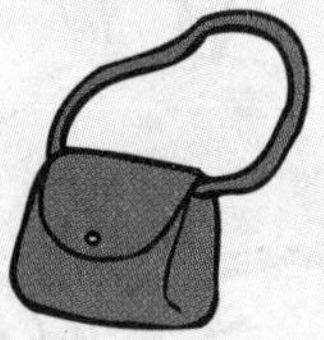

bride
bird
broil

herd
heel
hail

trudge
trophy
turtle

nozzle
nurse
night

## Fill It In

Write a word from the box in each sentence.

1. Mom does not want the candles to ________________ out.

2. Grandmother will let me ________________ the cake batter.

3. It is my ________________ to wash the dishes.

4. Mrs. Clark will ________________ tea and cookies at the party.

5. Amber is ________________ in line to get a drink of water.

6. The ________________ at the store was very nice to us.

| | |
|---|---|
| turn | serve |
| third | clerk |
| stir | burn |

# The Best Choice

______________________________
Name

## ▸Choose One

Circle the sentence that best describes the picture.

The gulls pulled Crusty's antennae.

Crusty shook a blue claw.

The bees flew away.

The bees swarmed around Crusty.

The two set off across the meadow.

Beetle Brightknee sang for Crusty.

The bees chatted with Flutterby.

Flutterby chased the bees away.

## ▸Choose Again

Circle ***T*** for true or ***F*** for false.

T F 1. Crusty was not afraid of the bees.

T F 2. The bees believed Flutterby.

T F 3. Crusty left in a huff.

T F 4. Flea, Beetle, and Flutterby went home.

T F 5. A fox can bark like a dog.

# Dear Hare, Deer Hair

## Match Them Up

Draw a line from each word to the picture with the same vowel sound.

pair

care

fear

bare

gear

cheer

stare

here

## Which One?

Fill in the circle beside the word that fits the sentence.

1. We will ____ for our team to win.
   - ○ cheer
   - ○ chime
2. It is rude to ____ at someone.
   - ○ stole
   - ○ stare
3. I like to walk in the sand with ____ feet.
   - ○ bare
   - ○ base
4. We will meet Dad ____ for lunch.
   - ○ here
   - ○ hope
5. Tom said he would ____ his cookies.
   - ○ shine
   - ○ share
6. Sandy found a ____ of socks under her bed.
   - ○ pair
   - ○ peer

Name ______________________________

## Watch Your Words

Draw a picture to match the words in each box.

| | |
|---|---|
| a cantankerous creature | a swarm of happy bees |
| an unbearably steep climb | an early bird with an idea |

## Choose and Write

Write the correct *a-* word in the sentence.

1. Dad leaned his ladder __________ the living room wall.

2. The bird flew __________ when we opened the back door.

3. My baby brother has been __________ for a few minutes.

4. Mrs. Clark planted flowers __________ the fence.

5. Uncle Rich read a book to us __________ our country.

6. Set the mixing bowl __________ for right now.

7. The puppy is __________ of loud noises.

8. The twins are dressed __________ for their picture.

# Creature Chatter

Name ____________________

## Pick a Character

Write the name of the creature who said each sentence.

|  |  |  |  |  |
|---|---|---|---|---|
| Crusty | Flea | Beetle | Flutterby | Fox |

"You do take the cake."

____________________

"But the sea's more for me;
I'm not built for land."

____________________

"Avaunt!"

____________________

"Flea saved you
from a terrible ride."

____________________

"You go to sleep,
and I'll give you a ride."

____________________

"Forgive my behavior;
can't I please make amends?"

____________________

"I know a few things
you might like to try."

____________________

"There is no big city."

____________________

# *Crusty and Friends*

## Find the Ones

Read these last lines from "The Cranky Blue Crab."
Draw a line under the sets of rhyming words.

Now when Beetle plays music
The crab hums along
And Fleabus is learning
To sing a whale song.
And Crusty's at home
Under Jaggedy Ledge,
Down by the sea,
By its rippling edge.

## Rhyme and Draw

Write a word that rhymes to finish each poem.
Choose one poem and draw a picture to go with it.

1. I jumped a rope, I climbed a tree,
   I ran a race and skinned my ____________.

2. While swinging in the sky so blue,
   I swung too high and lost my ____________.

3. When Granny drives her little car,
   She never drives it very ____________.

# Helping Hands

Name ______________________________

## Get in Line

Help Jan fix the dike. Number the sentences in story order.

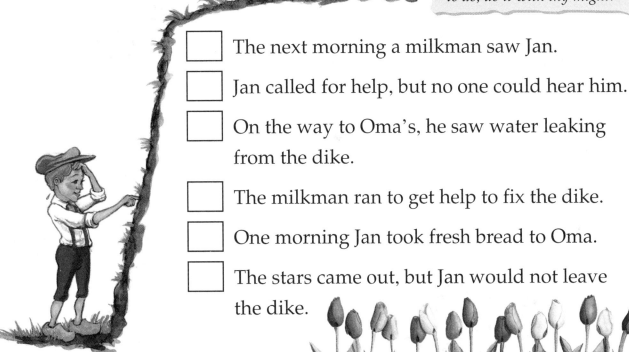

**ECCLESIASTES 9:10**
*Whatsoever thy hand findeth to do, do it with thy might.*

- ☐ The next morning a milkman saw Jan.
- ☐ Jan called for help, but no one could hear him.
- ☐ On the way to Oma's, he saw water leaking from the dike.
- ☐ The milkman ran to get help to fix the dike.
- ☐ One morning Jan took fresh bread to Oma.
- ☐ The stars came out, but Jan would not leave the dike.

## Find the Ones

Circle the hands next to the right answers.

**What three things are true about Jan?**

- ☞ He stayed all night at the dike.
- ☞ The water swept away his cap.
- ☞ Jan gave up and left.
- ☞ He stopped the water from flooding.
- ☞ Jan's mother scolded him.
- ☞ Oma told him many stories.

**What three things kept Jan from leaving the dike?**

- ☞ No one heard him call for help.
- ☞ His sister was mad at him.
- ☞ He had to fight the sea.
- ☞ He did not listen to his dad.
- ☞ There was a hole in the dike.
- ☞ Jan was afraid of the dark.

# Windmills and Wooden Shoes

## ▸ Order Them

Look at the second letter in each word.
Number the words in each group in alphabetical order.

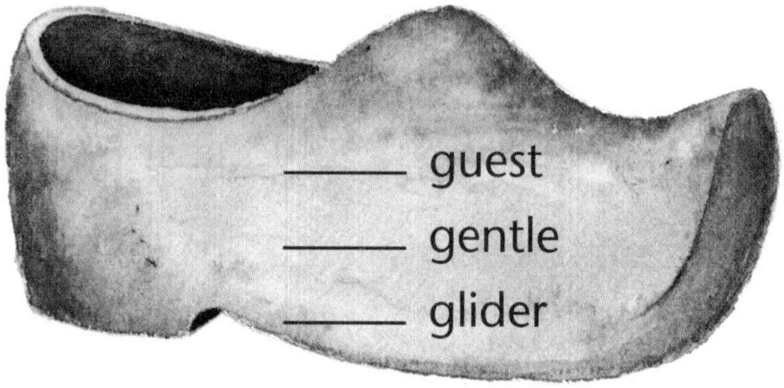

_____ guest
_____ gentle
_____ glider

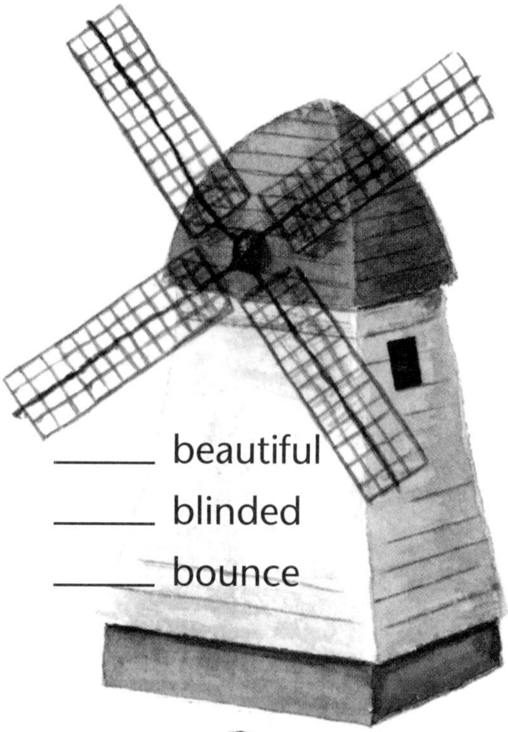

_____ beautiful
_____ blinded
_____ bounce

_____ month
_____ maybe
_____ mumble

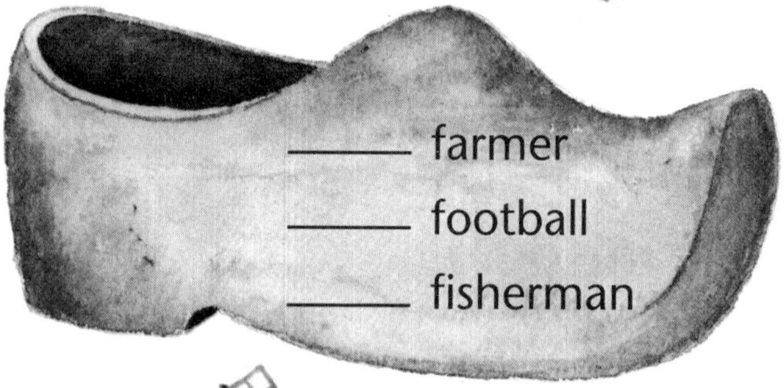

_____ farmer
_____ football
_____ fisherman

_____ steer
_____ snare
_____ several

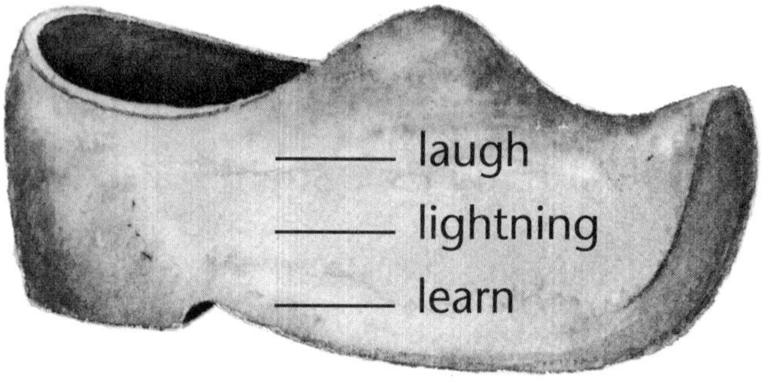

_____ laugh
_____ lightning
_____ learn

# So That Means...

Name ______________________________

## Think About It

Draw a circle around the picture that answers the question.

"Are we ready to go to church, Mom?" asked Kent.

"Yes," Mrs. Hines answered. "Dad is getting the car now. Will you get my Bible?"

Soon Mom and Dad and their three children were driving to church.

"I sure like our new car," said Kent. "The old one was too little for us."

Which is their new car?

Mr. Hines helps in the church. On Sundays he greets people as they come through the doors. He shakes hands with visitors and helps them find a place to sit. Sometimes Mr. Hines helps take up the offering.

Mr. Hines helps in the church on Mondays too. He cuts the grass in the churchyard and sweeps off the porches.

How does Mr. Hines dress on Sunday?

Kent loves God. He was saved when he was eight years old. Kent read a verse in the Bible that says, "Ye must be born again." Kent prayed to God and asked to be forgiven of his sin. God forgave him, and now Kent is a Christian.

When Kent was saved, he wanted everyone to know what had happened to him.

Who heard that Kent was saved?

# Fishy Fisherman

## Sort Them Out

Write the words from the net under the right title.

| Sea Creatures | Parts of a Fish |
| --- | --- |
| | |

## Dots and Circles

Put a big dot between the two words in each compound word.
Circle the right picture.

s a i l b o a t

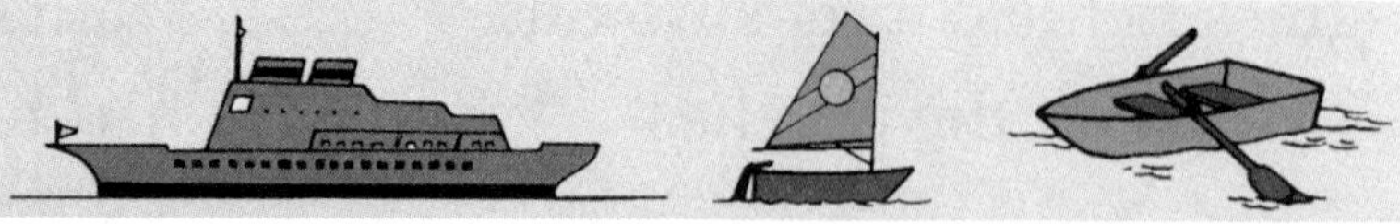

a i r p l a n e

p a n c a k e s

n e w s p a p e r

**Reading 2B: "The Old Fisherman,"** pp. 67-71, Lesson 108
Comprehension: classifying
Word work: dividing compound words between the base words

# The Question's Answer

Name ______________________

## Think and Write

Write the answer to each question.

1. Ben's castle was almost finished. Who had a castle?

2. The sun shone on Marty's book. What belonged to Marty?

3. The man's song floated toward them. Who sang a song?

4. Benjamin's name was from the Bible. Whose name came from the Bible?

5. The children listened to Daddy's rule. Who had a rule?

6. Daddy's children ran to his side. Who had children?

7. Marty wanted to hold Daddy's hand. Whose hand did Marty want to hold?

8. The man's fish were piled beside him. What belonged to the man?

# Come Along, Marker e!

## Choose One

Fill in the circle beside the word that goes in the sentence.

1. Scott got a new baseball ______ for his birthday.

   ○ cap ○ cape

2. My dog likes to ______ his tail.

   ○ wag ○ wage

3. We hung red and white candy ______ on the tree.

   ○ cans ○ canes

4. Brad wiped his feet on the ______.

   ○ mat ○ mate

5. Kay's brother ______ five cookies.

   ○ at ○ ate

## Choose Again

Write a word from the box under each picture.

| | | | | | |
|---|---|---|---|---|---|
| whale | snake | cake | grade | skate | gate |

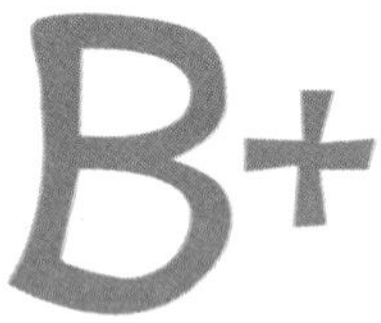


______

______

______

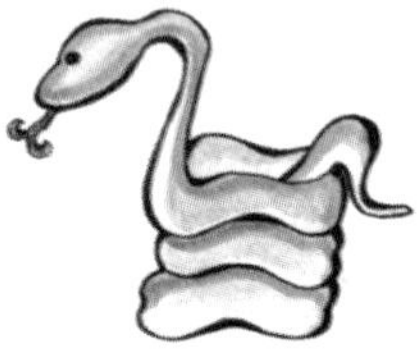

______

______

______

# Amusing Analogies

Name ______________________________

## Finish These

Circle the picture that best completes the sentence.

1. *Sea* is to *boat* as *sky* is to

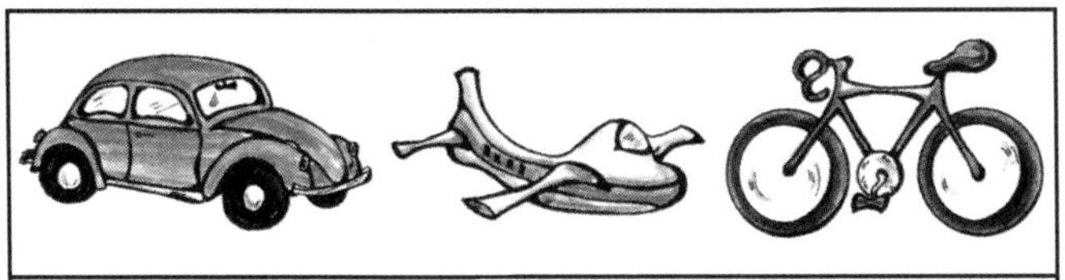

2. *Chirp* is to *bird* as *croak* is to

3. *Hot* is to *fire* as *cold* is to

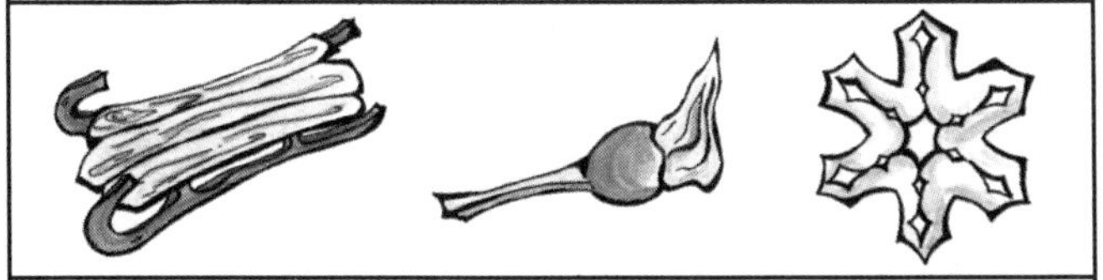

4. *Day* is to *sun* as *night* is to

5. *Hand* is to *mitten* as *foot* is to

## True or False?

Write *True* or *False* for each statement.

1. Marty and Ben heard Mr. Christian's testimony at church. ______________
2. Mr. Christian's mother taught him verses. ______________
3. Mr. Christian left home more than twenty years ago. ______________
4. Marty agreed with what Mr. Christian said about storms. ______________

# Beach Race

Miss Long is spending the day at the beach. Sometimes she and Miss Silent run along the water. They try not to get their feet wet. When Miss Long runs without Miss Silent, Marker *e* runs along with her.

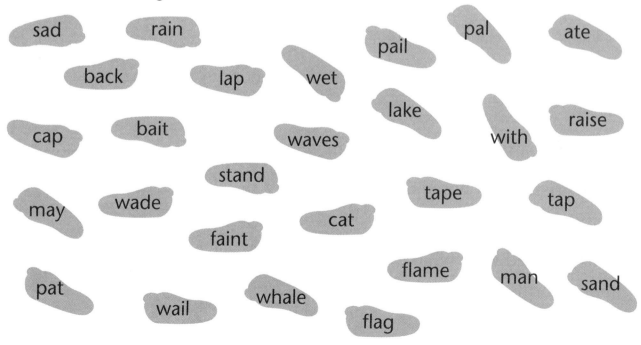

g r a i n          w a d e

## ▶Pick Them Out

Circle the footprints that Miss Long made when she was running with her friends.

sad    rain          pail    pal    ate

back    lap    wet    lake    raise

cap    bait    waves    with

stand

may    wade    tape    tap

cat

faint

pat    whale    flame    man    sand

wail    flag

**Reading 2B: "The Old Fisherman,"** pp. 77-82, Lesson 110
Phonics: using long vowel generalizations: vowel digraph and marker *e*

# Reel in the Answers

Name ______________________

## Work It

You have caught all the words that you need to do this puzzle. Read the clues and write each word where it belongs.

**EPHESIANS 2:8**
*For by grace are ye saved through faith; and that not of yourselves: it is the gift of God.*

### *Across*

1. The old man was catching ____ .
4. Ben made a ____ to hold water and alligators.
5. ____ flew around the children.
6. A saved person is called a ____ .
8. Mr. Christian wore a red ____ .
9. He was saved during a ____ .
10. The old man had ____ home many years before.

### *Down*

1. The children ran to their ____ .
2. Mr. Christian used to be a ____ .
3. The old man sang "____ Grace."
6. Ben built a sand____ .
7. John ____ wrote a song.

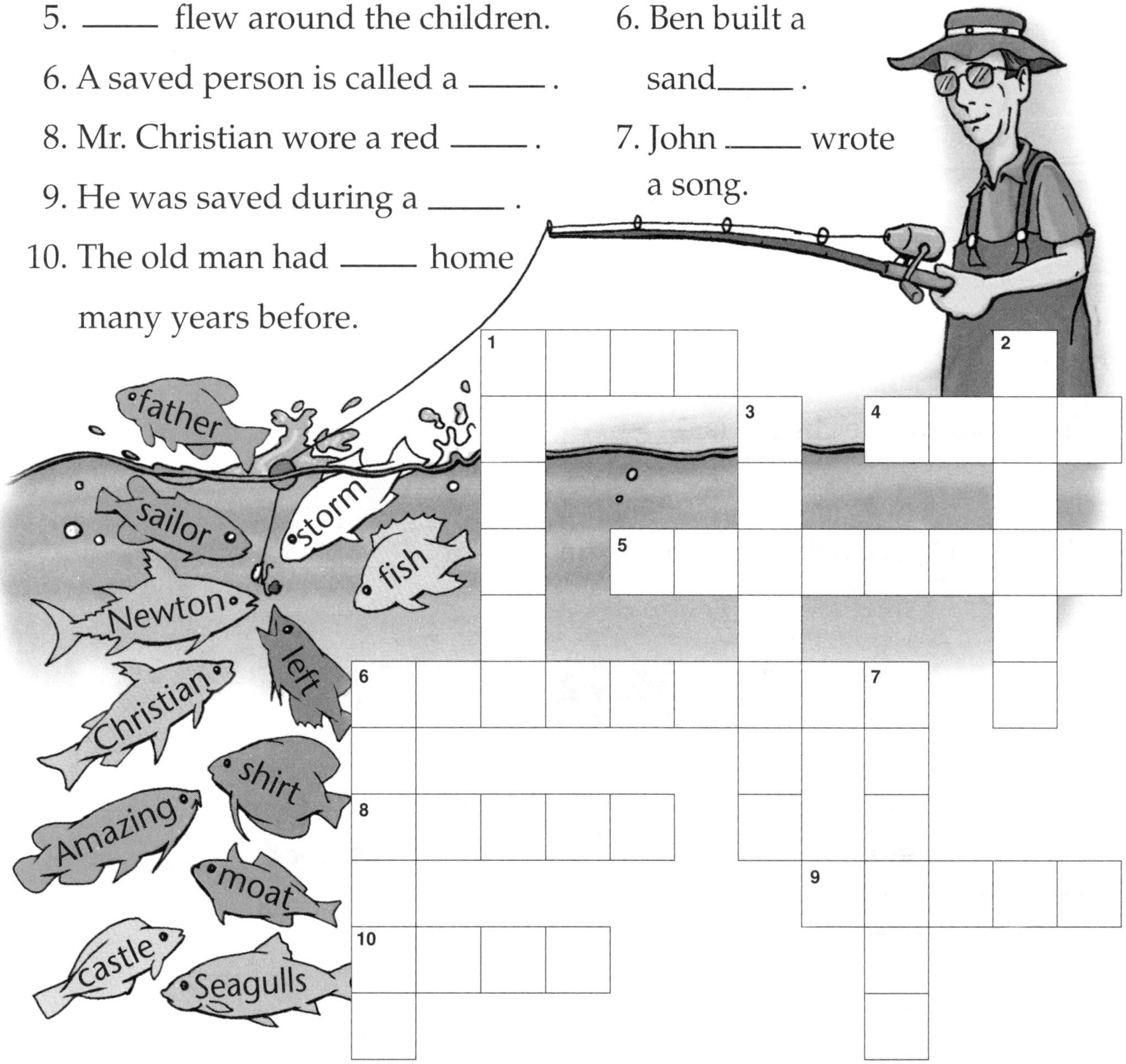

# Sandcastle St.

**Write One**

Choose the correct abbreviation from the sandcastle and write it in the correct sentence.

1. ______________ Brown is my grandfather.

2. The purse on the chair belongs to ______________ Brown.

3. The Browns live on Green ______________ in Flint.

4. ______________ Johnson set Billy's broken arm.

5. The pastor at the church is ______________ Samuels.

6. Have you been to the park that is on Aspen ______________?

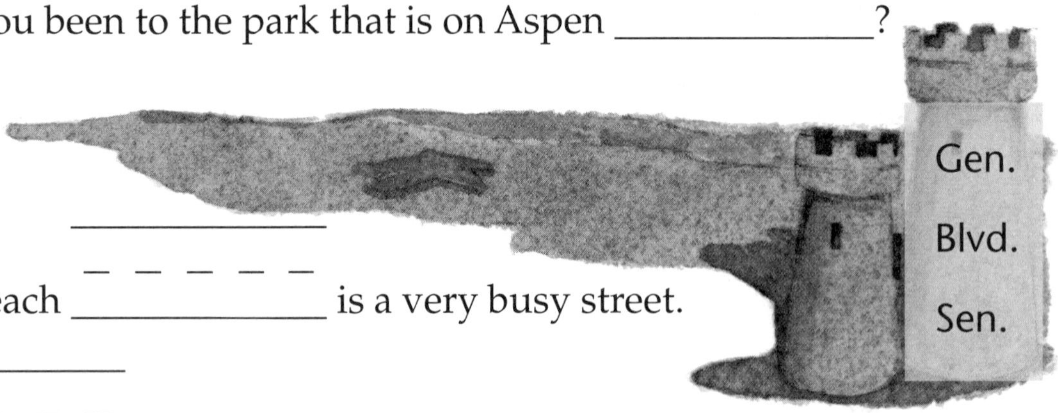


7. West Beach ______________ is a very busy street.

8. ______________ Smith helps to make the laws of our land.

9. ______________ Borders led the troops into the field.

# Just Like a Person

Name ______________________________

## Think About It

Read this line of poetry.

*I'd like to a be a lighthouse*
*With ships all watching me.*

Rachel Field, **"I'd Like to Be a Lighthouse"**

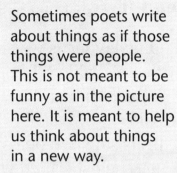

Sometimes poets write about things as if those things were people. This is not meant to be funny as in the picture here. It is meant to help us think about things in a new way.

Can ships really "watch"? __________

How did the artist make the ships look like people?

______________________________________________________________

______________________________________________________________

______________________________________________________________



## Picture It

Draw pictures to show these things acting like people.

| | |
|---|---|
| *In evening the city*<br>*Goes to bed.*<br><br>Langston Hughes, **"City"** | *Nobody else but the rose bush knows*<br>*How nice mud feels between the toes.*<br><br>Molly Chase Boyden, **"Mud"** |

# Classroom by the Sea

## Read It

Sometimes words with the same spelling can have different meanings.

One day Jesus was teaching beside the Sea of Galilee. The people wanted to be near Him and hear every word He said.

Jesus saw two boats beside the shore. The fishermen were washing their nets close by. Jesus sat **down** in a boat and taught the people who were standing on the shore.

When He had finished, Jesus said to a fisherman named Simon, "Take the boat to deep water and cast out your nets."

The nets caught so many fish that they began to break. The men in the other boat came to help. They pulled with all their **might**. Soon both boats were so full that they began to sink.

When Simon saw this, he knew Jesus could do great things. The first thing he did was **fall** on his knees in fear. Jesus told him and the other men not to be afraid. He told them that from now on they would catch men for the kingdom of God.

Simon and the other fisherman followed Jesus everywhere He went. They listened as He taught. They were able to **watch** as he showed His power.

(taken from Luke 5:1-11)

## Pick One

Look carefully at each colored word in the story.
Put an ***X*** by the definition that describes the word in the story.

**LUKE 5:10**
*Fear not; from henceforth thou shalt catch men.*

| | | |
|---|---|---|
| ______ | *down* | Soft, fluffy feathers of a young bird |
| ______ | *down* | Toward the ground, floor, or bottom |
| ______ | *might* | Strength |
| ______ | *might* | Possibly or probably will happen |
| ______ | *fall* | To drop to a lower position |
| ______ | *fall* | The season of the year that is also called autumn |
| ______ | *watch* | To look or observe carefully |
| ______ | *watch* | A small timepiece, usually worn on the wrist |

# A School of Words

Name ____________________

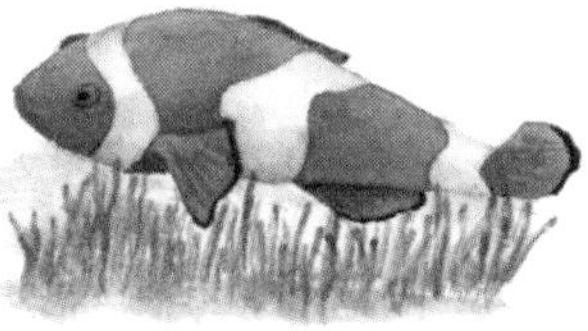

## Which Letter?

Write the letter of the correct definition in the blank beside the word.

| | | |
|---|---|---|
| _____ | tomorrow | a. use hands and feet to go up or over |
| _____ | village | b. went out of sight |
| _____ | climb | c. the day that comes after today |
| _____ | scales | d. a very small town |
| _____ | disappeared | e. These cover the skin of a fish. |

| | | |
|---|---|---|
| _____ | promise | f. say that you will keep your word |
| _____ | listen | g. the one you like best |
| _____ | collect | h. try to hear something |
| _____ | favorite | i. near the beginning |
| _____ | early | j. to gather things together |

## Match Them

Draw a line to match the name of the character with the story.

| | |
|---|---|
| Ben • | • "Hurricane!" |
| Jan • | • "The Old Fisherman" |
| Shanda • | • "Sea Island Mystery" |
| Marcus • | • "The Boy and the Dike" |
| Peter • | • "The Cranky Blue Crab" |
| Flutterby • | • "Fishers of Men" |

# Altogether Fishy!

## Make a Word

Use the prefix *al-* to complete the words in the fish.

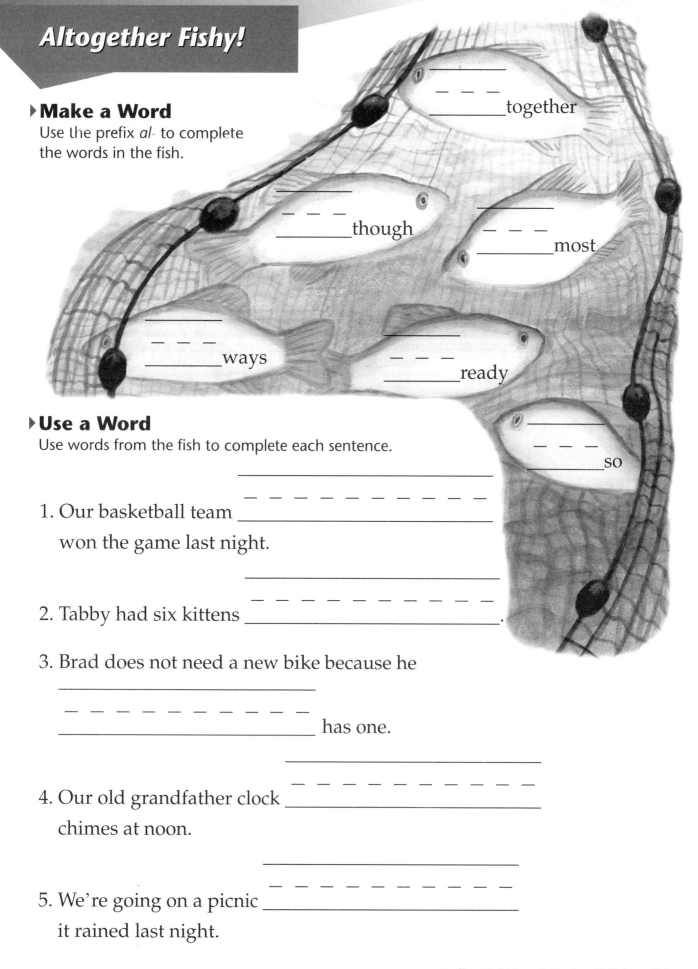

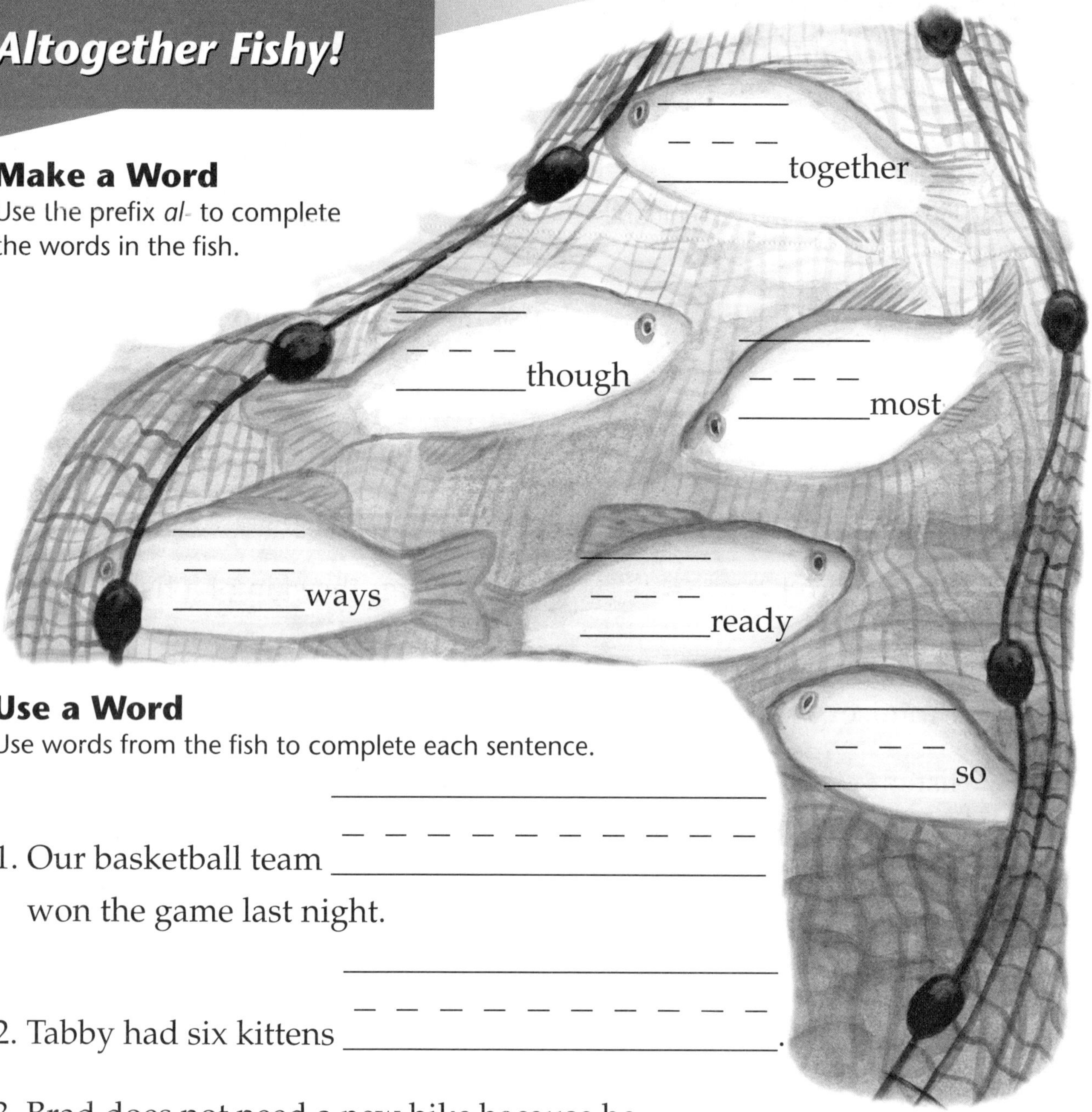


## Use a Word

Use words from the fish to complete each sentence.

1. Our basketball team ______________ won the game last night.

2. Tabby had six kittens ______________.

3. Brad does not need a new bike because he ______________ has one.

4. Our old grandfather clock ______________ chimes at noon.

5. We're going on a picnic ______________ it rained last night.

# Gather Them In

Name ______________________

## Get in Line

Number the pictures to show story order.

## Feelings

Circle the answer.

1. The disciples cast the net into the water. They did not catch any fish. How did the disciples feel?

   excited angry unhappy

2. Jesus told them to cast the net on the right side of the boat. This time the net was full of fish. How did the disciples feel?

   happy sad angry

3. John and Peter saw the Lord on the shore. Peter was excited. How did Peter show his feelings?

   He dragged the net to shore.
   He told the others to hurry.
   He quickly swam to land.

4. The Lord talked to the disciples. How did they show that they would follow the Lord?

   They wanted to tell the gospel.
   They caught more fish.
   They mended their nets.

# Four Little Fish

## Order It

Write a number on each bubble to show alphabetical order.

### *First Letter Work*

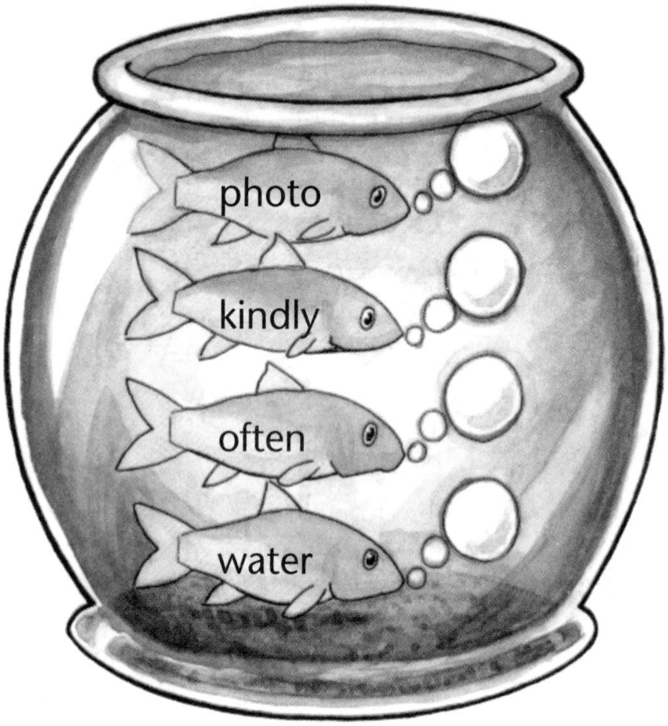


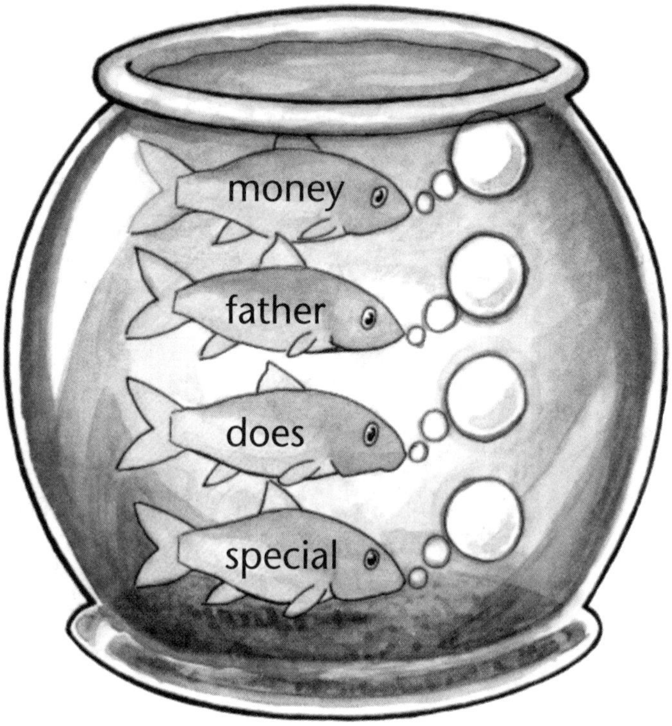


### *Second Letter Work*

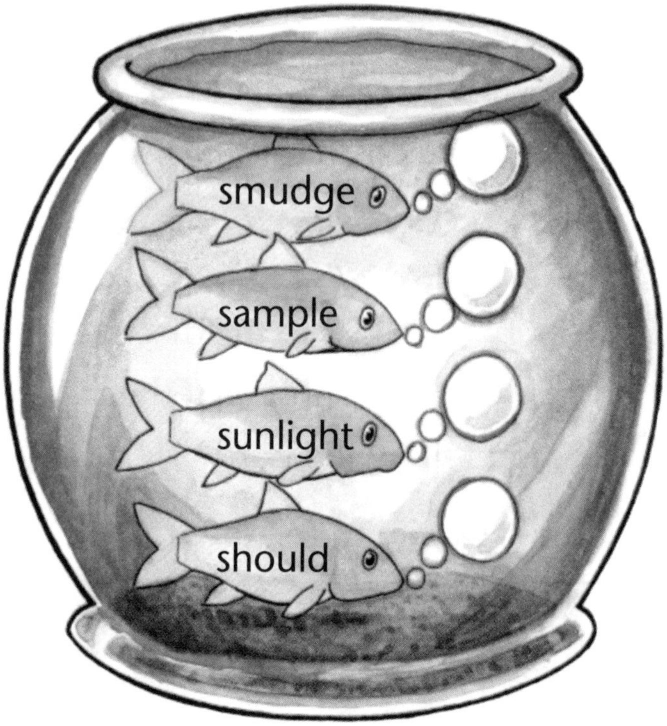


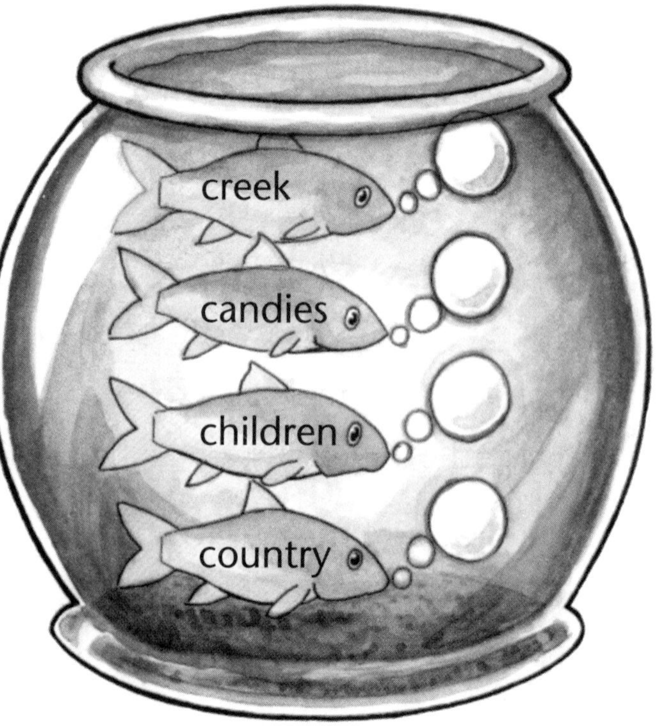

# The Stars and Stripes

Name ______________________

## Read and Do

Read the story. Then follow the directions.

**1** The American flag stands for many things. It makes us think of the love we should have for our country. It makes us think of the people who died to make this a free land.

**2** The first American flag was made many years ago. The leaders of our country planned the pattern for the flag. It had thirteen stars and thirteen stripes to stand for the first thirteen states. As more states joined our country, more stars were added.

**3** Our flag should be treated properly. It should never be allowed to touch the ground. It should be folded carefully when it is put away. We should be as proud of our flag as we are of our country.

Write the number of the correct paragraph beside each main idea.

______ the history of our flag

______ the meaning of our flag

______ the care of our flag

## What Does It Mean?

Fill in the circle beside the right answer.

1. In part **1** the word *land* means
   - ○ farm.  ○ country.

2. In part **2** the word *pattern* means
   - ○ how something looks.
   - ○ the sound that rain makes.

3. In part **3** the word *treated* means
   - ○ allowed.  ○ handled.

# Knocking Knees

### Paint It

Color the pencils that have /n/ spelled *kn* as in *knocking knees.*

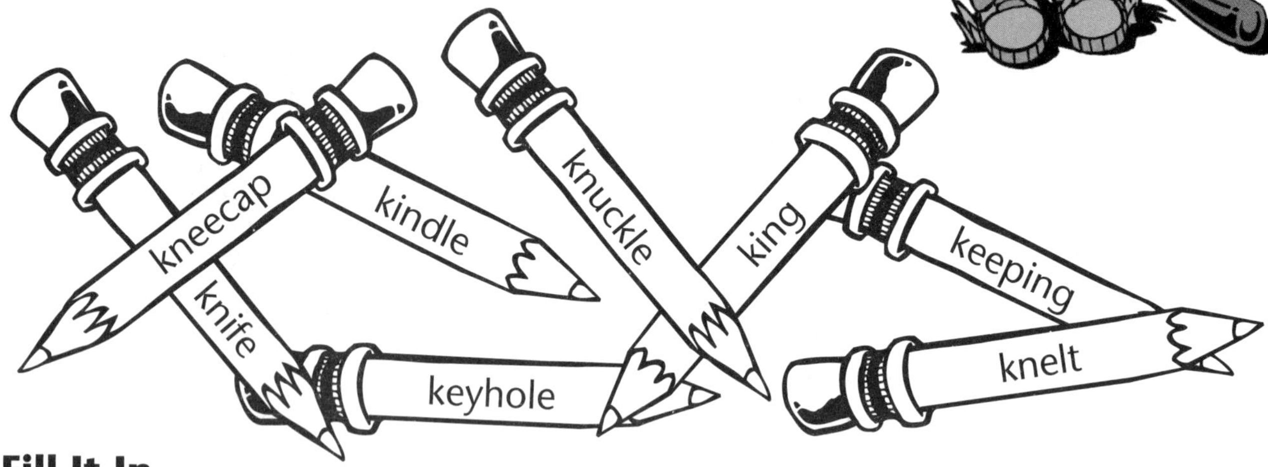


### Fill It In

Write a word from the box to complete each sentence.

| | | | | | |
|---|---|---|---|---|---|
| knapsack | know | knead | knee | knot | knight |

1. What did you pack in your ______________?

2. The ______________ rode the black horse into battle.

3. We must ______________ the clay to mix all of the colors.

4. I have a ______________ in my shoelace.

5. Do you ______________ the way to Mr. Bell's house?

6. Sue fell and scraped her ______________.

# True Friends

Name ______________________

## True or False

Write *T* in front of each sentence that is ***true.*** If the sentence is ***false***, write *F.*

___ America was Juanita's new country.

___ Kristy was a Spanish girl.

___ Kristy and Juanita ate tacos for dessert.

___ Juanita's Bible verse was Romans 5:8.

___ Kristy and Juanita prayed for their new friend every day.

___ The girl from the park came to the school program.

## Who Is It?

Read each sentence. Draw a line to the person that the word in the box tells about.

1. Juanita was thankful for her new Christian school.
2. Mother made something special, and she called it flan.
3. Kristy said that she would help Juanita.
4. Kristy skipped up to the swings, her red curls bobbing.
5. "Thanks for helping me," said Juanita.

# Take a Big Bite

## Mark the Spot

Read each word and put a big dot between the two syllables.

## Sort Them Out

Write the words with one syllable under *1*.
Write the words with two syllables under *2*.

pledge    dinner    Romans    friends    Spanish    verse

1

2

# Really? Fancy That!

Name ____________________

## Read and Think

Read each story. Draw a circle around the word that tells what kind of story it is.

### *A Tail Tale*

"Help! Help!" someone yelled.

A little squirrel popped his head out of his hole to see who was calling.

"Someone's making an awful racket!" he said to himself. Looking around, he saw a bear that had fallen into a hole.

"So you are the one who's shouting," the squirrel said. "Hang on to my tail, and I'll pull you out." The squirrel tugged and pulled and pulled and tugged. Out came the bear!

"Thanks for your help," said the bear. "You saved my life!"

real fanciful

### *Playing and Helping*

A brown turtle waved his legs wildly in the air. He had rolled onto his back and couldn't get back over. Just then a fox came close and sniffed him. Pulling in his legs, the timid turtle snapped his shell closed. The fox playfully batted him until he flipped the turtle back over! As the fox trotted away, the little animal poked his head out. Now he was ready to go on his way again.

real fanciful

# Sounds Silent to Me

### Find the Ones

Color the canteens that have words with silent consonants.

| | | | |
|---|---|---|---|
| tight | baby | fin | fork |
| write | knee | stop | lamb |
| fort | wren | bag | chalk |
| wind | light | risk | |

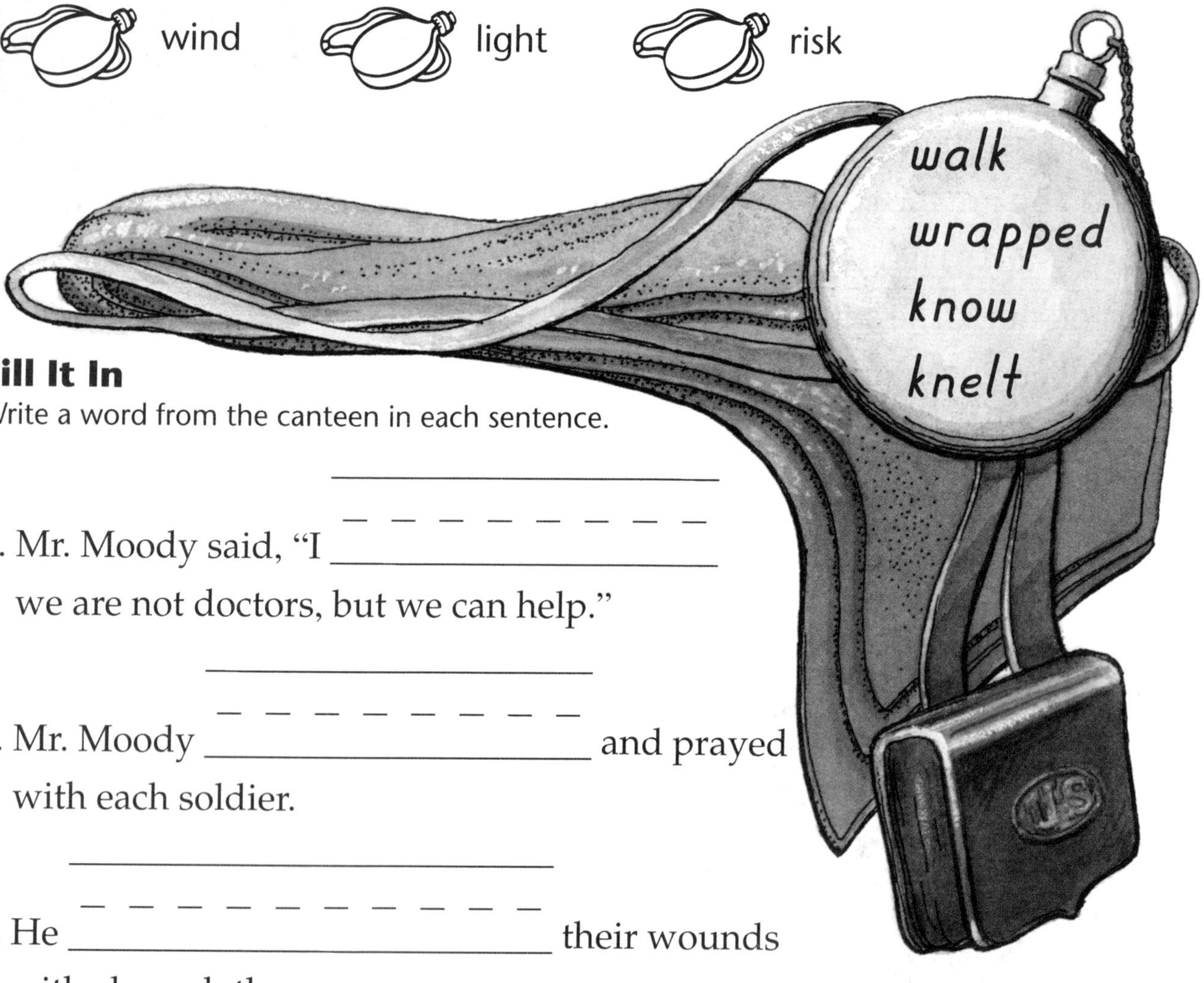


### Fill It In

Write a word from the canteen in each sentence.

1. Mr. Moody said, "I ________ we are not doctors, but we can help."

2. Mr. Moody ________ and prayed with each soldier.

3. He ________ their wounds with clean cloth.

4. The men had to ________ to the stream to get water for the soldiers.

# A Miracle for Mr. Moody

Name ______________________________

MATTHEW 6:11
*Give us this day our daily bread.*

## Get in Line

Number the sentences in story order.
The first one is done for you.

____ A wagon filled with bread stopped in front of the men.

__1__ The general asked Mr. Moody to help the soldiers.

____ The men gave the soldiers water from the canteens.

____ The young men took the canteens to the stream.

____ Mr. Moody thanked the Lord for the bread.

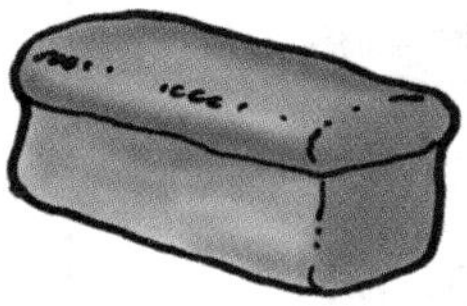

## Which One?

Fill in the circle beside the sentence that best describes each picture.

○ A man drove up in a wagon.

○ The men unloaded the wagon.

○ A man nearby raised up on one elbow.

○ Mr. Moody rolled up his sleeves.

○ He sat down.

○ He knelt on the ground beside the sheet of canvas.

○ Mr. Moody held out his hand.

○ Three men carried the bread.

# Compass Rose

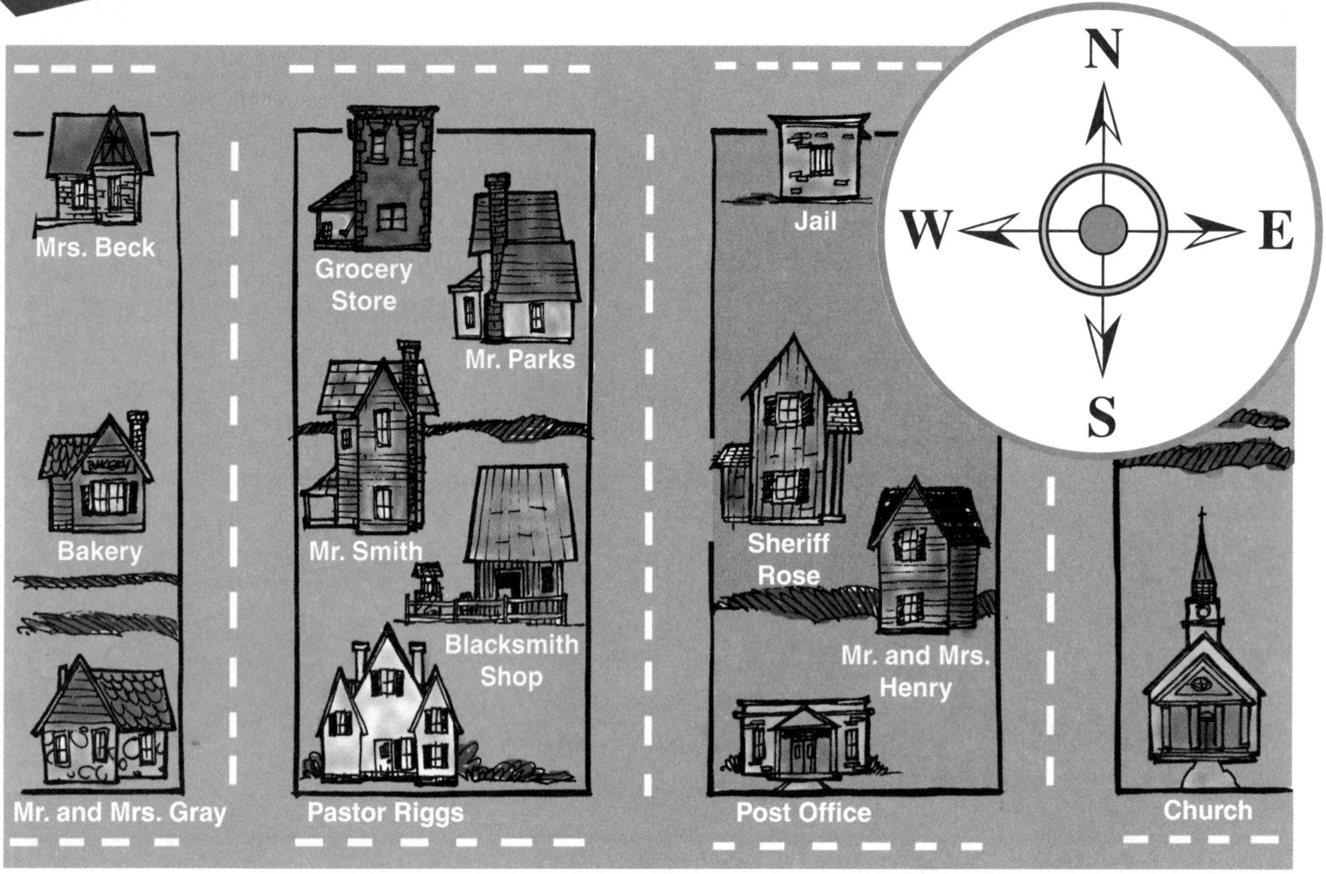


## ▸ Choose One

Notice the compass rose. Name the direction each character will take.

North, South, East, West

1. Mrs. Beck needs sugar. ____________
2. Mr. Smith, the baker, is late for work. ____________
3. Pastor Riggs will preach on Sunday. ____________
4. Sheriff Rose is headed for the jail. ____________
5. Mr. Parks has a letter to mail. ____________

## ▸ You Try

Make up a new question. Ask a friend to find a direction on the map.

# Surprise!

Name ______________________

## Choose Two

From the words on the cookies, choose a synonym and an antonym for the underlined word in each sentence.

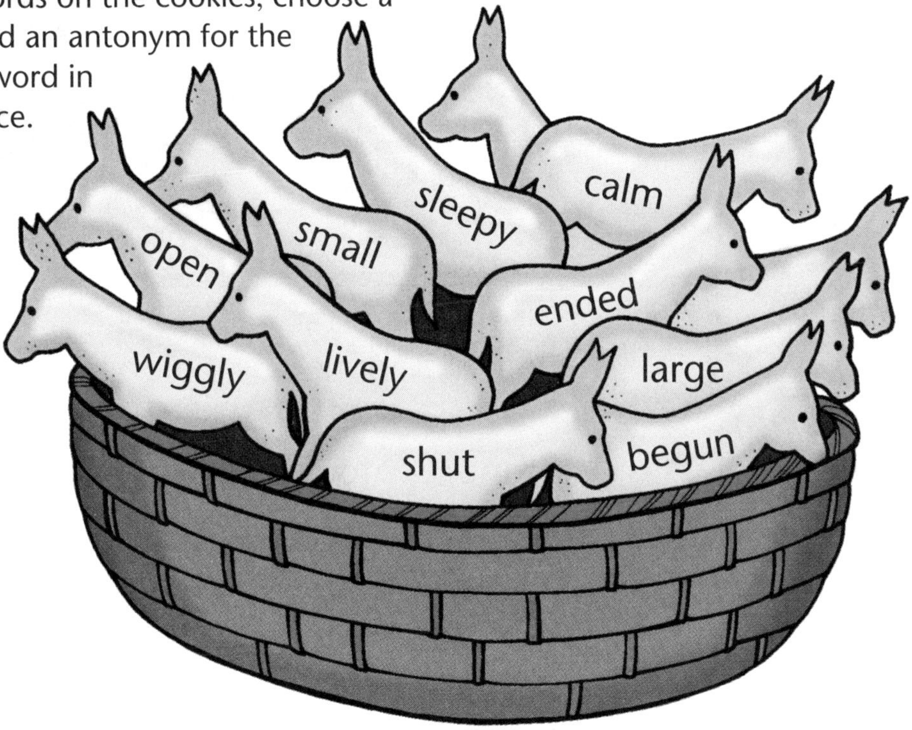


| | Synonyms | Antonyms |
|---|---|---|
| 1. "You look <u>tired</u> today," said the teacher. | | |
| 2. "Let's be <u>still</u> for a while," she told the class. | | |
| 3. "<u>Close</u> your eyes while I read a story." | | |
| 4. When they had <u>finished</u> their rest, the teacher called, "Surprise!" | | |
| 5. Then she gave everyone cookies that looked like <u>little</u> donkeys. | | |

# Glum Goes to Town

## Connect the Words

Help the farmer and his son take Glum to town. Draw a line to join the words with a long *o* vowel sound and marker *e* as in *note.*

rope

off broke globe scope

throne fog school

two

hope

code

slope could about joke

vote

town robe shone

country

spoke

you

tailor

stone

love woke son

home word those

# Rope the Answers

Name ______________________________

## Work It

Use the words inside the box to fill in the puzzle.

### Across

2. The farmer and his _____ took Glum to town.
4. The _____ said both should ride the donkey.
6. The farmer and his son carried Glum on a _____ .
8. The farmer wanted to _____ Glum in town.
9. The farmer tried to listen to everyone's _____ .
10. The _____ owned the donkey.

### Down

1. Glum's long ears were _____ .
2. A cobblestone _____ went through the town.
3. The townsfolk _____ at the farmer carrying the donkey.
5. The _____ carried a sack of wheat.
6. You cannot _____ everyone.
7. Glum was a _____ .

| | |
|---|---|
| donkey | son |
| advice | sell |
| miller | gray |
| farmer | pole |
| please | tailor |
| laughed | street |

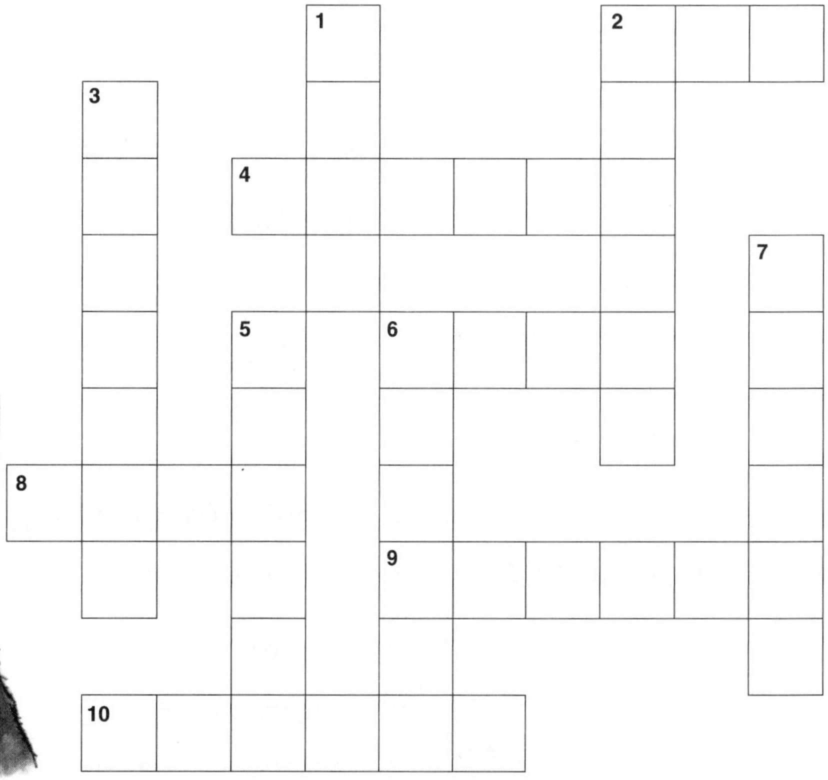

# Don't Be Glum

## Choose One

Circle the word that tells about each donkey.

rusted rested

squinted sparked

sneered splashed

shaded shocked

jolted jumbled

growled grinned

looked laughed

trotted twisted

## Choose Again

Fill in the circle beside the word that belongs in the space.

1. Brian was ______ that his teacher remembered him.

   ○ allowed ○ amazed ○ arrived

2. Lauren ______ at the funny story.

   ○ laughed ○ liked ○ locked

3. The cowboys ______ beside the stream.

   ○ counted ○ crushed ○ camped

4. The cow jumped over the moon while the cat ______.

   ○ finished ○ fiddled ○ frightened



**Reading 2B: "The Farmer and the Donkey,"** pp. 126-31, Lesson 122
Phonics: reading words with an *-ed* ending
Comprehension: recognizing emotional responses

# What a Hat!

Name ______________________

## Fold It

Read and follow the directions.

1. Start with a sheet of newspaper.
   Lay it flat.

2. Fold it from top to bottom.
   Press it flat. Leave it folded.

3. Fold it side to side and press
   it flat. Open this fold back up.

4. Bring each of the top corners to
   the center line you made in number 3.
   Press it flat.

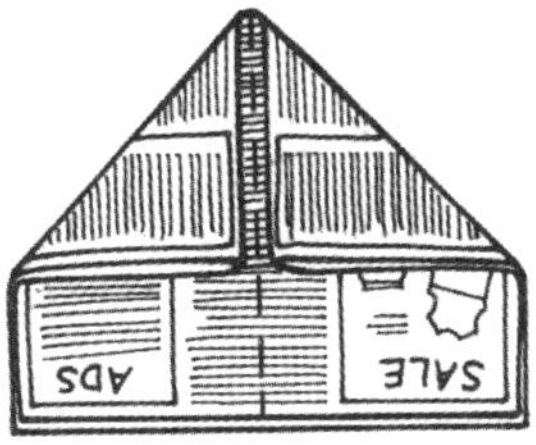


5. Fold one bottom edge up.
   Press it flat.

6. Turn the hat over and fold the other
   bottom edge up. Press it flat.
   Your hat is finished!

# Pedal Power

### Cut It Up

Put a large dot between the syllables.
Write one syllable on each wheel.

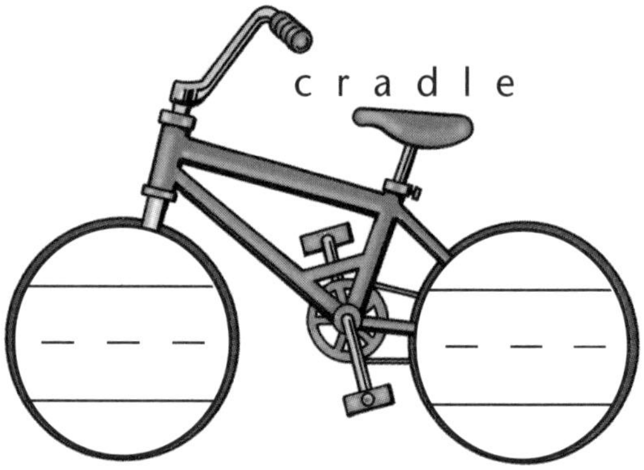

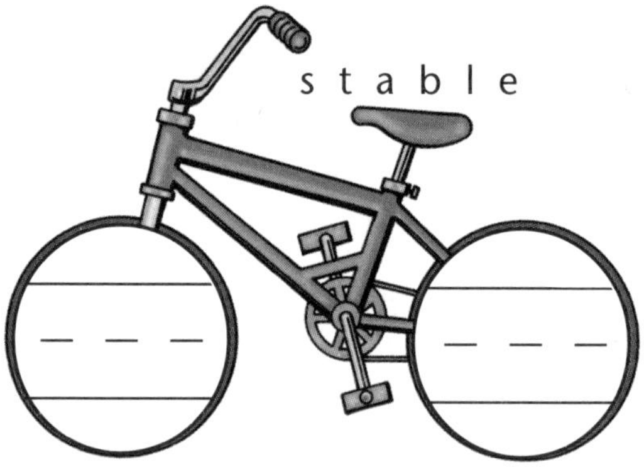

### Write It Down

Answer the questions. Use the words on the bicycles.

1. Which word names a place for horses? ____________
2. Which word names something that is round? ____________
3. Which word names something that gives light? ____________
4. Which word names something that makes a loud noise? ____________

**Reading 2B: "Have You Seen My Dog?"** pp. 132-36, Lesson 123
Word work: dividing words that end with a consonant + *le*
Comprehension: matching words and definitions

208

# Cat Tales

Name ____________________

## Who Said What?

Draw a line from the sentence to the person who said it.

*"Something must have happened to their mother."*

*"Why don't you telephone the newspaper office?"*

*"My curtains!"*

Mrs. Wei

Pete

Allen

*"We can take the kittens home in our bike baskets."*

*"How pretty. Where did you find them?"*

*"Lady sure looks lonely."*

## Fill It In

Write a word from the curtain in each space.

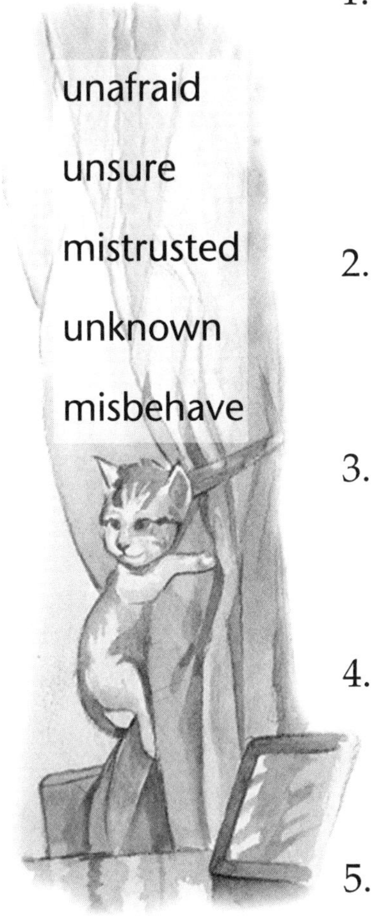

1. Lady often disappeared to an ____________ place.
2. The kittens began to ____________ as they got bigger.
3. Mrs. Wei was ____________ that a dog would adopt kittens.
4. The kittens were ____________ even when the dogs barked at them.
5. Mr. Wei ____________ the playful kittens.

**Reading 2B: "Have You Seen My Dog?"** pp. 137-42, Lesson 124
Comprehension: matching story characters and dialogue; getting meaning from prefixes *mis-*, *un-*

209

# The Dividing Line

## Mark the Spot
Put a dot between the syllables.

m e n d e d  u n w r a p  r e c a l l

s i n g i n g  p a i n t e d  m e e t i n g

u n p a c k  m i s t r u s t  l o c k e r

## Find the One
Use the above words to complete each sentence.

1. Uncle Bill ______________ the fence white.

2. Mother ______________ the tear in my shirt pocket.

3. We should ______________ the camper when we get home.

4. Do you want any help when you ______________ the gifts?

5. We're ______________ Dave at the park to play baseball.

# Write? Right!

Name ______________________

## Pick One

Look at the words and the pictures that show their meanings.
***Write*** the ***right*** word in the space.

hair

hare

1. The ______________ ran away from the hunter.

2. Betsy brushed her ______________ one hundred times.

3. Mary fed grass to her pet ______________.

knight

night

4. Alan didn't sleep well last ______________.

5. The ______________ rescued the queen from harm.

6. The ______________ was dark and dreary.

ring

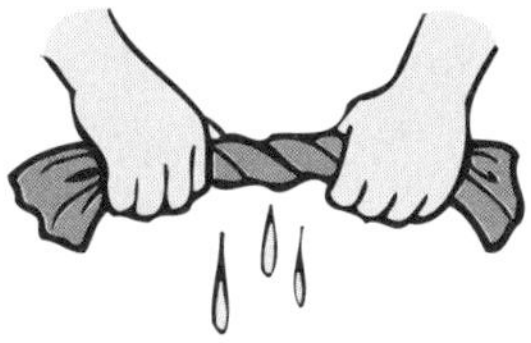
wring

7. Mother took her ______________ off before she did the dishes.

8. Shirley left her ______________ on the sink.

9. Mother had to ______________ out the towel.

# You Amaze Me!

## Find the Way

Help Naaman find the path to the Jordan River by drawing a line to connect the words with the long *a* two-vowel pattern.

pail

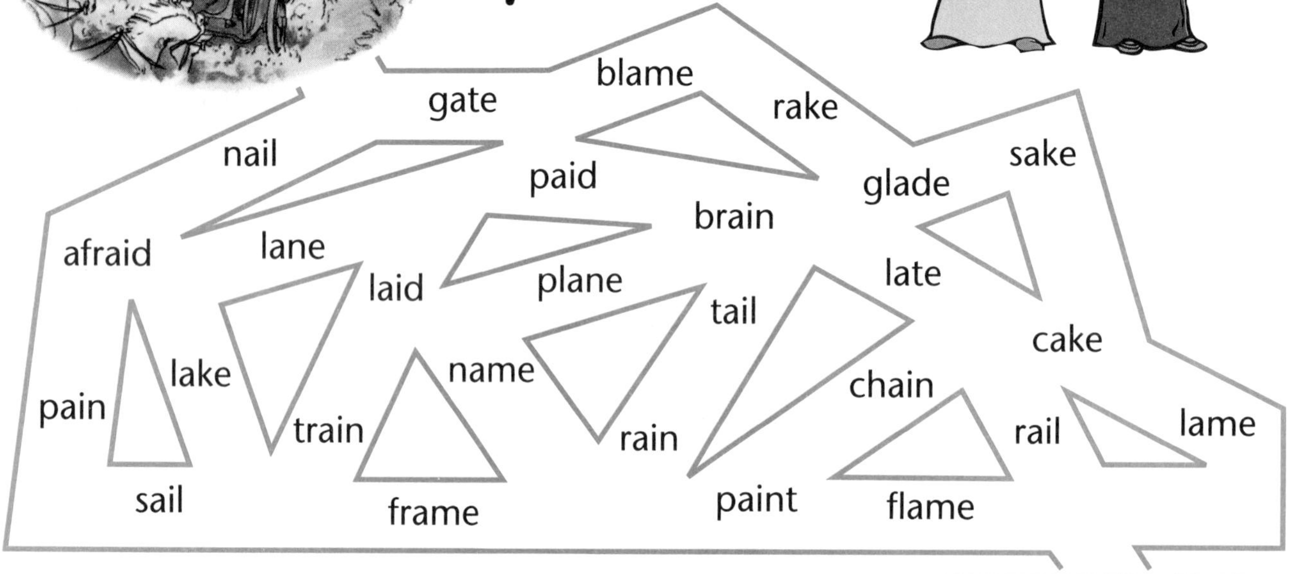

## Fill It In

Write one of the words you connected in each sentence.

1. John used green ______________ on the gate.

2. I must use my ______________ to learn.

3. Sarah ______________ her coat on the box.

4. The boat had a tall ______________.

5. The hammer hit the ______________.

*II KINGS 5:15*

*Behold, now I know that there is no God in all the earth, but in Israel.*





**Reading 2B: "The Little Maid,"** pp. 143-49, Lesson 125
Phonics: applying long vowel generalizations: vowel digraph for /ā/ as *ai* in *rain*

# Naaman's Cure

Name

## ▶ Choose One

Choose the best ending and write the letter in the space.

1. One day a little maid _____     a. had failed to heal Naaman.

2. The doctors in Syria _____     b. knew Elisha could heal Naaman.

3. But the little girl _____     c. found her mistress crying.

4. Captain Naaman _____     d. told Naaman to wash in the Jordan.

5. Elisha's messenger _____     e. traveled to Elisha's house.

6. That day the Lord _____     f. performed a great miracle.

## ▶ Find One

Write the answer to each question in the space.

1. The maid's tears showed her sadness. What belonged to the maid?

_____

_____

2. The horses pulled Naaman's chariot. Who had a chariot?

_____

_____

3. Naaman's chariot came to a stop at Elisha's door. What belonged to Elisha?

_____

_____

4. Elisha's servant gave Naaman a message. Who had a servant?

_____

_____

5. Naaman turned to leave Elisha's house. What did Elisha own?

_____

_____

**Reading 2B: "The Little Maid,"** pp. 150-54, Lesson 126
Comprehension: combining sentence parts; recognizing possessives

# Open Chariots

## Paint Some

Color the chariots that have words with a long vowel in the first syllable.

spider

candle

kettle

letter

paper

music

cattle

shiny

locate

## Use Some

Write one of the long vowel, open syllable words in each sentence.

1. "Write your name on your ________," said the teacher.

2. The pretty ________ made me want to sing.

3. A very ________ star led the wise men.

4. It is hard to ________ a needle in a haystack.

5. A tiny ________ made a huge web over my door.

# What Do You Mean?

Name ______________________________

### Match Them Up

Draw a line from each picture to the sentence that tells about it.

Each child is wearing a name *tag*.

The children are playing *tag* in the school yard.

---

Mr. Wilson brought home a bird with a large ***bill***.

Mr. Wilson got a telephone ***bill*** in the mail.

---

Mother is using a ***match*** to light a candle.

Mother bought a shirt to ***match*** my new pants.

---

The kitten began to ***lap*** up the milk.

The kitten sat quietly in Jan's ***lap***.

---

Angela ***can*** play the violin.

Angela is opening a ***can*** of soup.

# Twelve Tubas Twist and Tickle

## Match Them

Write the number of each phrase in the box beside the right picture.

1. a tuba in a pool
2. a tuba cooking
3. two tubas in the news
4. a tuba with a new tooth
5. a tuba drinking juice
6. two tubas pushing a buggy
7. a tuba with a sore foot
8. two tubas holding balloons

# In a Class by Itself

Name ______________________________

Here are some of the things Annie wanted to learn about.

| | |
|---|---|
| Flowers | Lights |
| Clothes | Jobs |

## Find the Title

1. Look at the two words in each book. From the box, write the title that best describes the words.

teacher
painter

flashlight
lamp

tulip
pansy

shoes
shirts

## Sort the Rest

2. From the box, write the words in the correct books.

| | | | |
|---|---|---|---|
| daisy | sun | candle | carpenter |
| mittens | hats | violet | fireman |

# A Splendid Ride

### Make a Word

Use the letters from the train to complete each word.

| | | |
|---|---|---|
| ______inter | ______eet | ______ow |
| ______ub | ______one | ______ing |
| ______ill | ______it | ______ape |

### Use a Word

Use words from above to complete the sentences.

1. My friend lives down the ____________.
2. The king sits on the ____________.
3. Dad pulled a ____________ out of my finger.
4. I will ____________ the pans for Mother.
5. Amber put the beads on a ____________.

# Two Friends

Name ____________________

## Who Is It?

Whom do these statements describe? Circle *Annie*, *Helen*, or both names if the statement tells about both.

| | | |
|---|---|---|
| She went to Perkins. | Annie | Helen |
| She was deaf. | Annie | Helen |
| She used the finger alphabet. | Annie | Helen |
| She lived in Alabama with her family. | Annie | Helen |
| She had an operation to make her see. | Annie | Helen |
| She was sent to a place for poor people. | Annie | Helen |

## Which One?

Fill in the circle beside the word that best fits the sentence.

1. Annie wanted to be able to ______.

   ○ sing ○ speak ○ read

2. In September, Annie went to Perkins School for the ______.

   ○ Deaf ○ Blind ○ Old

3. Annie wanted Helen to learn ______.

   ○ songs ○ poems ○ words

4. The first word Helen understood was ______.

   ○ water ○ cake ○ doll

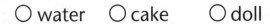

# Pair Them Up

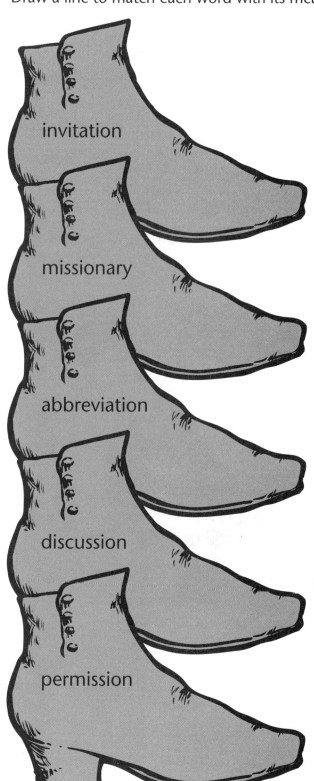

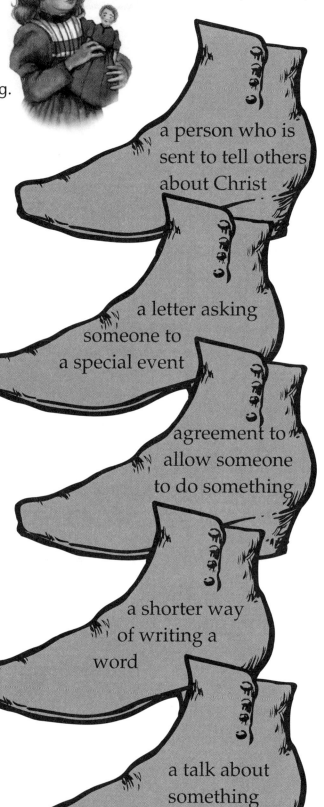

## Match It

Help Helen find the pairs of shoes for her doll.
Draw a line to match each word with its meaning.

| | |
|---|---|
| invitation | a person who is sent to tell others about Christ |
| missionary | a letter asking someone to a special event |
| abbreviation | agreement to allow someone to do something |
| discussion | a shorter way of writing a word |
| permission | a talk about something |



**Reading 2B: "Annie Sullivan,"** pp. 163-67, Lesson 130
Phonics: recognizing common suffixes: *-tion, -sion*
Comprehension: matching words and definitions; developing vocabulary

# What a Tail

Name ______________________

## Draw Some Tails

Draw a tail on the mouse next to each sentence that is true.

1. Mouse liked living alone.

2. He was an old gray mouse.

3. He wanted to help everyone.

4. Preston came to Mouse's house on a stormy day.

5. Mouse gave Preston some cheese.

6. Mouse wouldn't help Preston.

## Match the Tales

Write the number of the title that matches each picture.

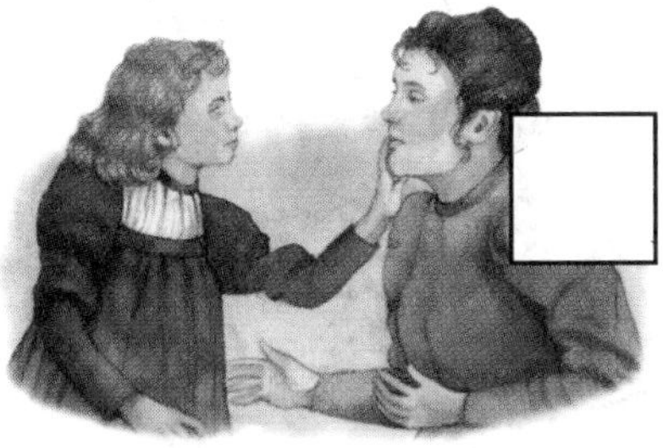

1. "New Friends"
2. "Bread From Heaven"
3. "Just Mouse"
4. "The Farmer and the Donkey"
5. "Annie Sullivan"
6. "The Little Maid"

# Contraction Action

## Make Contractions

Make contractions out of the words.

I will ______

she will ______

they will ______

you have ______

we have ______

I have ______

## Use Contractions

Make a contraction to complete each sentence.

They will

1. ______ eat the cheese for lunch.

I have

2. ______ started eating my lunch.

She will

3. ______ sing a song for us.

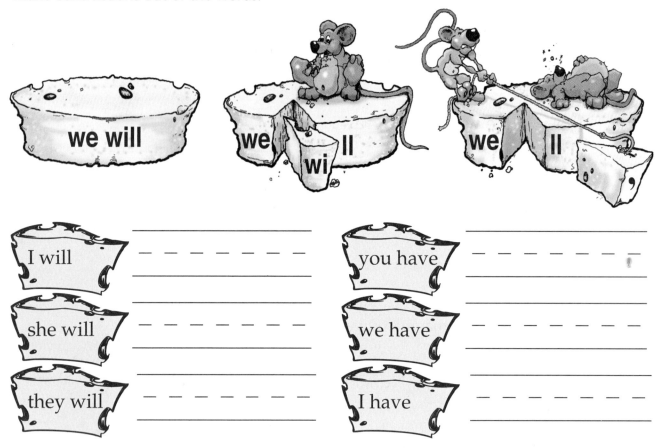

# Draw Your Own Conclusions

Name ____________________

## Read and Think

Read each story. Fill in the circle beside the correct answer to each question.

Patton heard a tapping sound as Granddaddy Mouse limped from the kitchen to the living room. He sat in his chair and propped up his sore leg.

"I'm glad the doctor gave you something to help you walk," Patton said.

Granddaddy Mouse leaned his "extra leg" against the chair. "My legs just aren't enough," he said.

What is Granddaddy Mouse's "extra leg"?

- ○ his tail
- ○ his cane
- ○ his chair

★ ★ ★ ★ ★

Thunder crashed. Lightning lit the sky. The five little mice snuggled close to Granddaddy Mouse on the chair. Granddaddy Mouse read a book to them. The wind howled outside, but inside, the mice were cozy and safe.

What caused the noise outside?

- ○ a cat fight
- ○ a football game
- ○ a storm

Preston sniffed. The smell of cheese seemed to tickle his nose. He peeked around the wall. A thick slice of cheese lay on the floor. Quickly, Preston scampered across the room and grabbed the cheese.

Snap!

Preston tried to dash away, but he found that he couldn't.

What had snapped?

- ○ a trap
- ○ the plate
- ○ the cheese

# A Few Clues

## Color the Ones

Color each new broom that has a word with the same vowel sound as *new* or *broom*.

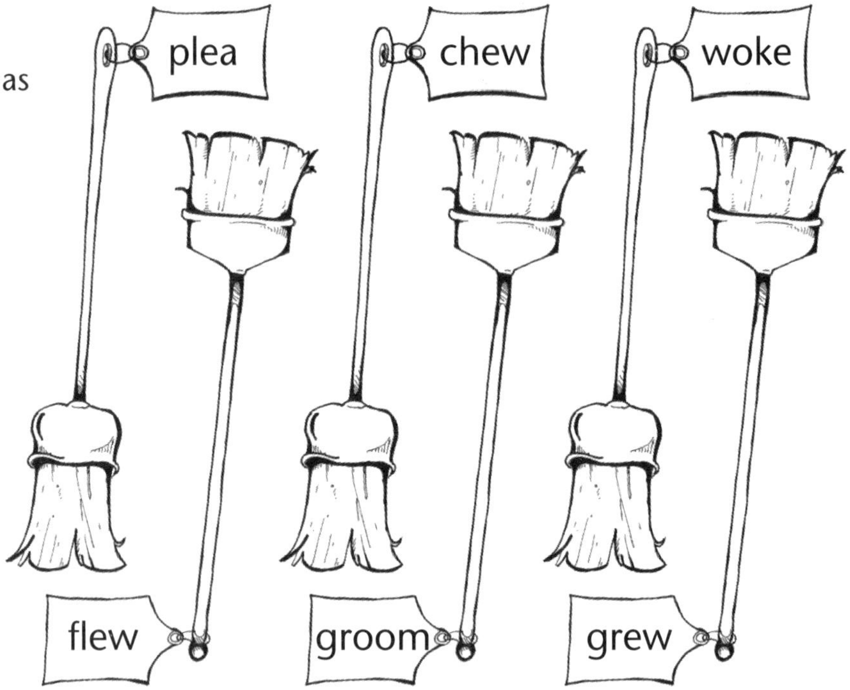


## Riddle Time

Draw a line from the riddle to the word.

*Squeeze me out on paper and watch the paper stick;*
*Or seal up an envelope with me and just one lick.*

*I am a pretty color and as bright as day.*
*If you let go of me, I'm sure to float away.*

*I may be an apple, a pear, or a peach.*
*I'm up in a tree, just out of your reach.*

*I may be as round as a big apple pie.*
*But sometimes I'm only a smile in the sky.*

*I'm what the wind did when it brought the leaves down.*
*I'm what the wind did when it went through the town.*

*I'm not morning, and I'm not night.*
*When it's my time, the sun is bright.*

balloon

glue

noon

fruit

moon

blew

# They Finished the Job

Name ______________________________

## Draw It

Follow the directions to finish the picture of the Wright brothers' first flight.

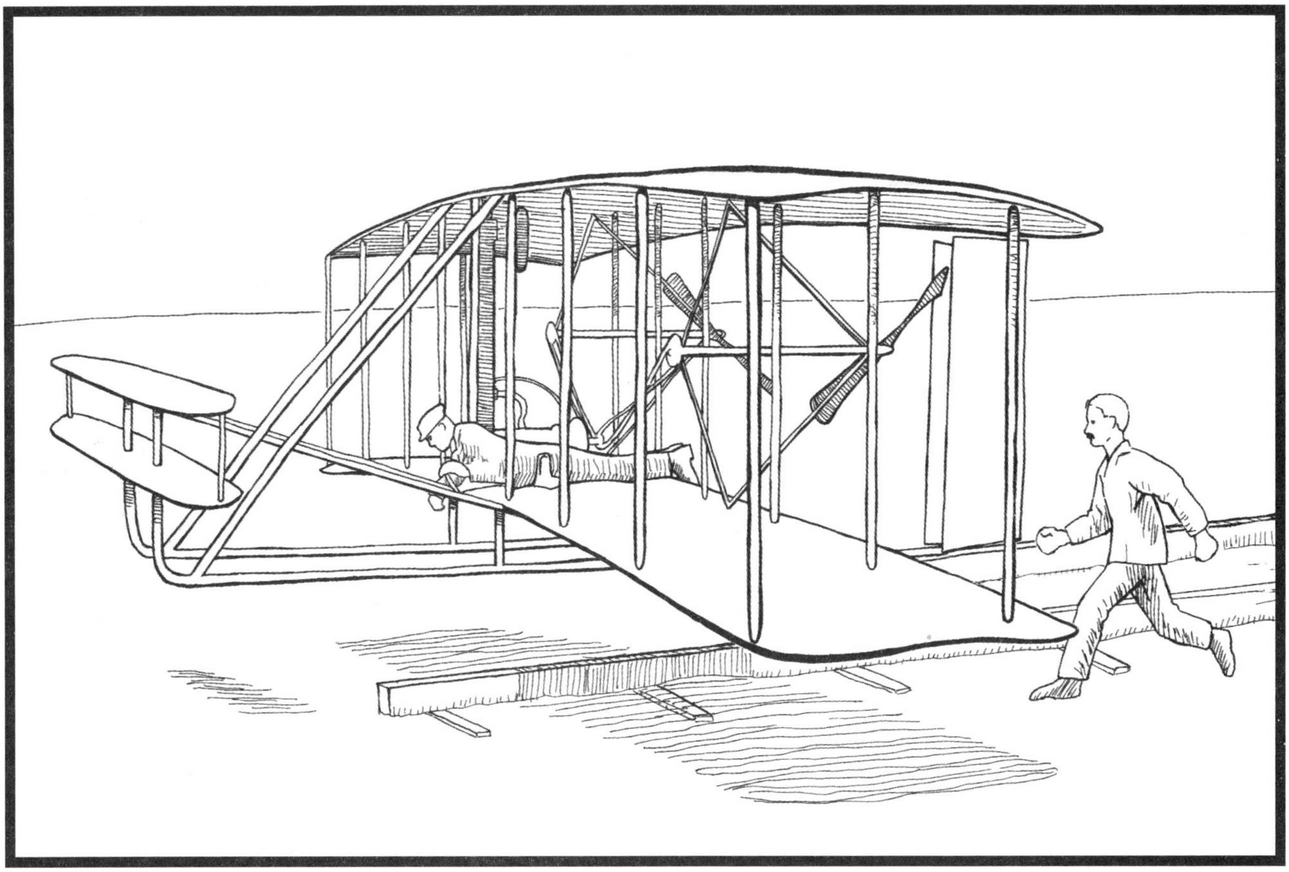

1. Add clouds hanging low in the sky.

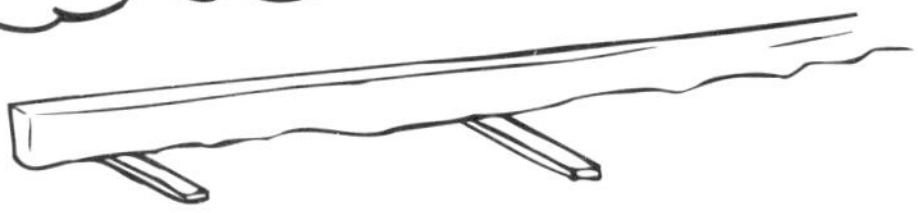

2. Draw one more track for the airplane to follow.

3. Add two helpers by the track.
4. Draw a cap and a scarf on Wilbur Wright.

5. Draw a bird in the sky.

## Color It

Use crayons to color the picture.

# Plain and Simple

Homonyms sound alike but have different spellings and meanings.

The *maid made* the bed.

### Match It

Draw a line to match the pictures with the words.

| | |
|---|---|
| blue ● | ●  |
| blew ● | ● 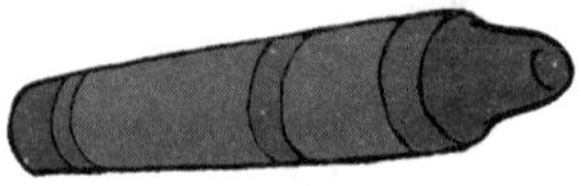 |
| sail ● | ● 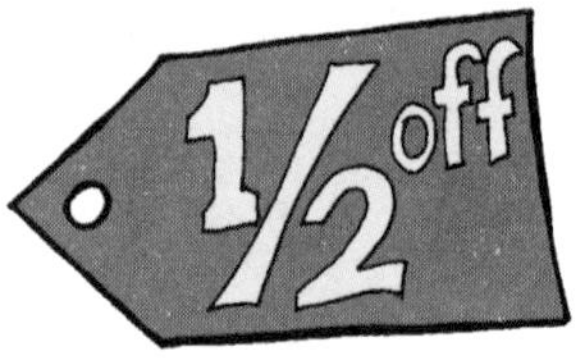 |
| sale ● | ●  |



### Circle It

Circle the word that best completes each sentence.

1. I (sent, cent) a letter to my grandfather.
2. He lives far away across the (see, sea).
3. When I am (ate, eight), we will go visit him.
4. We will have to fly in a (plane, plain) to get there.
5. My sister wishes we could go (right, write) now.
6. I (no, know) we will have fun visiting Grandfather.

# Timber!

Name ____________________

**Pick One**

Put an ***X*** by the correct answer.

1. When did the lumberjacks climb into the trees?
   - _______ at the first flurry of snow
   - _______ after the big snowstorm
   - _______ before they dropped their axes

2. When did Johnny Inkslinger fall asleep?
   - _______ before the snowstorm ended
   - _______ when the dinner bell rang
   - _______ after he climbed into a tree

3. When did the lumberjacks wave their hats and cheer?
   - _______ when their camp disappeared under the snow
   - _______ before they climbed into the trees
   - _______ as soon as they saw Paul

4. When did the cooks know it had snowed?
   - _______ when they looked outside
   - _______ when Paul told them
   - _______ when they heard the wind

5. When did Paul and the lumberjacks begin to work?
   - _______ as soon as Paul arrived
   - _______ after Paul talked with the cooks
   - _______ when the snow began to melt

# Flipping Flapjacks

## Join Them

The cooks are making pancakes for Paul Bunyan. There are seven compound words on the griddle.

1. The first part of each compound word is on a shovel. Color each shovel a different color.
2. Find the pancake with the second part of the compound word and color it the same color as the shovel.

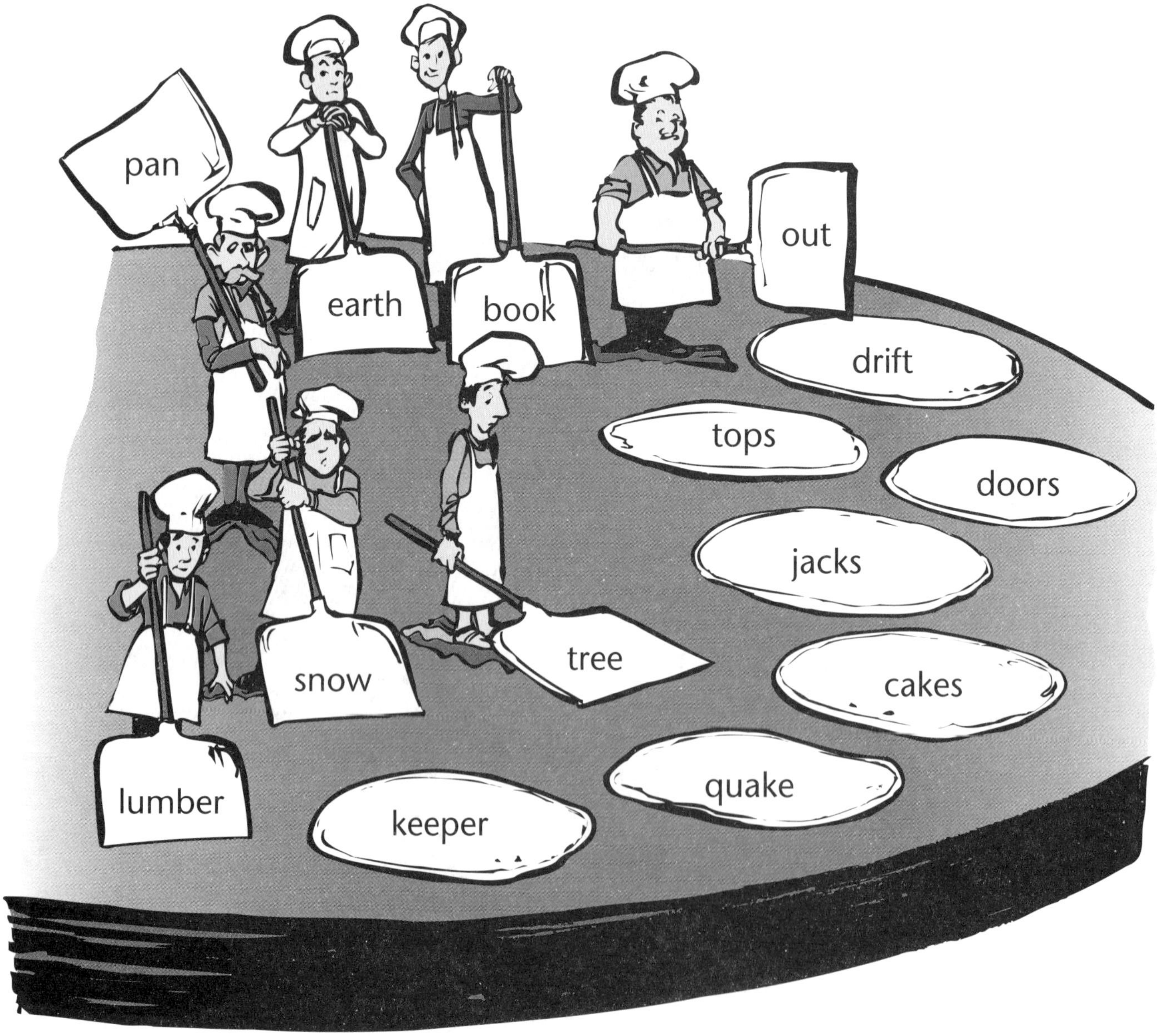

# I Don't Believe It!

Name ______________________________

## Read

Read about tall tales.

"The Pineyridge Snowstorm" is a tall tale. Sometimes tall tales started as true stories. In a tall tale, things happen that cannot really happen. People told them over and over again. Every time a tale was told, it got farther from real people and things.

Tall tales have people in them who can do things that people really cannot do. They have things in them that cannot be real. When the United States was newer, cowboys, lumberjacks, sailors, steelworkers, and riverboat men all had tall tales they liked best.

## Choose

Fill in the circle beside the answer you choose.

What kind of person would like Paul Bunyan for a tall-tale hero?

○ a sailor ○ a steelworker

○ a lumberjack ○ a cowboy

## Mark the Ones

Put an ***X*** beside the things that could not really happen.

______ Paul walked slowly, taking mile-long steps.

______ The cooks were too busy to see the snow.

______ The boys skated around the griddle with slabs of bacon strapped to their feet.

______ Babe hit the ice on the river so hard that it fell as hail all the way to Boston.

______ The logs floated down the river to the sawmill.

______ Babe drank all the water in the river.

# Float the Logs

Vowel sounds can be spelled in different ways.

## Color It

Color the end of each log to match the log above.

# Read a Recipe

Name ______________________

## Read and Think

Read the recipe. Write your own answer in each blank.

### *Cinnamon Muffins*

**Muffins**

1 box white cake mix
½ teaspoon nutmeg
1 cup milk
2 eggs

**Topping**

½ cup sugar
½ teaspoon cinnamon
¼ cup melted butter

Heat oven to 350°. Line 24 muffin cups with paper baking cups. In a large bowl, mix everything for the muffins. Put the batter into the 24 muffin cups. Bake muffins for 20 minutes. Mix sugar and cinnamon in small bowl. Take muffins out of the pan. Dip tops of muffins in melted butter and then dip in sugar and cinnamon.

1. Write a shopping list of the items you will need to make the muffins.

______________________

______________________

2. How hot will your oven need to be in order to bake these muffins? ______________

3. How long will the muffins have to bake inside the oven? ______________

4. Circle what you will do first.

   Bake muffins for 20 minutes.    Dip tops of muffins in butter.

# Fun with Phil and Phun

## Match Them

Draw a line to the sentence that matches each picture.

Phun is stuck in a telephone booth.

Phil's small car has a large telephone.

---

Phil writes his autograph for Stephanie.

Phun gives Phedra his photo.

---

Phun feeds the hungry elephant.

Phil teaches Ophelia the alphabet.

---

Phil threw the ball to Fido.

Phun showed the trophy to Phyllis.

---

Phun is playing with his nephew Ralph.

Phil is talking to his guppy Gill.

# A Story Sandwich

Name ______________________

## ▸ Tell It

Write one or two sentences to tell what happened just before the picture and one or two sentences to tell what happened after the picture.

***Before:***

***After:***

# Worthy Word Work

PROVERBS 17:22
*A merry heart doeth good like a medicine.*

## ▸Work It

Find the *wor* word for each clue and complete the puzzle using words from the pot.

***Down:***

1. The Bible tells us not to ______.
3. Grandpa keeps his tools on his ______.
5. The Bible is the ______ of God.
6. Dad uses ______ to catch fish.

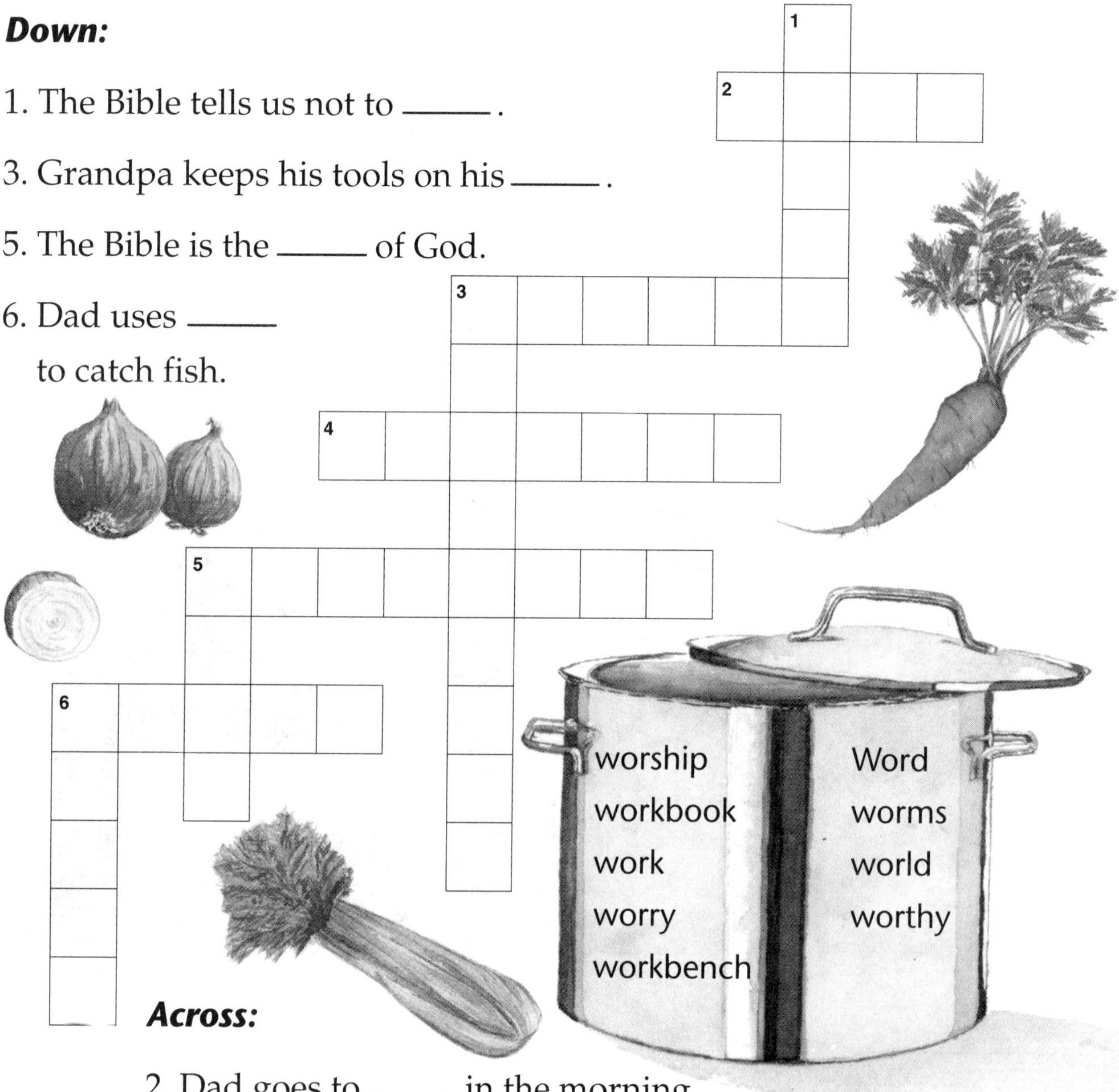


***Across:***

2. Dad goes to ______ in the morning.
3. God is ______ of our praise.
4. We go to church to ______.
5. I like to do pages in my ______.
6. God loved the ______ and gave His Son.

# That's Really Fantastic!

Name ______________________________

## Read and Decide

Read each story and decide if it is real or fanciful. Use your *yellow* crayon to color the box to show the one you chose.

The shy nightingales hide in the forest. There they whistle pretty songs. Nightingales grow to be only six inches long, and their brown feathers blend in with tree branches and leaves. Some have bright red tails that show where they are hiding.

| real |
| --- |
| fanciful |

After spending the winter in a warm place, the nightingale returns to her home. She builds a nest near the ground and lays five or six little eggs in it. All summer the baby birds grow. Then, during the cold winter, they and their mother fly to warmer weather again.

| real |
| --- |
| fanciful |

Nathan Nightingale flitted around hunting for insects. "Aha!" he laughed as he grabbed an insect with his sharp beak and swallowed it in a gulp. Quickly he tried to pick up another. Crack! Something went wrong! The insect was a pebble and not a juicy bug after all. Now he would have to get a new beak.

| real |
| --- |
| fanciful |

# Sweet Syllable Songs

## Show How Many

Color 1, 2, or 3 birds to show how many syllables you hear in each word.

nightingale

court

wonderful

China

## Mark the Spot

Divide each word by putting a dot between the syllables.

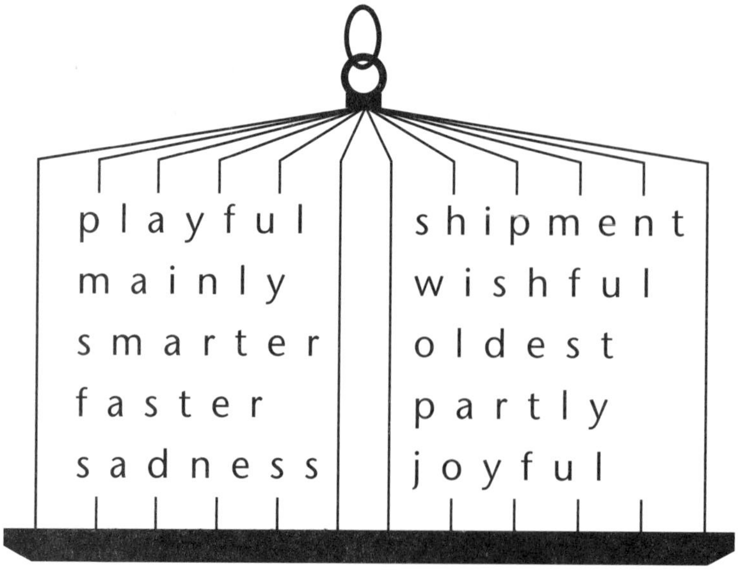

# A Bird in the Hand

_______________________
Name

## ▸What Order?

Number the sentences in story order.

_____ The real nightingale had flown out of the window.

_____ The emperor became very ill.

_____ The golden nightingale sang the same song thirty-three times.

_____ The watchmaker fixed the golden bird.

_____ The real nightingale was banished from the empire.

_____ The real bird's song helped the emperor get well.

## ▸Which One?

Fill in the circle beside the word that best fits the sentence.

1. The court musician ____ the golden bird.
   ○ praised ○ laughed at

2. Everyone in the kingdom ____ the golden nightingale's song.
   ○ forgot ○ learned

3. The watchmaker said the bird's ____ were wearing out.
   ○ jewels ○ gears

4. The emperor said that the golden bird could be played only ____ a year.
   ○ once ○ twice

# A Mystery for You

## Long or Short

Color the real nightingale or the golden nightingale to show whether the **y** in the <u>word</u> is a short or long *i*.

1. The baby began to <u>cry</u> when the dog barked.
2. The boys played basketball in the <u>gym</u>.
3. We sang a <u>hymn</u> in church.
4. The <u>shy</u> little girl hid behind her mother.
5. Kathy helped Lori wash and <u>dry</u> the dishes.

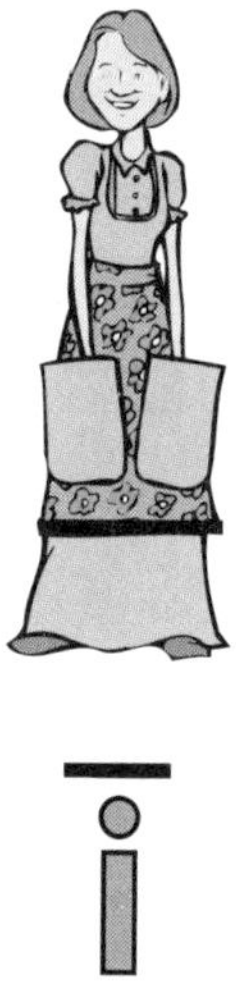

## Fill It In

*Y* is sometimes a consonant. Write a word from the birdcage in each sentence.

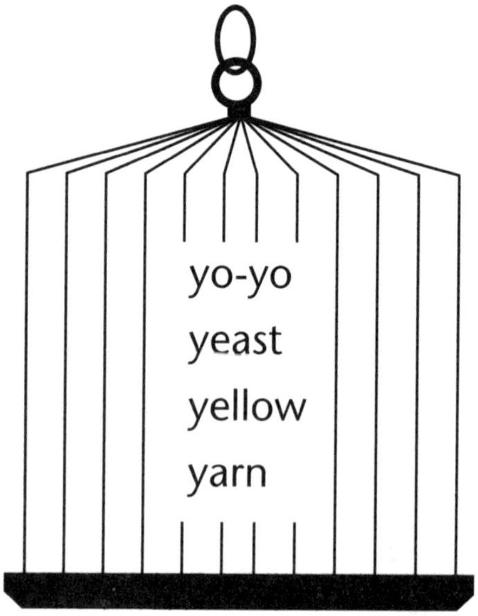


1. Grandma uses ______________ to make the bread rise.
2. The kitten likes to play with a ball of ______________.
3. We painted the hallway ______________.
4. Cally showed me how to make the ______________ go around in a circle.

# O Say, Did He Say?

Name ____________________

## Match Them

Match the person with his speech bubbles by writing his number in them.

"I brought some letters from British soldiers." ____

"There is the British fleet now." ____

"Dr. Beanes is a friend of yours, isn't he?" ____

"We must catch up to the British fleet. Dr. Beanes is in British hands!" ____

"When I heard he had been arrested, I went to see President Madison." ____

"I'm glad we're flying the truce flag!" ____

"The doctor was kind enough to treat the wounded on both sides of a battle." ____

Francis Scott Key | Colonel Skinner | Captain of the ship

# Beginnings and Endings

## Where Is It?

Read each word. Draw a musical note around the prefix or suffix.

| | | |
|---|---|---|
| jumping | replace | cheerless |
| pretest | untie | clearer |
| unfair | kindness | unlock |
| fearless | preheat | singing |
| unlock | playing | unhappy |
| preview | helpless | cheerful |

## Which One?

Fill in the circle beside the word that best completes each sentence.

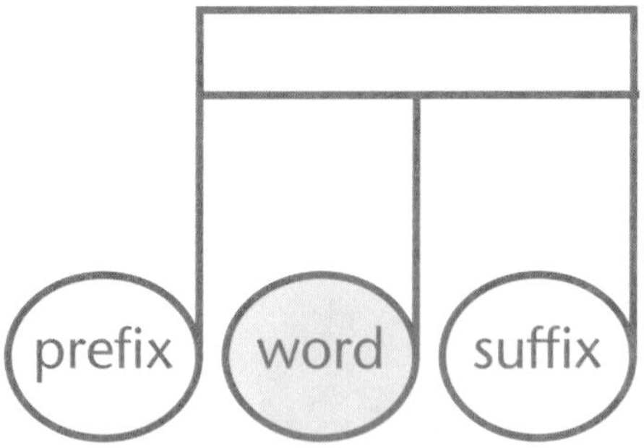


1. Our teacher gave us a spelling ____.
   ○ preheat ○ pretest ○ unlock
2. We sang ____ songs all the way home.
   ○ cheerless ○ unfair ○ cheerful
3. "If you're ____, you'll break those dishes."
   ○ careless ○ careful ○ clearer
4. Our cat was ____ when he got tangled in the yarn.
   ○ cheerful ○ helpless ○ replace
5. Mother had to ____ the oven before baking the Christmas cookies.
   ○ unlock ○ untie ○ preheat

# O Say, What Did He Do?

Name ______________________

## Match them

Put an ***X*** in the box under the character the sentence tells about.

| | Francis Scott Key | Colonel Skinner | Dr. Beanes | Captain of the ship |
|---|---|---|---|---|
| 1. He sailed the ship that took Key to the British admiral. | | | | |
| 2. He brought along letters about Dr. Beanes. | | | | |
| 3. He asked President Madison if he could go and ask for Beanes's release. | | | | |
| 4. He helped British and American soldiers during a battle. | | | | |
| 5. He asked the British for permission to come aboard. | | | | |
| 6. He went aboard the British ship with Key. | | | | |
| 7. He wrote a poem about the flag. | | | | |

# You Said It!

## Which Part?

Read the sentences below. Circle just the words that the person said.

1. “Have you seen my teddy bear?” Kyle asked.
2. Kayla said, “I don’t know where it is.”
3. “Maybe you left it in the park,” Keisha said.
4. “I’ll go look for it,” Kyle said.
5. “We’ll go too!” Kayla and Keisha said.
6. “I see it beside the swing!” Kyle said when they reached the park.
7. Kayla and Keisha shouted, “Hooray!”
8. Kyle smiled. “Thank you for coming with me to find Teddy,” he said.

## How About You?

Write your answer and your name in the right spaces.

“What game do you like best?” asked the teacher.

“I like to play ______________________________,”

answered ______________________________.

# Note These Words

Name ____________________

## Fill It In

Write a word from one of the notes to complete each sentence.

majesty | wicked | capital | invading | messenger

1. The palace was in the _ _ _ _ _ _ _ city of Jerusalem.

2. The _ _ _ _ _ _ _ _ _ knelt before King Jehoshaphat.

3. The people of Judah were worried about the _ _ _ _ _ _ _ _ armies.

4. Your _ _ _ _ _ _ _, the people are waiting for you to speak.

5. The _ _ _ _ _ _ people of Moab and Ammon were coming to fight the people of Judah.



## Write the Ones

Write each colored letter on the matching space to show what the people did as King Jehoshaphat prayed. This word is not found on a note.

_ _ _ _ _ _

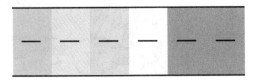

# See Two, Say One

## Choose Two

In each sentence, circle two words that have a long vowel sound spelled with two vowels. Remember that *y* can be a vowel.

| | |
|---|---|
|  The rain washed off some of the red paint. | Why is there a stack of hay on Mom's silver tray?  |
|  There are three birds sitting in the tree. | A leaf fell off the peach in the basket.  |
| Why is there a goat standing on our boat?  |  Dad dripped apple pie on his best tie!  |

## Choose Again

Circle the word that best completes each sentence.

1. Granny made a (roast, rain) for Sunday dinner.
2. There was enough food to (fail, feed) ten hungry men.
3. We ate warm apple (pain, pie) and ice cream after dinner.
4. Now I wish we had a (may, maid) to wash all the dishes.

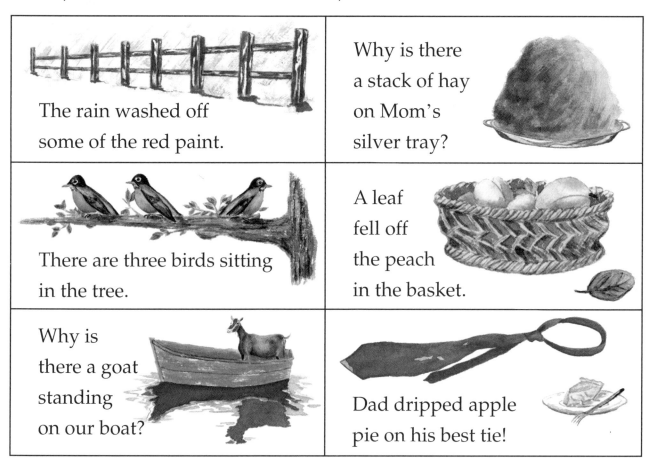

# Victory!

Name ____________________

**PSALM 107:1-2**

*O give thanks unto the Lord, for he is good: for his mercy endureth for ever. Let the redeemed of the Lord say so, whom he hath redeemed from the hand of the enemy.*

## Mark Them Out

Put an ***X*** on the ones that are **not** true answers.

1. Who did God say would fight for the people of Judah?
   Jehoshaphat　　God　　Jahziel
2. What did the king and the people do before the battle?
   pray to God　　sing praise songs　　sharpen spear
3. What did the king tell the people on the day of battle?
   stay home　　sing praises　　believe God
4. What did the people take with them to battle?
   swords　　spears　　shields
5. What did the enemy armies do?
   ran away　　fought　　killed each other
6. What did the people of Judah do when they returned to Jerusalem?
   built walls　　sang praises　　found a new king

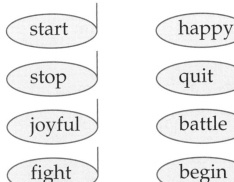

## Match Them Up

Draw lines to match the synonyms.

| | |
|---|---|
| start | happy |
| stop | quit |
| joyful | battle |
| fight | begin |

Draw lines to match the antonyms.

| | |
|---|---|
| valley | city |
| morning | evening |
| whisper | mountain |
| country | yell |

# Chosen Choir

## Same Sound

Read each sentence. Circle the picture that has the same beginning sound as the word in dark print.

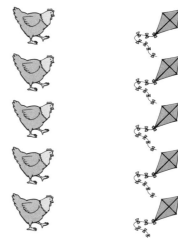

1. Father read the **Christmas** story. 
2. We went to the dentist for a **checkup.** 
3. **Chris** studied hard for his spelling test. 
4. A mouse ate the last piece of **cheese.** 
5. The **chrome** on Missy's bike is scratched. 
6. We read a **chapter** from the Bible each day. 
7. The children sang the **chorus** three times. 

## What Is It?

Circle the phrase that tells about the picture.

a chattering chipmunk
a silly chimpanzee
a sleeping child

a fast chase
a chilly wind
a fat cherry

a cheerful bug
a boy named Chris
a yelling chief

a china cup
a chocolate cake
a broken chain

a chewy gumdrop
a Christmas wreath
a chirping bird

a checker game
a happy Christian
a treasure chest

# The Very Best Way

Name ____________________

## Fill It In

Write the words from the box in the puzzle.
These words go only across.

| | |
|---|---|
| five | Becky |
| verse | Greene |
| learned | faces |
| song | when |
| told | |

1. The Greenes wrote a ______.
2. In a class, ______ heard about obeying.
3. Mrs. ______ sang the song for the judge.
4. "To obey" means to do what I'm ______.
5. Becky was ______ years old.
6. Obeying also means to obey ______ I'm told.
7. Becky ______ a lesson.
8. We should obey with a "happy" on our ______.
9. I John 2:3 is a ______ about obeying.

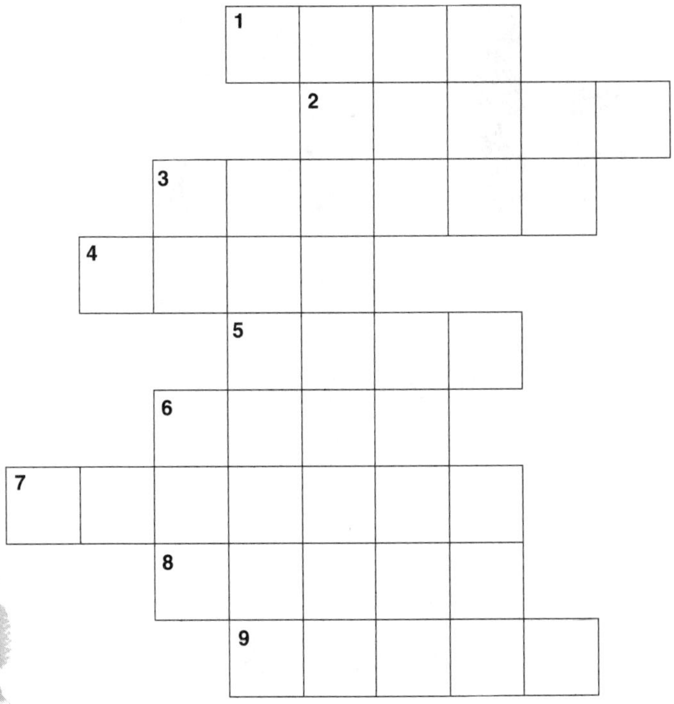

## Find the Word

Find the title to the song hidden in the puzzle.
Draw a red circle around it. Write it here.

______________________________________________

# Who Can Compare?

tall
(describes one)

taller
(compares two)

tallest
(compares three or more)

**Choose One**

Circle the word that best completes the sentence.

1. That is the (older, oldest) building in our town.
2. Is your bike (bigger, biggest) than mine?
3. My brother is (stronger, strongest) than I am.
4. Of all my teddy bears, this is the (softer, softest).
5. That is the (cuter, cutest) kitten I have ever seen.
6. That shirt is (whiter, whitest) than the other one.
7. The sun is (brighter, brightest) than the moon.
8. I smiled at the (shorter, shortest) of the three girls.

# Whose?

Name ______________________

## ▸ Whose Is It?

Circle the picture of the owner of the underlined word in each sentence.

1. Granny's <u>cabin</u> is up the trail.

2. The squirrel's <u>home</u> is in the tree.

3. Tansy's <u>eyes</u> opened wide.

## ▸ It's the Same

Write the words from the dulcimer that mean the same as the words in dark print. The first one is done for you.

1. **The mitt that belongs to Ben** is too large for his little brother.

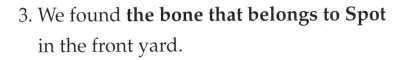

   Ben's mitt

2. **The present that belongs to Mom** is wrapped in bright red paper.

   ______________________

3. We found **the bone that belongs to Spot** in the front yard.

   ______________________

4. Scott shined **the shoes that belong to Dad** for a birthday surprise.

   ______________________

# Inspector Vector, Private Detector

## Fill It In

Help the inspector find a word from the footprints to complete each sentence.

pastor doctor conductor tailor sailor

1. The nurse helped the ______________ put a cast on Granny's broken arm.

2. Mr. Barber took his slacks to a ______________ to have them shortened.

3. The ______________ watched for the lighthouse as his ship neared the rocks.

4. Our ______________ preached about the lost sheep.

5. The music stopped, and the ______________ took a bow.

## Which One?

Fill in the circle beside the words that tell about the picture.

- ○ brown bear
- ○ polar bear
- ○ black bear

- ○ skater
- ○ baker
- ○ beggar

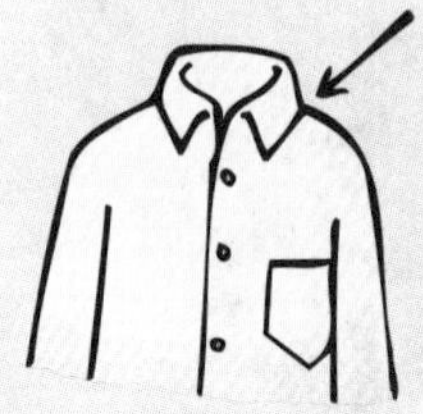

- ○ collar
- ○ sweater
- ○ jumper

- ○ pennies
- ○ dollar bill
- ○ dimes

# More Than Guessing

Name ______________________________

## Read and Think

Read each group of sentences. Fill in the circle beside what you know without the writer telling you.

The woman plucked the strings with something that looked like a feather. The music made Tansy think of sunshine and laughter and faraway places.

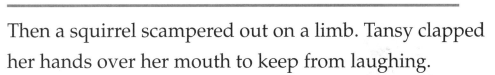

- ○ The music made Tansy sad.
- ○ The music made Tansy angry.
- ○ The music made Tansy happy.

---

Then a squirrel scampered out on a limb. Tansy clapped her hands over her mouth to keep from laughing.

- ○ Tansy did not want Granny Nell to see her laugh.
- ○ Tansy did not want to scare the squirrel away.
- ○ Tansy does not like to laugh.

---

Granny nodded to herself as the notes faded. "I've never had anyone learn to play the dulcimer as fast as you have."

- ○ Granny is pleased with Tansy.
- ○ Granny thinks Tansy doesn't try hard enough.
- ○ Granny has not taught many people to play the dulcimer.

---

There was a sudden flash of blue, and the little blue jay dashed about her head, scolding loudly. "What's wrong with you?" Tansy asked.

- ○ The blue jay is acting just the way he always does.
- ○ The blue jay is acting like a robin.
- ○ The blue jay does not usually act this way.

# They're Playing Their Song

## Choose One

As you read each contraction, pronounce both words that make it. Circle the right word in each box.

your
you're book

Their
They're twins.

Its
It's cold.

who's
whose car

## Choose Again

Write one of the words from the box in each sentence.

| its | you're | who's | their |
|---|---|---|---|

1. Sam and Chad are going to visit ________ uncle on his farm.

2. Mom said, "I think ________ going to have fun."

3. They enjoyed watching a calf kick up ________ heels.

4. I wonder ________ going to want to visit the farm again.

# What's the Big Idea?

_______________________________
Name

## Read and Think

Read each story. Put an ***X*** by the main idea.

Jenny set the dulcimer on her lap. She brushed the goose quill over a string. A low, clear note sounded. She pressed the strings down with the chicken bone and plucked one of them with the goose quill. A higher note sounded. Before long she was playing a tune!

_______ Jenny has a chicken bone and a goose quill.

_______ Jenny learns to play a dulcimer.

_______ A dulcimer has many notes.

---

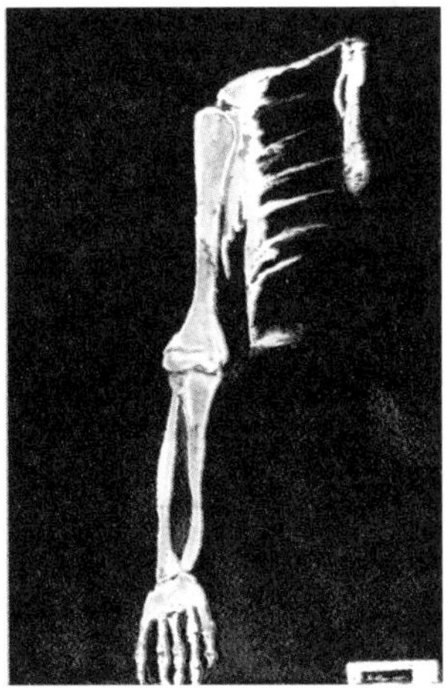

Dale had slipped on the icy walk and fallen on his arm. At the hospital he sat on a table after being x-rayed. The doctor studied the x-ray carefully. "Well, Dale," he said. "It's broken. You need a cast."

_______ Dale shovels an icy walk.

_______ The doctor studies x-rays.

_______ Dale breaks his arm.

---

People crowded in on every side, but the fair was too exciting for Henry to mind. He stopped to hear the music contest and to see the sheep-shearing contest. Then he came to the best contest—the pie-eating contest. That was the contest where Henry always won first place!

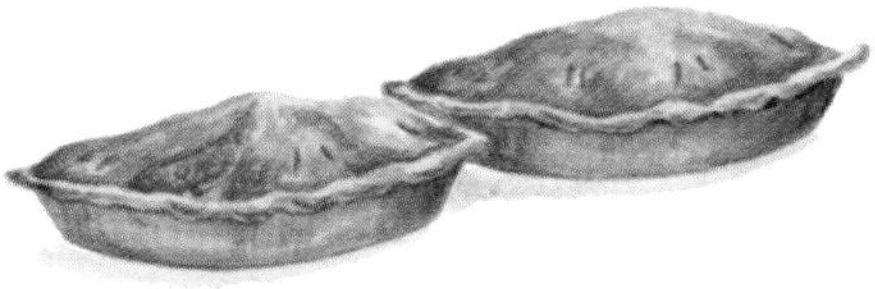

_______ Henry goes to a music contest.

_______ Henry sees a sheep-shearing contest.

_______ Henry has a good time at the fair.

# A Few Family Photos

**Draw It**

Draw a picture for each sentence.

Dad and Sam waxed the new car.

Brad threw the baseball to Thad.

Lisa made a crown with big jewels.

Mom made beef stew for supper.

Grandfather flew a plane during the war.

Kim drew a picture of her cat, Fluffy.

# It's a Contest!

Name ______________________

## Wanted: cakes, cookies, pies, and breads!

### *What do you like best?*

Bake a cake, some cookies, a pie, or some bread for this year's baking contest.

**Bring your goodies to the fair.**

### Draw It

Read the baking contest ad. If you were to enter the baking contest, what would you bake? Draw what you would bake. Put it on the table with the other baked goods.

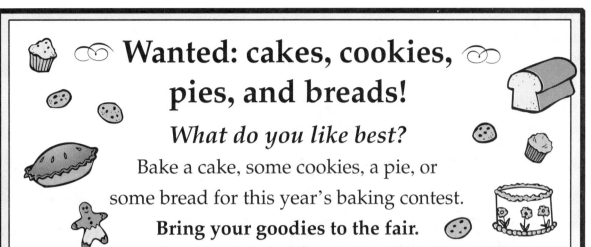

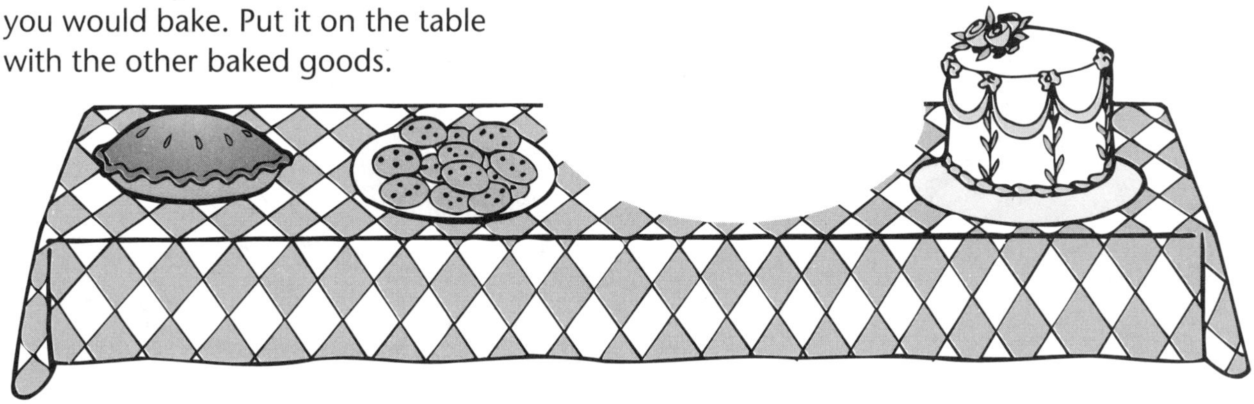

### Tell It

Write a sentence or two telling about what you baked.

# Bird Calls

## Paint It

Read the word beside each bird. Color each bird the same color as the matching birdhouse.

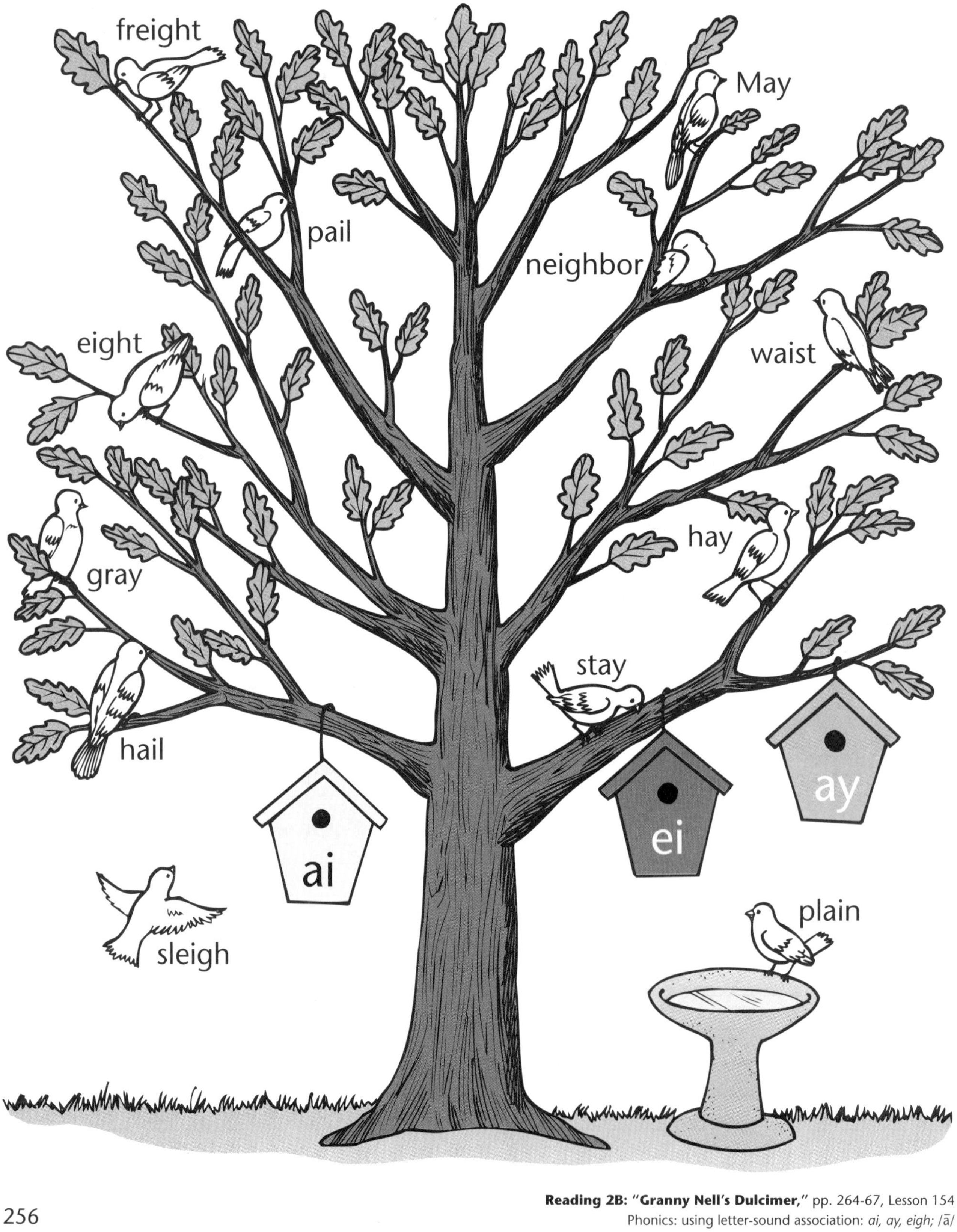

# Don't "Fret"

Name ____________________

**Work It**

Use the words next to the OONEE-CAN to complete the puzzle.

***Across***

3. You can use a _______ stick and guitar pick to play the OONEE-CAN.

4. A pattern of pitches is called a _______ .

5. The _______ are made of metal.

7. You can relax as you play the _______ .

8. The frets are spaced along the board to make a pattern of _______ .

***Down***

1. The Magees have a shop in the _______ Mountains.

2. "The _______ " is just the right size to carry with you on a hike.

6. There are only three _______ on "The Hiker" dulcimer.

9. The can helps make the sound _______ .

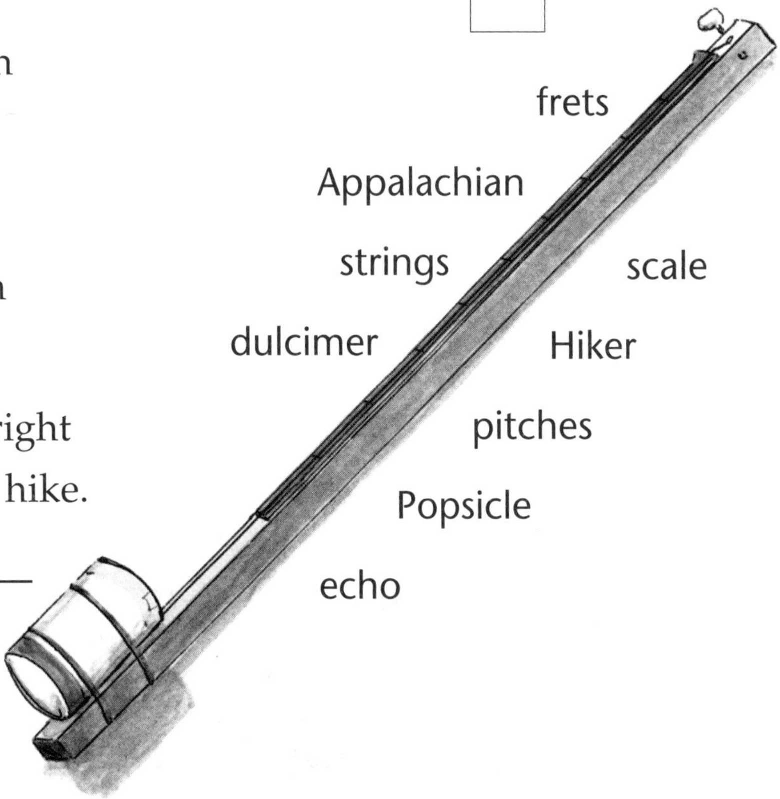

frets

Appalachian

strings

scale

dulcimer

Hiker

pitches

Popsicle

echo

# A New Song

## Pick One

Circle the word that best completes the sentence.

1. "Our (town, tower) is having a music fair," said Miss Snyder.
2. "We have been asked to have boys and girls sing on (bold, both) days."
3. Miss Snyder (told, toil) the second-grade class that they would have to work hard.
4. They (rejoiced, enjoyed) singing the songs in music class.
5. "You (sound, shout) great," said Miss Snyder, "but we need something special."
6. Just then Mr. Ray, the principal, came (joining, strolling) by.
7. "Mr. Ray, will you be in (your, our) singing group?" asked the girls and boys.
8. Mr. Ray (frowned, joined) in to sing with them.
9. "We will be the only (fold, folks) with a principal in our group!" cried Miss Snyder.

The boys and girls and Mr. Ray all laughed.

**PSALM 40:3**

*And he hath put
a new song
in my mouth,
even praise
unto our God:
many shall see it,
and fear,
and shall trust
in the Lord.*

# Praise the Lord with Harp

Name ______________________

## Read and Think

Write the letter of the instrument on the line beside the sentences that tell about it.

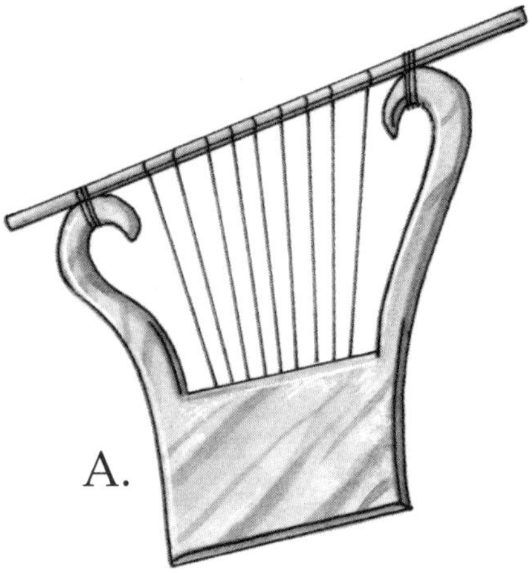

A.

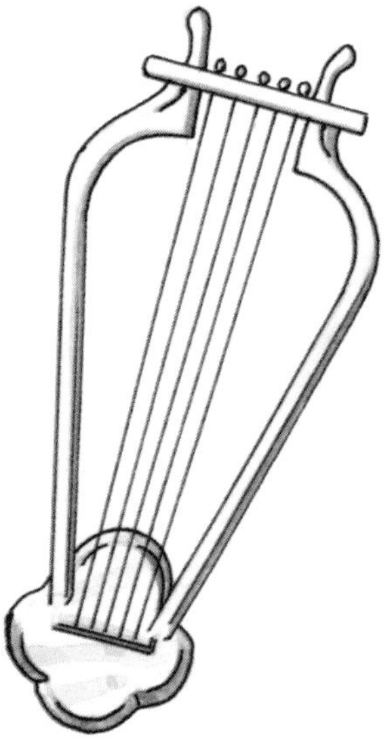

B.

C.

______ The *psaltery* was a harp with a long, slender shape. It had only a few strings. A quill or a piece of bone was used to pluck the strings.

______ The *instrument of ten strings* was a kind of harp. It had a large sounding board at the bottom. The strings were stretched around a large peg across the top. Knobs on each end of the peg were used to turn it so that all the strings were tuned together.

______ The *harp* was shaped like a bow. The ends curved in and were bound to the long cross piece at the top. Most harps had nine strings. The bottom was flat so that it could be held on the lap or set on a table.

# Keeping Time

**PSALM 69:30**

*I will praise the name of God with a song, and will magnify him with thanksgiving.*

### Count Them
Count the syllables.

| | | | |
|---|---|---|---|
| ___ pitch | ___ pitches | ___ watch | ___ watches |
| ___ dish | ___ dishes | ___ push | ___ pushes |
| ___ pass | ___ passes | ___ bus | ___ buses |
| ___ fix | ___ fixes | ___ box | ___ boxes |
| ___ waltz | ___ waltzes | ___ buzz | ___ buzzes |
| ___ dime | ___ dimes | ___ kite | ___ kites |
| ___ joke | ___ jokes | ___ wipe | ___ wipes |

### Talk About It
When is *es* a separate syllable?

___

### Fill It In
Make these words mean more than one. Add *s* or *es*.
Watch for *ch, sh, s, x,* or *z*.

hymn______ church______ harp______ hand______

1. In Bible times, worship music was played with ______________.

2. Most ______________ today have a piano and an organ.

3. The song leader uses his ______________ to keep time.

4. God is pleased with our ______________ of praise.

# It's Classy

Name ______________________

## Sort Them

Look at the words on the piano keys.
Write each word in the correct box.

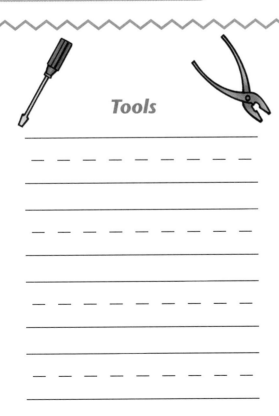

- dulcimer
- hot dog
- hammer
- tuba
- banjo
- ax
- steak
- drill
- peas
- bagpipe
- corn
- wrench

**Instruments**

______________________

______________________

______________________

______________________

______________________

**Tools**

______________________

______________________

______________________

______________________

______________________

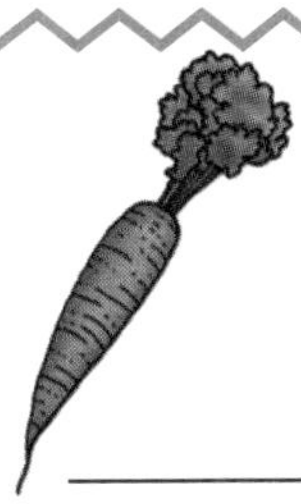

**Food**

______________________

______________________

______________________

______________________

______________________

# Check Your Mail

## Use One

Add a suffix from one of the letters to make a new word.
Write the new word in the space. Read the sentence.

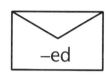

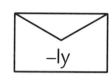

–ing    –ed    –ly    –ness

listen
1. The doctor ______________ to Fanny's heartbeat.

short
2. "Fanny should be well ______________," said the doctor.

blind
3. Fanny's ______________ did not stop her from having fun.

climb
4. Fanny liked ______________ trees.

brave
5. Fanny walked ______________ beside her mother.

## Choose One

Write the letter of the meaning in the space beside the word.

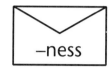

| | |
|---|---|
| ____ 1. mistreat | a. open |
| ____ 2. unhealthy | b. sick |
| ____ 3. unlock | c. different |
| ____ 4. ungrateful | d. to be unkind to |
| ____ 5. untrue | e. without thanks |
| ____ 6. unlike | f. false |

# Fanny's Story

Name ____________________

## Which One?

Circle the ***T*** if the sentence is True.
Circle the ***F*** if the sentence is False.

> PROVERBS 3:6
> *In all thy ways acknowledge him, and he shall direct thy paths.*

T F 1. Fanny Crosby was born blind.

T F 2. Fanny's grandmother read the Bible to her almost every day.

T F 3. Fanny memorized whole books of the Bible.

T F 4. Dr. Mott was able to help Fanny see.

T F 5. Many of Fanny's poems became gospel songs.

T F 6. Fanny did not want to marry Mr. Van Alstyne.

## Get in Line

Number the sentences in story order.

_____ At the New York Institute for the Blind, Fanny learned to read Braille.

_____ Mr. and Mrs. Crosby followed the doctor's directions closely.

_____ While Fanny wrote poems, Mr. Van Alstyne wrote music for them.

_____ Dr. Mott carefully checked Fanny's eyes to tell if he could help her see again.

__1__ Fanny Crosby's mother bundled her up in a thick quilt.

_____ Fanny asked the Lord to forgive her sins and to be her Savior.

# Reading Braille

## Choose One

Fill in the circle beside the word that belongs in each sentence.

1. When my dad asks me to do something, I always say "Yes, ______."
   ○ sir ○ stir
2. I gave my money to the ______ to pay for the gum.
   ○ nurse ○ clerk
3. I drink water to take away my ______.
   ○ thirst ○ first
4. I threw the paper in the fire, and it began to ______.
   ○ burn ○ turn
5. I looked out my window and saw a blue ______.
   ○ third ○ bird

## What Is It?

Use the Braille letters to find the name of one of Fanny Crosby's most famous hymns.

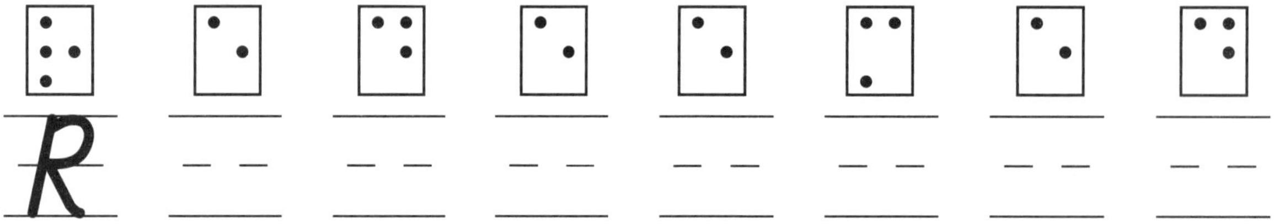


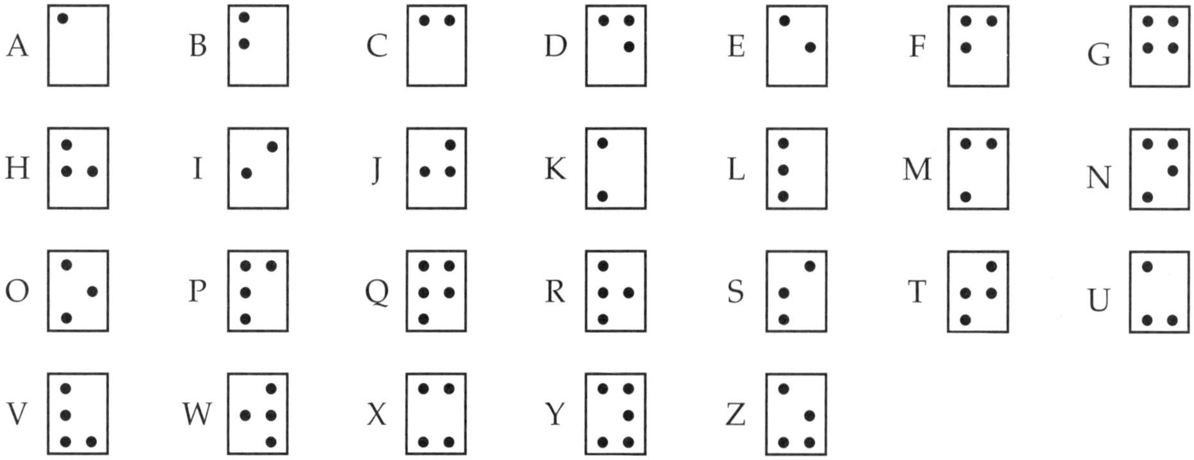

# Making Melody Again

Name ____________________

## What to Do

Read each sentence. Fill in the circle beside the best thing to do.

1. The day was too cold for bread to rise. What should the baker do?
   - ○ wait for warm weather
   - ○ put the rolls in a warm oven

2. The shoemaker dropped his tacks. What should he do?
   - ○ pick up the tacks
   - ○ wait to get tacks at a lower price

3. The weaver's reeds were too brittle. What should the weaver do?
   - ○ soak the reeds in water
   - ○ close up shop because he may never have soft reeds

4. Mr. McDoogle saw the sad workers. What should he do?
   - ○ scold them
   - ○ help them know what to do

## Which Is It?

Read the list of words in each box. Write the number of the correct title in the blank.

1. "O Say, Can You See?"
2. "The Nightingale"
3. "Song of Faith"
4. "Fanny Crosby"
5. "Obedience"
6. "Granny Nell's Dulcimer"

| | | |
|---|---|---|
| ____ armies<br>king<br>Judah | ____ blind<br>poems<br>songs | ____ bird<br>emperor<br>China |
| ____ song<br>verse<br>revival | ____ taxes<br>contest<br>broken arm | ____ flag<br>British<br>battle |

**Reading 2B: "The Song of the Happy People,"** pp. 285-92, Lesson 160
Comprehension: identifying problems and solutions; matching facts and details to story titles

265

# ANTonyms

## Work It

Choose an antonym for each word from the anthill and write it in the puzzle.

***Across***

1. short
3. low
4. mend
6. float
8. shy
9. old
10. wrong

***Down***

1. thin
2. follow
5. sow
7. far
8. straight

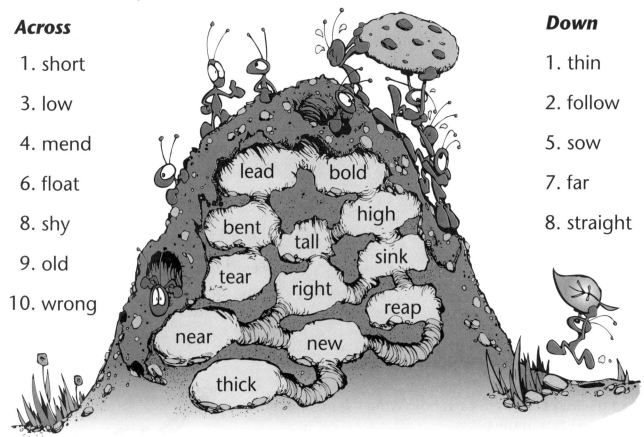

# Poetry Time

Name ______________________

PSALM 147:16
*He giveth snow like wool.*

## Read and Write

Read the poem and write the three pieces of clothing that the poet used to help you "see" the snowy picture.

### *On a Snowy Day*

by Dorothy Aldis

*Fence posts wear marshmallow hats*
*On a winter's day,*

*Bushes in their nightgowns*
*Are kneeling down to pray,*

*And trees spread out their snowy skirts*
*Before they dance away.*

______________ ______________ ______________

## Read and Paint

Read the poem and color the "feet" of the carrot green. Color the "head" of the carrot orange.

### *Mister Carrot*

by Dorothy Aldis

*Nice Mister Carrot*
*Makes curly hair,*
*His head grows underneath the ground—*
*His feet up in the air.*

*And early in the morning*
*I find him in his bed*
*And give his feet a great big pull*
*And OUT comes his head!*

# Word Beats

## Pick One
Read the words in the harmonicas and match them with a rule. Write one word beside each rule.

1. Divide words between double consonants. ______________

2. Divide words that end in *le* by putting a consonant with the *le*. ______________

3. Divide compound words between base words. ______________

4. Divide words between the prefix, base word, and suffix. ______________

## Mark the Spot
Put a ` in each underlined word to divide it into syllables.

1. Vanessa found many shells along the <u>s e a s h o r e</u>.

2. She placed them in a cloth inside her yellow <u>b a s k e t</u>.

3. She made four piles of shells on the kitchen <u>t a b l e</u>.

4. It is <u>u n l i k e l y</u> that Vanessa will keep all of the shells.

# Picture It

Name ____________________

## Read and Paint

Color the picture that shows what the writer really meant.

"This box is really heavy," said Dad. "Can you lend me a hand?"

Mandy cried and cried when she dropped Paul's present and broke it. Mandy was beside herself.

Alex was in stitches as he watched the clowns at the circus.

Hal broke the kitchen window this morning, and now he's in the doghouse.

Bill thought the joke was very funny. He laughed his head off.

# What in the World!

## Choose and Tell

Circle the word that best describes each picture. Answer each question with another word.

color

coming

What do you like to draw?

learn

hear

What sound do you like?

minute

month

When is your birthday?

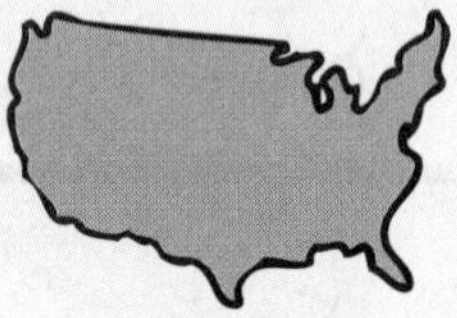

enough

country

What state do you live in?

door

done

What could be inside?

during

music

What do you like to sing?

money

whose

What would you buy?

picture

brought

What is hanging on your wall?

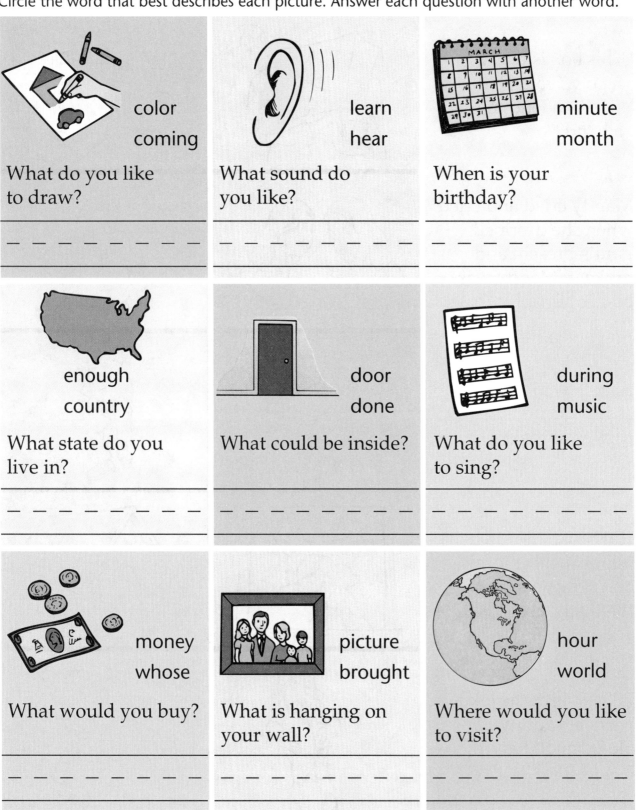

hour

world

Where would you like to visit?

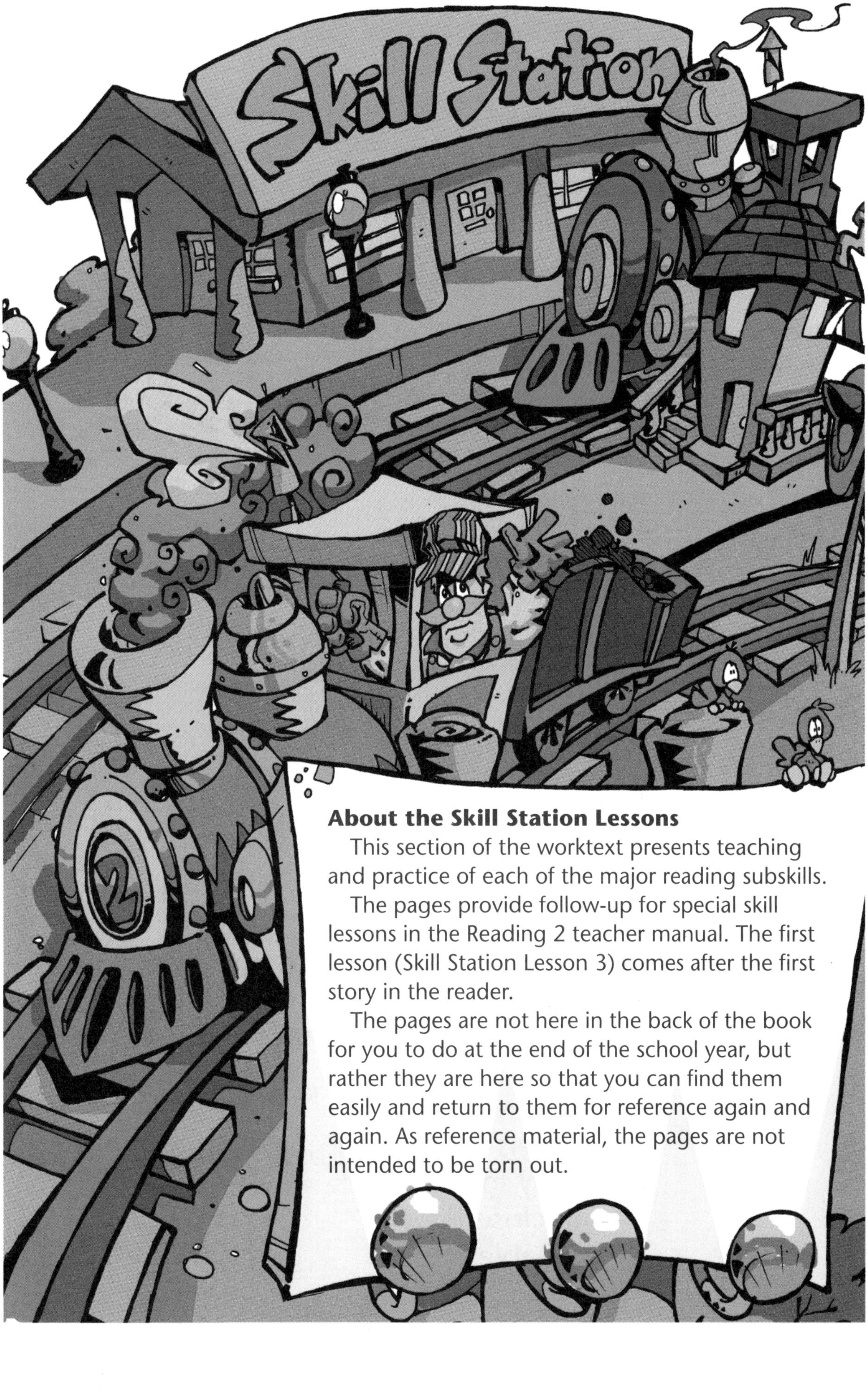


**About the Skill Station Lessons**

This section of the worktext presents teaching and practice of each of the major reading subskills.

The pages provide follow-up for special skill lessons in the Reading 2 teacher manual. The first lesson (Skill Station Lesson 3) comes after the first story in the reader.

The pages are not here in the back of the book for you to do at the end of the school year, but rather they are here so that you can find them easily and return to them for reference again and again. As reference material, the pages are not intended to be torn out.

# The Shorts: At Home in Closed Syllables

## Let's Talk About It

What is the same in this set?

| | | |
|---|---|---|
| wet | gum | fan |
| him | dot | cut |

They have one vowel letter.
After the vowel is a consonant letter.

Are these words the same?

| | | |
|---|---|---|
| went | gust | band |
| hill | miss | ping |

After the vowel are two consonant letters.

The vowels are the ladies, and the consonants are the men.

**wet** **band**

Mr. and Mrs. Short are a closed syllable.

Mr. and Mrs. Short and Uncle Short are a closed syllable.

Short vowels are usually found in closed syllables.

## Ring It

Circle the Short family in each word.

stop lock

fed kick am

it trust

gum shut jump

## Fall In

Write the words in the correct column.

map
west
bell
big
pin
ox
shock
band

# Give It a Title

## Let's Talk About It

Batter's Up!
Bugs, Bugs, Bugs
The Cat Nap
Penny Pals

## Think of One

This story has no title. What title will fit?

A bug sat on his rock. "I will go west on a trip," said Bug. "I will pack a backpack. I have a tent to rest in and a blanket for a bed. I have a net to fish with and ham and buns in a box. I have a map." Bug could not pick up the backpack. It was too big. "I will not go west," said Bug. "This rock is better."

A story title gives a hint of what a story will be about. It invites us to read.

## ▸ Picture This

Write the number of the title that matches each picture.

1. "At the Temple"
2. "The Sun Stands Still"
3. "A Den of Lions"
4. "The Last Supper"
5. "Drinking from the River"
6. "Ten Lepers"

## ▸ Match Up!

Draw lines to match each story title with something you might read about in the story.

| | |
|---|---|
| "Pond Pals" | six robin eggs |
| "A Little Bus" | a trip to school |
| "Lunch to Munch" | a frog and a fish |
| "The Nest" | a vest and a black hat |
| "A Happy Cat" | a sandwich and an apple |
| "The Dressed-Up Man" | seven little kittens |

## What Happened?

### Let's Talk About It

Number the events in story order.

Details tell the story.

## ▸ Read and Think

Read the stories. Fill in the circle next to the correct answer.

The fox huddles next to a rock, resting. He wants to be in his den on the hill. Hunters are coming.

Hunting dogs smell the fox in the clover and run to the rock. The bugle blasts, and the fox runs. He jumps over a rock and runs fast.

The hunt is fun for the fox. He gets in the stream and rests under some branches. He runs through the grass. The panting dogs run here and there. The fox is too much for them.

Why did the fox huddle next to the rock?

- ○ He was fast.
- ○ He was resting.
- ○ He was panting.

Why did the dogs not get the fox?

- ○ The fox was angry.
- ○ The fox was tricky.
- ○ The fox was winning.

---

Summer is fun! It is the time for trips and planting. In summer you smell fresh cut grass and stinky skunk!

There is no school in summer. It is filled with anthills and fishing and bumblebees. In summer, cats have kittens, and nesting robins catch bugs. In the summer it is fun to get in the water of a stream. It's best when you jump in and get wet!

What can you slip on in the water?

- ○ You can slip on fish.
- ○ You can slip on rocks.
- ○ You can slip on robins.

What is not seen in summer?

- ○ Robins are not seen in summer.
- ○ Bumblebees are not seen in summer.
- ○ Blankets are not for summer.

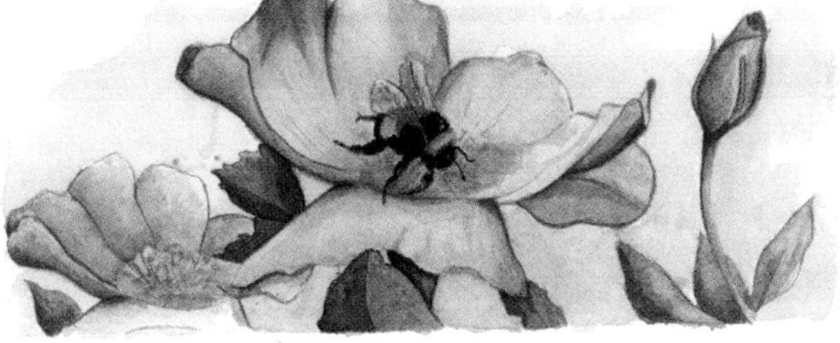

## Let's Talk About It

Where is Miss Long in these words?

These words end with Miss Long.
She is the long vowel.

These words are open syllables.

go

my

I

How are these words alike?
They all end in a consonant + *le.*
Add dots before the consonant + *le* to make syllables.

candle

puzzle

grumble

Are the vowels in these syllables long or short?

How can you tell?

Open syllables have long vowels.

Bible

title

able

## Mark It Off

Cross out words without Miss Long.

trap she

fly cat

I me

so bad

## Mark The Spot

Add dots to make syllables.
Use the words to complete the sentences.

| | | |
|---|---|---|
| l i t t l e | c r a d l e | n o b l e |
| m i d d l e | c a n d l e | g i g g l e |

1. The king is a ____________________ man.

2. The little one sleeps in a ____________________.

3. Flip the pancakes on the ____________________.

4. Bob will ____________________ when I tickle him.

5. That click, click, clicking is from a ____________________ cricket.

6. Mom gets a ____________________ when she puts a wick in wax.

**Reading 2A: Skill Station Day,** Lesson 7
Word work: distinguishing between long and short vowel words;
dividing words ending with a consonant + *le* into syllables; developing sentence meaning

279

# Miss Long and Friends

**Let's Talk About It**

One of Miss Long's friends is in these words. Who is it?

greet team pie

Yes, the friend is Miss Silent.
She tells us that the first vowel is Miss Long.

Another of Miss Long's friends is in these words. Who is it?

cake gate drive

Yes, this friend is Marker *e*.
He too tells us that the first vowel is Miss Long.

---

When you see one of these friends, who is close by?

team

cake

When you see Miss Silent or Marker *e* in a word, that word usually has a long vowel.

## Sort Them

Put the words under the correct characters.

| | | | | | |
|---|---|---|---|---|---|
| nail | smoke | drop | I | flip | my |
| toast | blue | mule | den | bone | no |

# *Where Are You, Cousin?*

## Thinking Together

Some words are related to each other. They can be put into the same set. Which word belongs in the family?

lad beetle quail

| | | |
|---|---|---|
| bumblebee | dentist | kingfishers |
| ant | locksmith | eagles |
| roach | uncle | geese |
| ________ | ________ | ________ |

## Sorting Together

Think of words that go in these sets.

| Names | Fish | Pies |
|---|---|---|
| ________ | ________ | ________ |
| ________ | ________ | ________ |
| ________ | ________ | ________ |
| ________ | ________ | ________ |

Related words can be put into sets.

## Sort It
Write the words that go in these sets.

| | | |
|---|---|---|
| crust | black | hen |
| red | cheese | duck |
| gull | green | crumb |

## Write It
Put the names of your friends in a set with your name.

# Bossy R in Charge

## Let's Talk About It

Find the words with Bossy *R*.
Underline the *ar* in each Bossy *R* word.

| | | |
|---|---|---|
| art | have | card |
| band | farm | bar |
| shark | cat | harm |

What sound does *ar* make?
Who makes *a* say something new?

## Mark One

Mark the one that matches each picture.

○ Art sees a big shark in the dark barn.

○ The angry chicken darts and pecks at Art in the barnyard.

○ Carl hits his arm on a bar and drops the feed pan.

○ The dog starts to bark when Carl ties him up with yarn.

○ Bossy *R* parked his car in the barnyard.

○ Art got a scar when he tripped over a rock in the marsh.

When *r* follows a vowel, it usually influences the vowel's sound.

## Pick One

Mark the correct answer.

○ Dad drove us in the car to the park.

○ Do you think there were sharks in the ark?

○ Someone sent you a card in the mail.

○ I will get to act like a farmer in the play.

○ That star is part of the Little Dipper.

○ An angry whale charged at the men on the whaleboat.

○ The smart dog plays a bugle while standing on two legs.

○ Sam sprained his ankle hopping over a cart.

# Get the Message?

## Let's Talk About It

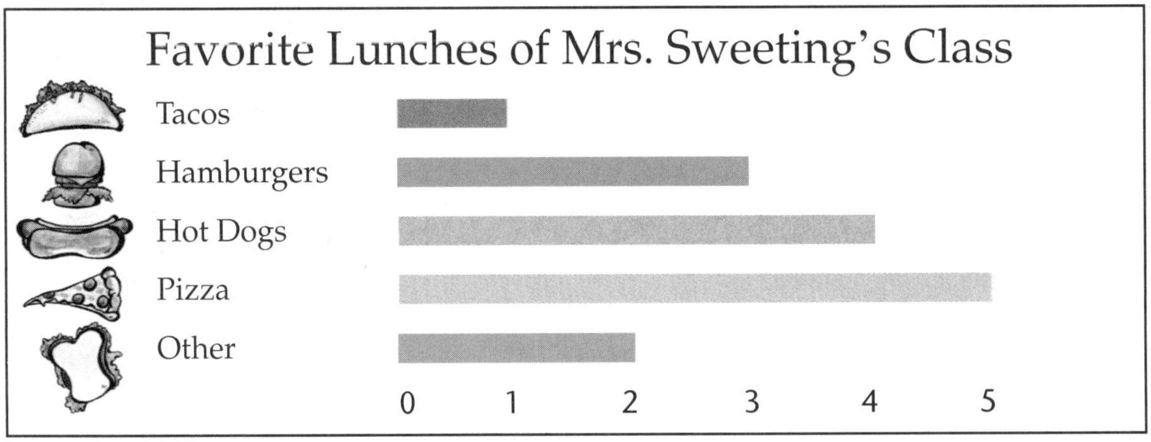


Whom or what is this about?

What is the special message?

What is the main idea?

## Let's Write It

Joan just got a bike. The bike is red and white and has a star it. Joan's dad gave her the bike, and she likes it.

Whom or what is this about?

What is special about her?

What is the main idea?

To find the main idea, find whom or what the paragraph is about and what is special about them.

## Read and Think

Read the story. Circle the answer to each question.

God wanted Jonah to preach to the wicked people of Nineveh. But Jonah did not want to go to Nineveh. He got on board a ship going the other way.

God sent a big storm because He was unhappy with Jonah. Jonah could see that this storm was to punish him. He did not want the others to be punished also. So he asked the sailors to cast him overboard. When Jonah landed in the water, a big fish that God had prepared came along and swallowed Jonah. Inside the fish, Jonah prayed. He asked for forgiveness for his sins.

1. Whom or what is this about?

   Jonah Nineveh

2. What is special about him?

   He did not obey God and was punished.

   He did not like to ride on big ships.

3. What is the main idea?

   Jonah did not obey and was punished.

   Jonah will take a ship to Nineveh.

After Jonah prayed, God caused the fish to spit him up on dry land. Then Jonah went to Nineveh and preached to the people. The people prayed and asked God to forgive them for their sins. Jonah pleased God because he did what God said.

1. Who or what is this about?

   Jonah fish

2. What is special about him?

   The sailors pray to God.

   He obeyed and pleased God.

3. What is the main idea?

   The sailors ask God to forgive them.

   Jonah pleased God by obeying.

# Characters

## Main Characters

1. The story tells much about them.
2. They sometimes change or learn something.
3. Many times we feel and think the same way they do.

Think about the story "Little Bug's Trip."
Who was the main character?

## Lesser Characters

1. The story tells less about them.
2. They stay the same.
3. Many times we do not feel or think the same as they do.

Who were the lesser characters in "Little Bug's Trip"?

To find the main character in a story,
find the one whom you know much about,
who changes, and who you feel the same as.

## ▸ Name Them

Write the name of the main characters next to the title of the correct story.

"A Night to Remember" ______________________

"Someone My Age" ______________________

"The Tuna Tangle" ______________________

"Seth and the Angry Bug" ______________________

"Sticky Fingers" ______________________

crook

Donna

Seth

Rags and Jingle

Randy and Ben

# What Made That Sound?

## Listen to the Sounds

### Listen and Write

Write the word in the blank that has the same vowel sound as the picture.

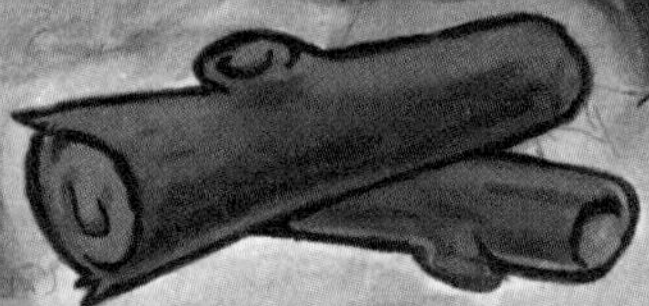

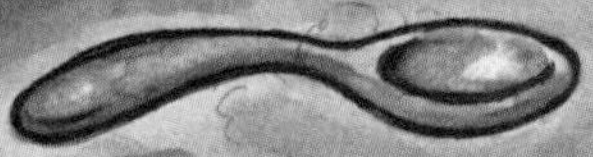

Sometimes letters have special sounds when they are with other letters.

## Choose One

Write the words beside the correct definitions.

1. ______________ name of a man

2. ______________ a baby deer

3. ______________ rules one must follow

4. ______________ not big

5. ______________ time of day when the sun comes up

6. ______________ something to play with

7. ______________ grass in the yard

fawn
small
ball
Paul
lawn
laws
dawn

## Choose Again

Read each question. Circle the best answer.

1. What is your toe on?
   foot boot soot

2. Which is a dog?
   poodle tool broom

3. What is a horse's foot?
   woof hoof crook

4. Which is a time of day?
   food noon spool

5. What will catch a fish?
   spoon moon hook

6. What can you swim in?
   cool pool coon

### Let's Talk About It
What is this word?
Which letters are silent?
Which letters are not silent?

# high

### Let's Read and Do
Find the silent letters.
Find the vowel.
Read the words.

| | |
|---|---|
| bright | lightning |
| fight | tonight |
| fright | flashlight |
| might | nightstand |
| night | sunlight |
| right | spotlight |

When *gh* follows an *i*, it is silent and the *i* is long.

## Read and Draw

Complete the pictures. Make them match the sentences.

This robe is just the right size.

Tonight we will see many bright lights.

We stayed up very late one night.

We drove on the highway to Grandmother's.

After eating too much pie, I sighed.

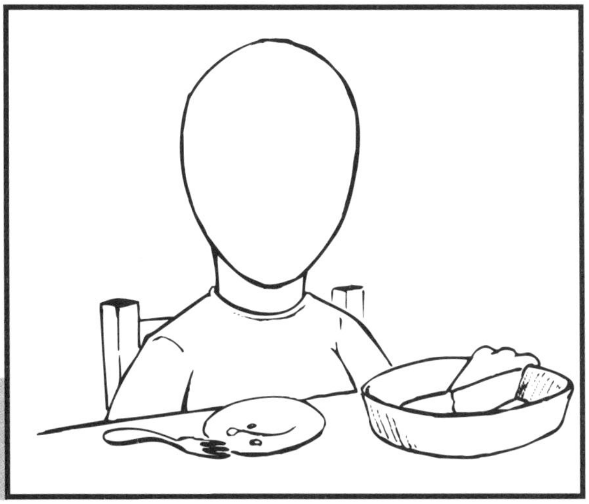

# Two Words in One

**Talking Together**

cupcake

**Making More Words**

Put words from the top row with words from the bottom row to make compound words.

| | | | | | | |
|---|---|---|---|---|---|---|
| mail | snow | rain | corn | sea | milk | light |
| flake | drop | shell | man | house | horse | ball |

Two words put together make another word called a compound word.

## Match Up!
Draw lines to form compound words.

| | |
|---|---|
| sun | man |
| milk | tan |
| pop | yard |
| barn | corn |

## Write It
Write the compound words you made.

## Make a Word
Use two of the words from the box to make a compound word for each picture.

| | | | | | |
|---|---|---|---|---|---|
| boat | fish | mail | steam | star | box |

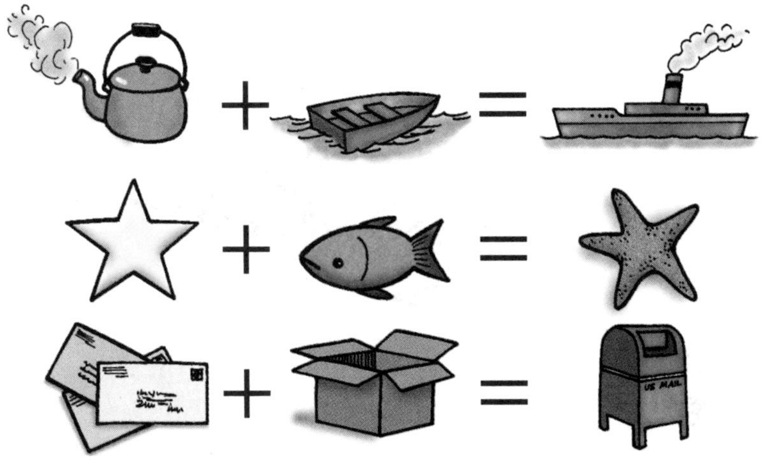

# What Do I Do?

## Let's Talk About It

To follow directions,

1. Read each step carefully.
2. Do each step in order.
3. Read the steps again if you need to.

## Polar Bear Ice Cream

½ cup of milk
¼ teaspoon of vanilla
1 tablespoon of sugar
1 pint-sized sealable bag
1 gallon-sized sealable bag
ice
6 tablespoons of salt
a hand towel

## Follow the Steps

**1** Mix the milk, vanilla, and sugar in the smaller bag and seal it.

**2** Fill the larger bag half full of ice. Also put in the salt and the small bag. Seal the big bag.

Follow the directions to complete something correctly.

**3** Wrap the big bag in a towel. Shake it for 5 minutes.

**4** Take out the little bag and wipe it off with the towel. Eat the ice cream.

## Follow Again

Follow these instructions to make a dog.

1. Lay a square sheet of paper on your desk.

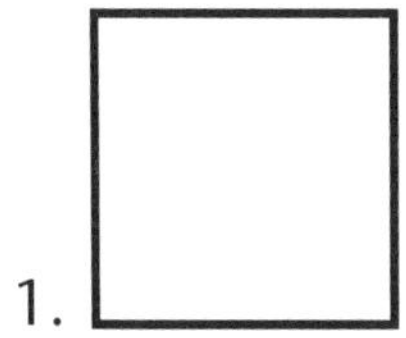

2. Turn the paper so that one corner points to you and one corner points away from you.

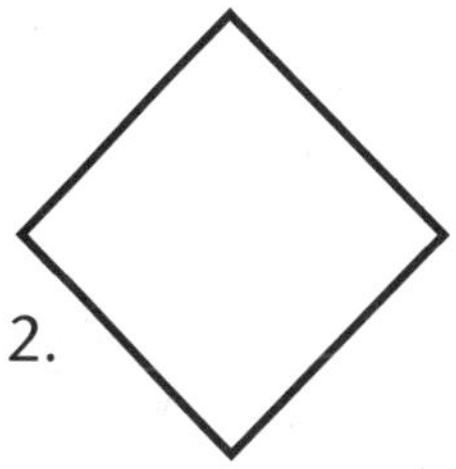

3. Fold the right corner over to meet the left corner. Press to make a fold line.

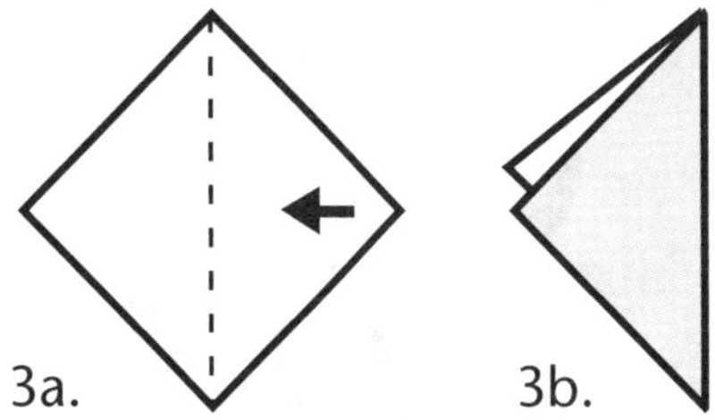

4. Unfold the paper.

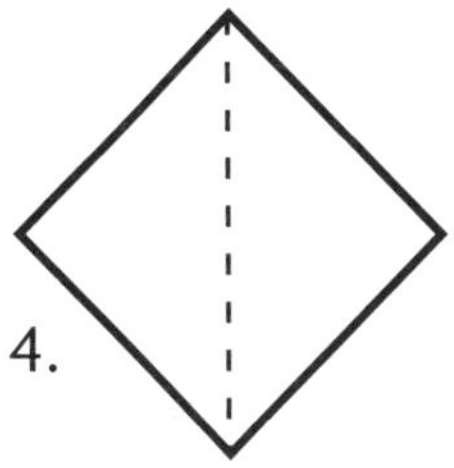

5. Fold the top corner down to meet the bottom corner. Leave the paper folded.

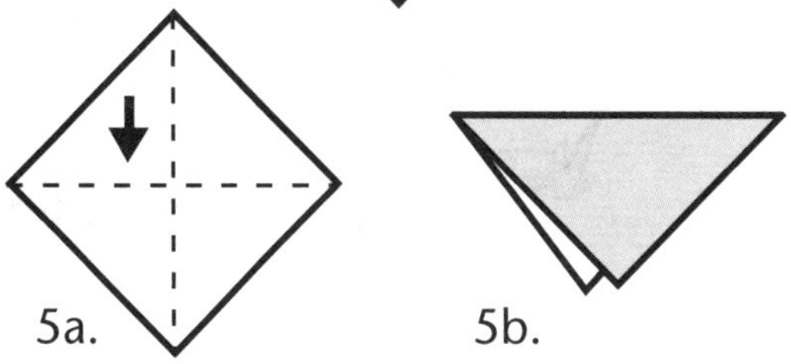

6. Fold up the bottom corner of the top sheet.

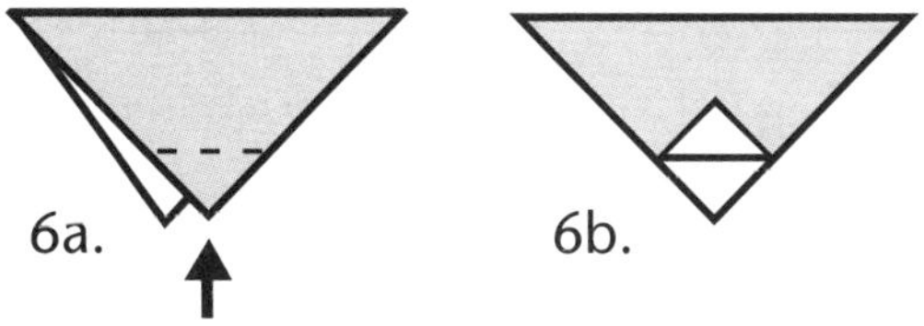

7. Fold the two side corners down.

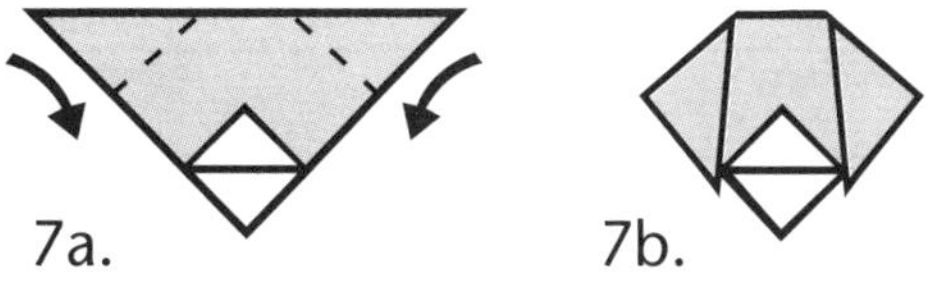

8. Draw a dog's face on your paper.

# Shout Ouch!

## Listen to Some

Find the letters that make the /*ou*/ sound.
Circle them.

out

our

owl

Find the letters that make the /*oi*/ sound.
Circle them.

coin

enjoy

## Add Some

Add more words to these families.

| out | owl | oil | joy |
| --- | --- | --- | --- |
| | | | |
| | | | |
| | | | |

**Some letters have special sounds when they are with other letters.**

# Read and Do

Follow the directions under each picture.

1. Color the kangaroo brown.
2. Make a black line for a pouch.
3. Draw shoes on the kangaroo's feet.

1. Draw a trout coming out of the water.
2. Color the trout green.
3. Draw a boy in the water.

1. Draw a toy in the baboon's mouth.
2. Draw a crown on the baboon.
3. Color the baboon brown.

1. Draw clouds over the hound.
2. Color the sky blue.
3. Make the hound howl.

# Around the World

## Let's Talk and Think

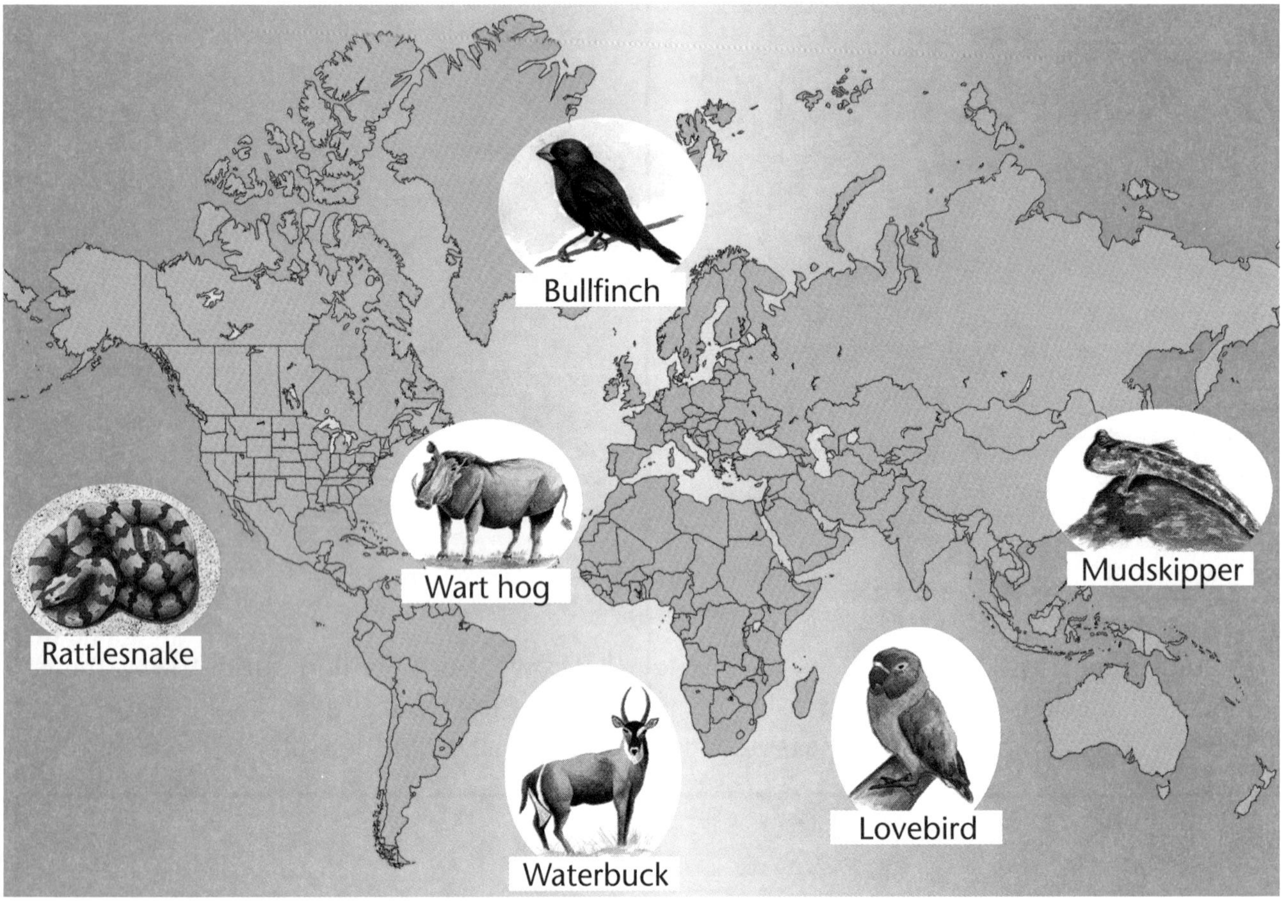


Both are useful. Which should you use?
Think about what you need.

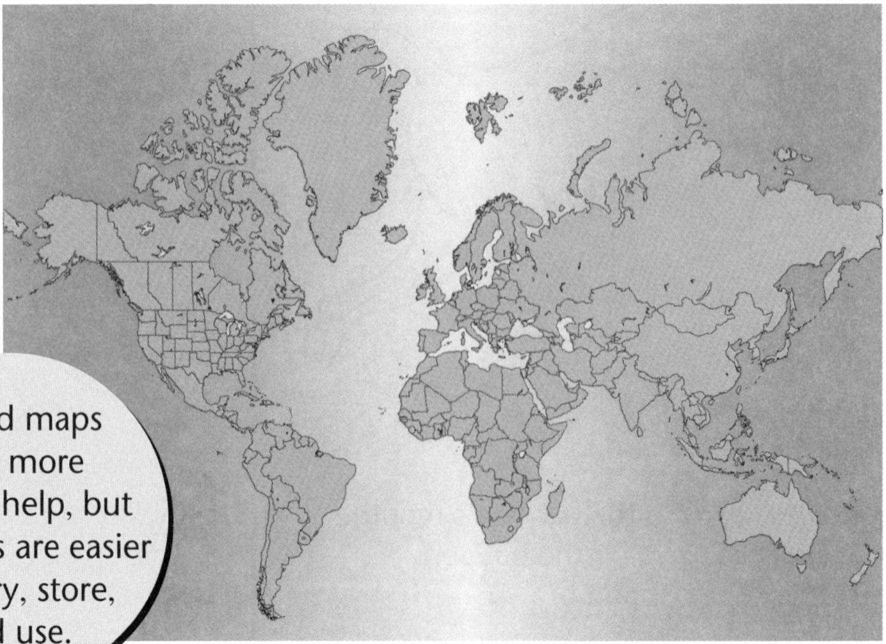

Round maps give more correct help, but flat maps are easier to carry, store, and use.

## ▸ Match Them Up

Match the descriptions with the correct animal. Write the correct letters in the circles. Notice where each animal lives.

A. a flat fish with a long, pointed tail
B. a hunter with a dark mask and fur
C. a bird that is only three or four inches long
D. a long-nosed animal that eats ants

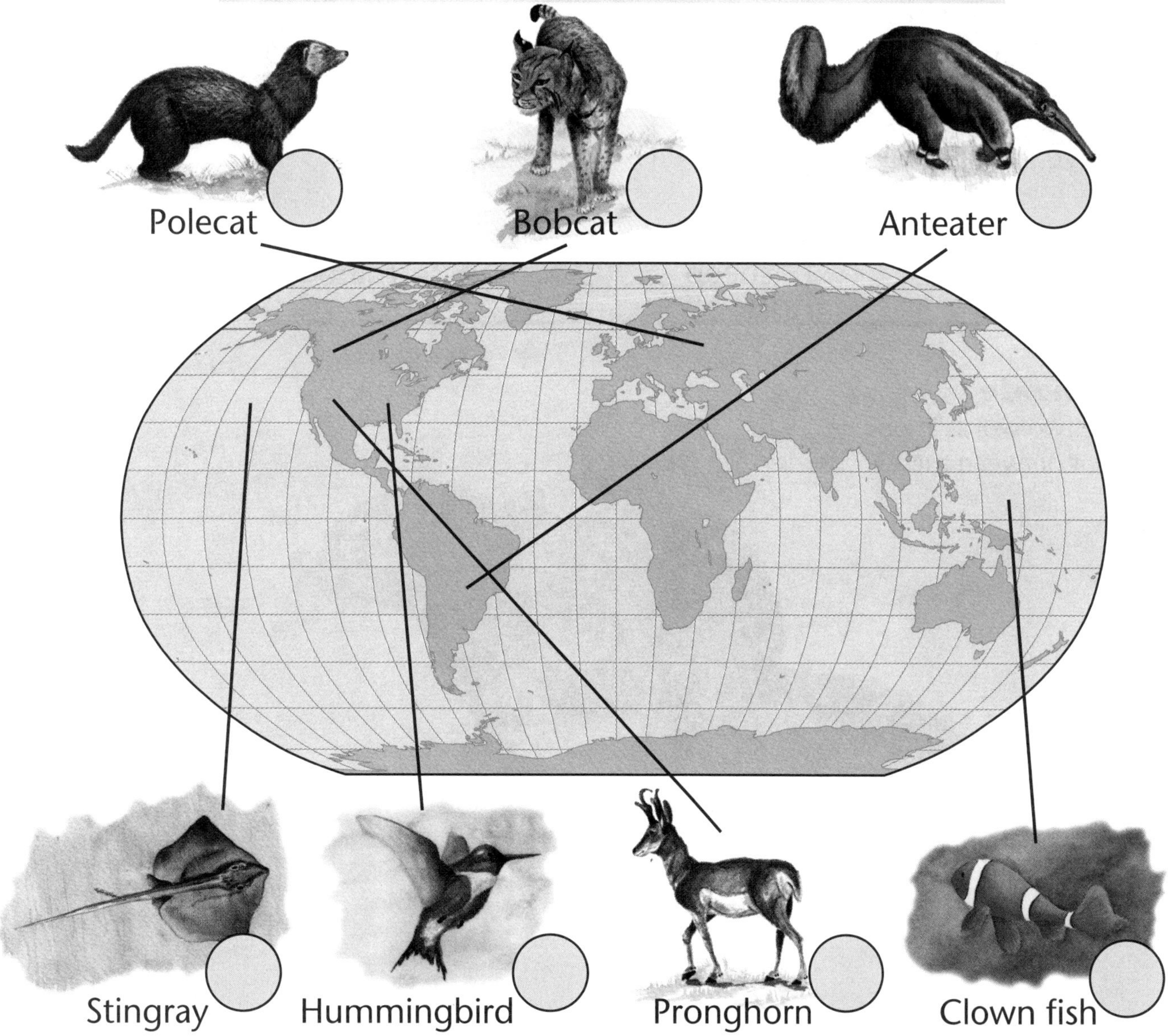


E. an orange fish with bands of white and black
F. a wild cat with a stumpy tail
G. a big animal with funny horns

# Animal Syllables

## Listen and Count

How many syllables do you hear?
Write an answer.

baboon ______

sheep ______

rhinoceros ______

## Let's Divide

Find the two words in one.
Put a dot between the two words.

g r o u n d h o g

Put dots between the two words in each of these.

| | | |
|---|---|---|
| f i r e f l y | s t a r f i s h | l o v e b i r d |
| b u l l f i n c h | p r o n g h o r n | w a t e r b u c k |

## Dot and Circle

1. Put a dot between the two words in each compound word.
2. Circle each compound word that is the name of an animal.

| | | |
|---|---|---|
| jellyfish | cowbell | blackbird |
| horsefly | anthill | butterfly |
| bobcat | mousetrap | toadstool |
| fishhook | catfish | birdbath |
| bluebird | bumblebee | doghouse |

# Problems, Problems, Problems!

## ▸Thinking Together

Think about the verse. Read each problem and solve it the best way.

**PHILIPPIANS 4:13**
*I can do all things through Christ which strengtheneth me.*

Kelly could not read the writing on the chalkboard. What should she do? Fill in the circle next to the correct answer.

- ○ Whisper to a friend to ask what it says.
- ○ Ask the teacher to move her desk closer to the chalkboard.
- ○ Do what she thinks the writing says.

Gail lost a button on her coat and could not find it. What should she do? Fill in the circle next to the correct answer.

- ○ Sit down and cry until someone finds it.
- ○ Blame her mother for not sewing it on well.
- ○ Ask if she could check the lost and found box.

Bobby's bike had a flat tire. What should he do? Fill in the circle next to the correct answer.

- ○ Ask someone to help him fix it.
- ○ Keep putting air in and hope it will stay.
- ○ Take the tire off his brother's bike and use it.

God's Word helps us solve problems.

## ▸Thinking Alone

Read the story. Then answer the questions.

1 For forty days and forty nights, the mighty storm had pounded the ark. Noah and his family had stayed safely inside. Now the rain had stopped, and the ark had come to rest on the top of Mount Ararat.

2 Noah looked out the window. All he could see was water everywhere. "I must see if the ground is getting dry," he said. He could not leave the ark to find out himself. So he began to think about what he could do.

3 Noah sent a bird out of the ark, but it came back because it could not find a dry spot to rest. Seven days later he sent a bird out again. This time it came back with a leaf in its mouth. Noah understood that the waters were going down. Soon they would be able to leave the ark.

1. Which paragraph tells Noah's problem? ______

2. Which paragraph tells the answer to Noah's problem? ______

## Soft or Hard?

### Let's Find the Pattern

The letter *c* can say /s/ or /k/.
How can you tell which sound it is saying?
The letter that follows *c* tells you when to say /s/.

c i t y     f e n c e
m i c e     c e n t
l a c y     c i n d e r

*C* usually says /s/ when followed by ____, ____, or ____.

The letter *g* can say /j/ or /g/.
How can you tell which sound it is saying?

b u d g i e     g e m
g y m     g i a n t
b a d g e r     E g y p t

*G* usually says /j/ when followed by ____, ____, or ____.

*C* and *g* usually say their soft sounds when followed by *e*, *i*, or *y*.

## ▸ Work It

Use words from the word box to complete the puzzle.

### *Across*

1. Part of you
4. You ride this
5. A kind of school
7. Someone not met
9. Something round

**Word Box**

| | |
|---|---|
| stranger | face |
| bicycle | rice |
| cyclone | cage |
| college | circle |
| gerbil | fudge |

### *Down*

1. A sweet food
2. A small pet
3. A mighty wind
6. A place to keep a mouse
8. Another food

# Little Owls Laughed

## Let's Talk About It

What are some words that have similar meanings?

little

laughed

Look at the title of this page.
Use the words above to make new titles.

______ Owls ______

______ Owls ______

Here are synonyms for *eat*.

| | |
|---|---|
| nibble | snack |
| gobble | dine |
| feast | devour |

Which would a hungry lion do?
Which does a mouse do?
Which do you do?

Synonyms are words that have similar meanings.

## ▸ Read and Think

Read each line of the poem carefully. Decide which word above the stanza best describes how each animal moves. Write the correct synonym for ***move*** in the blank.

# *Jump or Jiggle*

by Evelyn Beyer

**jump** **hump**

Frogs ________________.

Caterpillars ________________.

**leap** **creep**

Mice ________________.

Deer ________________.

**jiggle** **wiggle**

Worms ________________.

Bugs ________________.

**bounce** **pounce**

Puppies ________________.

Kittens ________________.

**clop** **hop**

Rabbits ________________.

Horses ________________.

**walk** **stalk**

Lions ________________,

But I ________________!

**slide** **glide**

Snakes ________________.

Sea gulls ________________.

# "I" What?

## Marking Together

Contractions are formed from two words. Some letters have been left out. Which letters were left out of these contractions? Circle the letters that were left out.

| | |
|---|---|
| I'm | I a m |
| I'll | I w i l l |
| I've | I h a v e |
| I'd | I w o u l d |

## Picking Together

Which word is the right one?

○ I'm
○ I'd
like to hear an owl laugh at the children.

○ I'll
○ I've
ride on a camel if my brother will.

○ I'll
○ I'm
going to give Mr. Moose an ant farm.

○ I've
○ I'm
trained my dog to obey me.

## Pick One

Circle the correct word to complete the sentence.

1. I've / I'd like another slice of peach pie, please.

2. I hear the telephone ringing. I'll / I'm answer it.

3. I've / I'd read eight pages for the reading contest.

4. I've / I'll heard many stories of Christ's love for us.

5. Someday I've / I'm going to drive my very own car.

6. Mother says I'll / I'm grow to be much taller than she is.

7. I've / I'd love to see my friend become a Christian.

8. I'm / I'll going to move to a house only one mile from yours.

# What's the Big Picture?

## Working Together

Find the main idea.
What is the story about?
What is special about them?

**GENESIS 1:25**

*And God made the beast of the earth after his kind, and cattle after their kind, and every thing that creepeth upon the earth after his kind: and God saw that it was good.*

When enemies come, a beaver will flip his tail up high. Then he will slam it down with a smack on the water. The other beavers dive to safety when they hear that loud sound. In the water, their enemies cannot catch them.

What is the story about?

water safety beavers enemies

What is special about them?

They dive for food.
Their tails give warnings.
Their tails are flat.

Write the main idea.

________________________________

________________________________

To find the main idea, find whom or what the paragraph is about and what is special about them.

## ▸Choose and Write

Read the story and answer the questions.

Polar bears are *big* animals of the *north*. Many polar bears are seven feet tall, but the biggest ones stand nine feet tall. A fat polar bear may be more than 900 pounds! A 900-pound polar bear does not get *cold* living on an *iceberg*. His fat is like a thick winter *coat*.

1. What is the story about?
   - Polar bears
   - Animals of the north
   - Icebergs

2. What is special about them?
   - They get fat eating fish.
   - They live in the north.
   - They are big animals.

3. Write the main idea.

______________________________________________

______________________________________________

## ▸Find the Facts

Use the words in the story to finish the sentences.

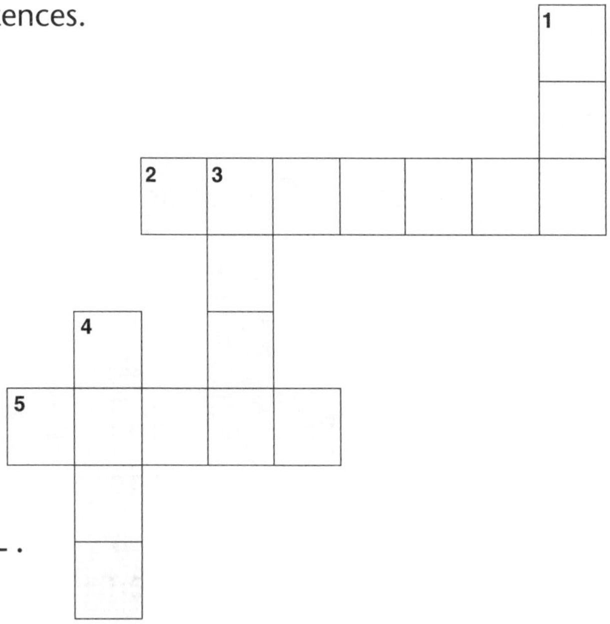


***Across***

2. A big mass of floating ice is called an ______ .
5. The polar bear lives up ______ .

***Down***

1. If the bear is large, we say it is ______ .
3. The bear's fur is called its ______ .
4. If ice is there, it must be ______ .

# Steadfast and Ready

## Reading Together

Listen to the sound of the vowel in the words in the box. They rhyme with *red* and *bed*. Use words from the list to fill in the sentences.

| | |
|---|---|
| head | bread |
| dead | thread |
| lead | spread |

Raleigh cocks his ______________. His legs are ______________.

In some words *ea* has a short *e* sound. The rest of the sentence can help you tell which sound to use.

## More Meanings

Look at these dictionary entries.

**head** *[hĕd]* 1. The top part of the body, containing the brain, eyes, ears, nose, and mouth. 2. A person who is in charge; a leader.

**leather** *[lĕther]* A material made from hide.

**spread** *[sprĕd]* 1. To open or to cause to open wide. 2. A cover. 3. To scatter.

**threat** *[thrĕt]* A person or thing regarded as dangerous.

Which word has the most meanings? ______________________

Some words have more than one meaning.

## Find More

Use more words with the short *e* sound spelled *ea*.
Think about the listening story your teacher read.

| | |
|---|---|
| ahead | heavy |
| ready | instead |

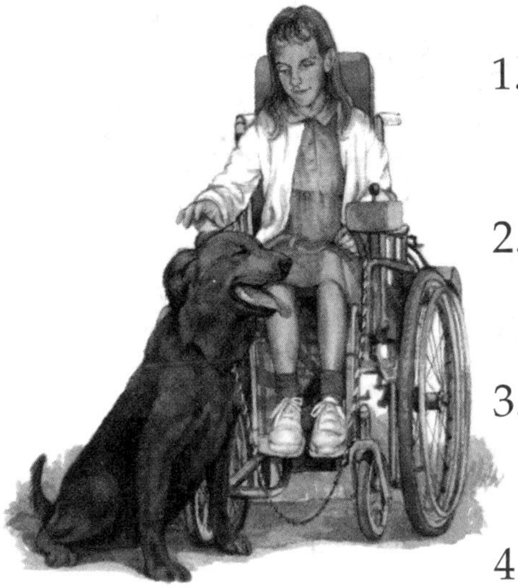

1. Raleigh is getting too ______________.
2. He needs to be ______________ to help.
3. Will he walk ______________ of resting?
4. Raleigh will not go ______________.
   He will stay by Molly's side.

## Fill It In

Use the words in the box to solve the puzzle.

| | | |
|---|---|---|
| stretch | black | dad |
| blanket | attacking | leash |

### *Down*

2. An _____ dog was a *threat* to Molly.
4. Raleigh lifted his big _____ *head*.
5. Raleigh picked up his *leather* _____ and handed it to Molly.

### *Across*

1. Molly's _____ is the *head* of her family.
3. Raleigh *spread* his legs to _____ and wake up.
6. Raleigh used Molly's old *spread* for his _____.

# Find the Treasures

## Hunting Together

## Make a Word

Add the treasures to the correct buckets to make words.

## Match Up!

Draw a line from each word to the correct picture.

captain

mountains

curtain

fountain

# Alike and Different

## Thinking Together

Match the sentences to the correct pictures.

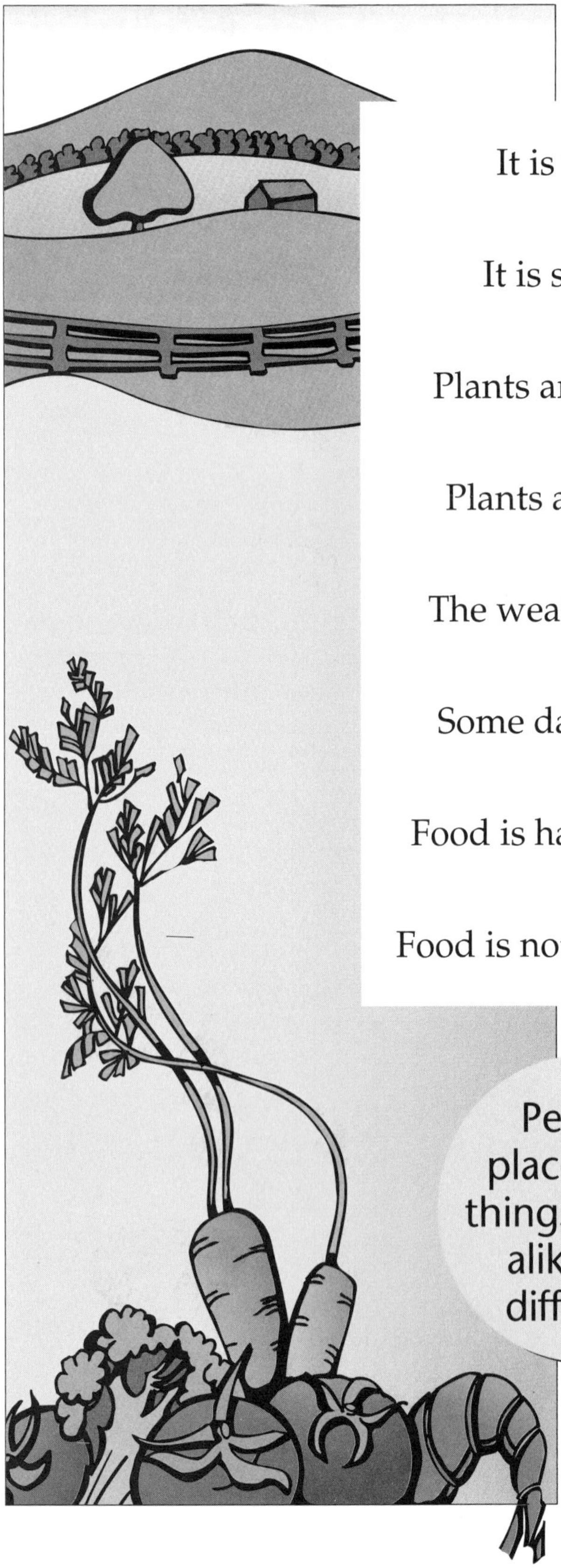

It is winter.

It is summer.

Plants are growing.

Plants are resting.

The weather is cold.

Some days are hot.

Food is harder to find.

Food is not hard to find.

People, places, and things can be alike and different.

## ▸Read and Do

Read the story and follow the directions.

God had told Abraham that he must leave his homeland. So Abraham herded together his many sheep and cattle and packed up his tents. Lot would be going with his Uncle Abraham. He would bring his many sheep and cattle too.

Together Lot and Abraham traveled far away from Ur, their home. At last they reached the land that God had chosen for them.

Abraham gave Lot a choice. Lot could choose between the bare and rocky land or the lush, green plains. Lot looked at the plains. He selfishly chose the best land for himself. Abraham took the bare and rocky land.

God said that He would bless Abraham and one day give him all the land that he could see. Abraham thanked God.

Whom do these statements describe?
Draw a line to Abraham, to Lot, or to both.

Abraham

had many sheep and cattle

went with his uncle

left his homeland

chose the lush, green plains

took the bare and rocky land

blessed by God

Lot

# Meet You There

### Let's Work Together

Use your compass rose to follow these instructions. Where do you end up?

1. Start at the stone wall.
2. Walk east to Acorn Hill.
3. Turn north and walk over Acorn Hill to High Water Bridge.
4. Turn east and cross High Water Bridge.
5. Walk north and follow the path through the briar patches.

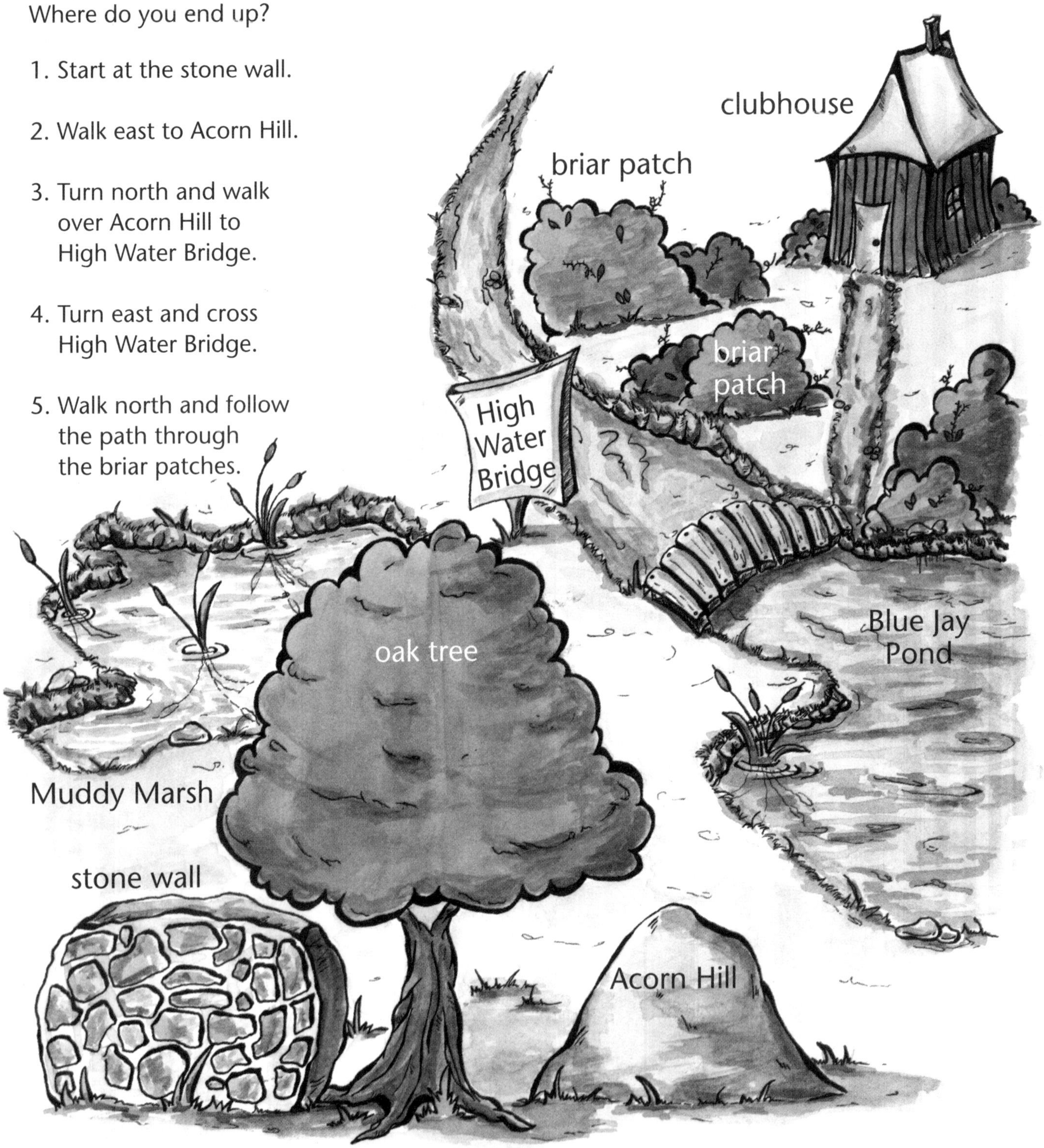


A compass rose shows the directions on a map.

## Which Way?

Pretend you are standing in the middle of the map. Place your compass rose over the outline and use it to answer the questions. Write the correct direction to answer each question.

north
south
east
west

Where are the sea gulls? ______________

Where is the cabin? ______________

Where are the orange trees? ______________

Where are the bikes? ______________

Where are the children? ______________

Where is the snake? ______________

# Ends and Beginnings

## Let's Talk About It

What happens before the cat adds a suffix to short vowel words?

| | |
|---|---|
| cross | shop |
| crossed | shopper |
| smash | thin |
| smashed | thinned |

If the base word ends with only one consonant, add another one.

limp ____________ drum ____________

What happens before the cat adds suffixes to these long vowel words?

hope—hoping

bake—baker

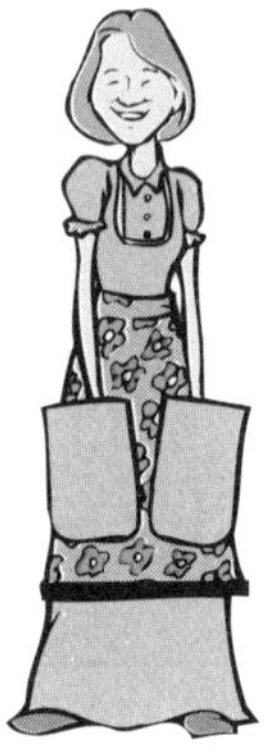

If the base word ends with Marker *e,* drop the *e.*

boat ____________ ride ____________

A prefix is added to the beginning of a base word. One prefix is *a*-.

cross—across

Did the prefix change the base word's spelling? Prefixes do not change the base word's spelling.

Do prefixes add syllables? Prefixes do add a syllable.

Prefixes are added to the beginning of words. They do not change the base word's spelling, but they do add a syllable.

## Pick One

Use words from the chests to complete the sentences.

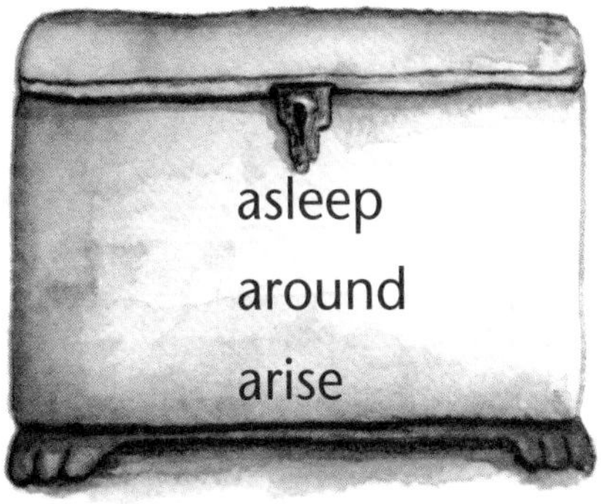


1. Christ said He would ________________ on the third day, and He did.

2. I fall ________________ when the lights are turned down low.

3. The button fell off my coat. Will you look ________________ on the playground for it?

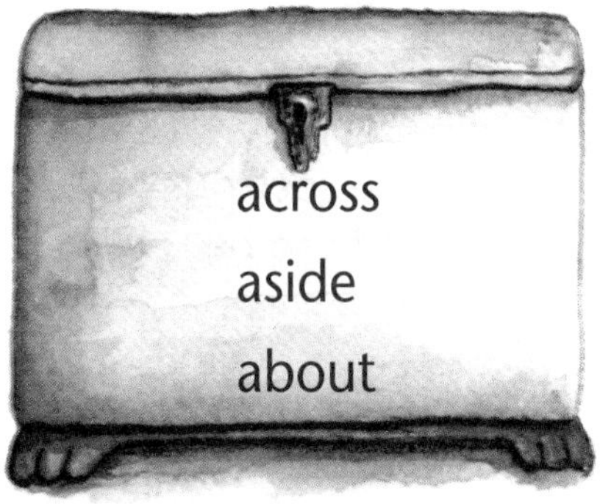


4. The stream was too deep to wade through, so I walked ________________ on a fallen log.

5. When my older sister runs for the phone, I step ________________.

6. This story was great! May I tell you ________________ it?

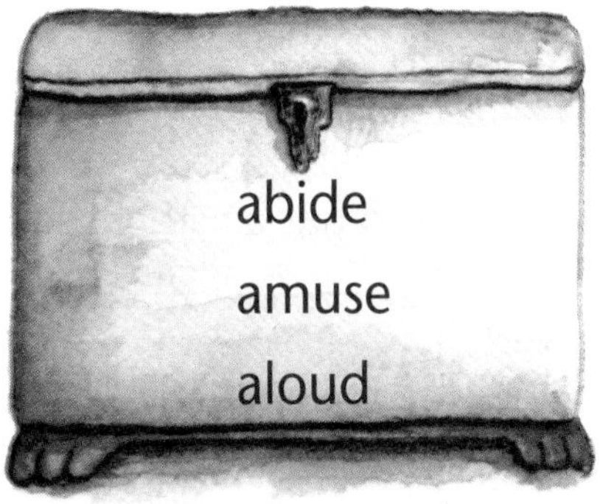


7. For homework tonight, I am going to read ________________ to my mother.

8. My sister and I watch the baby make funny faces. His faces ________________ us.

9. The law says we must pay taxes. We will ________________ by the law.

# The Sound of Bear

### Listen and Look

These words have a sound that is the same.
What other words have the same sound?

care

bear

<u>*Bear*</u> being a <u>*bear*</u>.

Look at the spellings of your words.
One sound can be spelled many ways.

| pair | pare | pear |
|---|---|---|
|  | 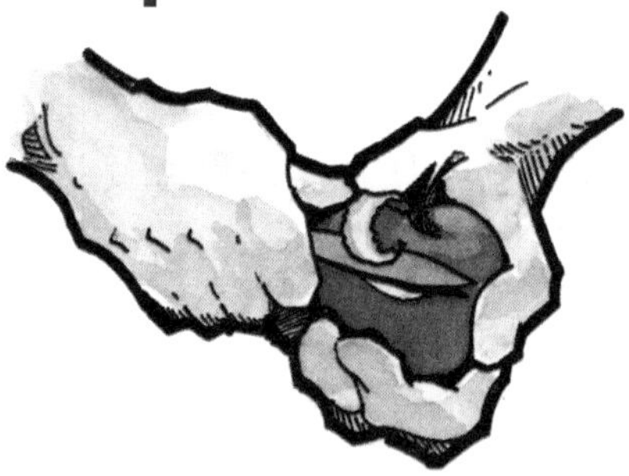 |  |

The last spelling, *-ear*, can make another sound.
This sound has another spelling too.

| | |
|---|---|
| hear | fear |
| dear | gear |
| ear | near |

| | |
|---|---|
| cheer | sheer |
| deer | sneer |
| jeer | steer |

When *r* follows a vowel, it usually influences its sound.

## Draw It

Look carefully at the picture. Then follow the directions.

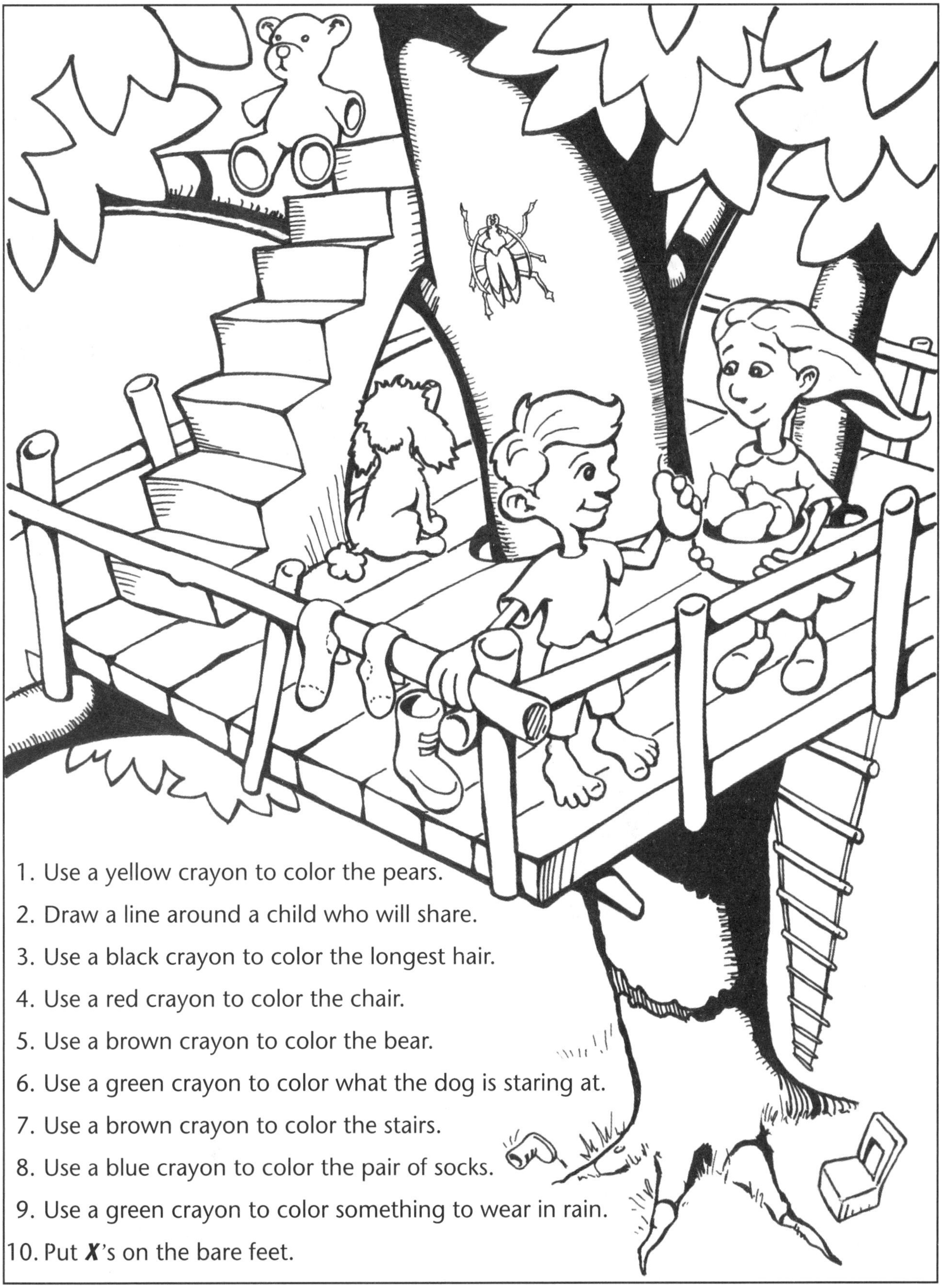

1. Use a yellow crayon to color the pears.
2. Draw a line around a child who will share.
3. Use a black crayon to color the longest hair.
4. Use a red crayon to color the chair.
5. Use a brown crayon to color the bear.
6. Use a green crayon to color what the dog is staring at.
7. Use a brown crayon to color the stairs.
8. Use a blue crayon to color the pair of socks.
9. Use a green crayon to color something to wear in rain.
10. Put ***X***'s on the bare feet.

# Are You with Me?

## Match It Up

Match these analogies with the right picture.

1.  ring is to 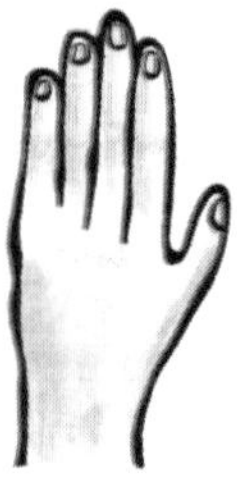 as  earring is to  bird

2.  day is to  as  night is to  moon

3. 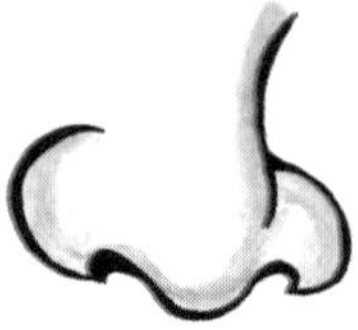 nose is to  as  beak is to  ear

4.  snow is to  as  rain is to  umbrella

## Fill It In

Use the words in the word box to complete the analogies.

| | |
|---|---|
| cry | glass |

1. *Food* is to *plate* as *drink* is to ______________.

2. *Big* is to *little* as *laugh* is to ______________.

Analogies compare words or ideas to show their relationship.

## ▸ More Matches

Write the correct word in the blank.

1. *Up* is to *down* as *in* is to ________________.

2. *Hand* is to *arm* as *foot* is to ________________.

3. *Dog* is to *doghouse* as *bird* is to ________________.

4. *Crayon* is to *color* as *pencil* is to ________________.

5. *Warm* is to *hot* as *cool* is to ________________.

| |
|---|
| out |
| cold |
| write |
| leg |
| nest |

6. *Knife* is to *cut* as *brush* is to ________________.

7. *Room* is to *house* as *page* is to ________________.

8. *Hen* is to *chick* as *cat* is to ________________.

9. *Young* is to *old* as *first* is to ________________.

10. *Laugh* is to *happy* as *cry* is to ________________.

| |
|---|
| book |
| kitten |
| paint |
| sad |
| last |

## ▸ Working Together

Read the first two words.
Add the prefix *un-* to the words.
*Un-* can mean "not."

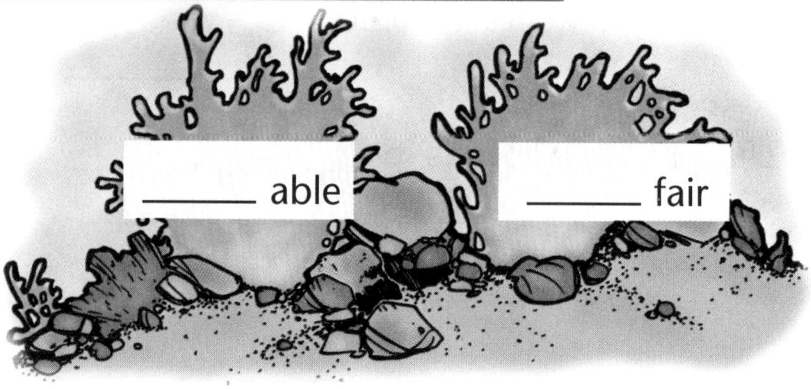


Read the next two words. Add *un-* to these words.
*Un-* can also mean "do the opposite of."

______ wrap ______ tie

Add the prefix *mis-* to the words.
*Mis-* means "bad or wrong."

Study these words so that
______________________
you do not ______________________
them on the test.

Add the prefix *re-* to the words.
*Re-* means "to do again."

This roast is cold.

Please ______________________ it.

**Adding a prefix changes the meaning of the word.**

## Choose a Prefix

Circle the correct prefix to complete the sentence.

1. The sponge is (un / re) able to walk.

2. This sponge will (un / re) grow its missing part.

3. The color of the coral is (un / mis) important.

4. Someone must (re / mis) string the coral beads.

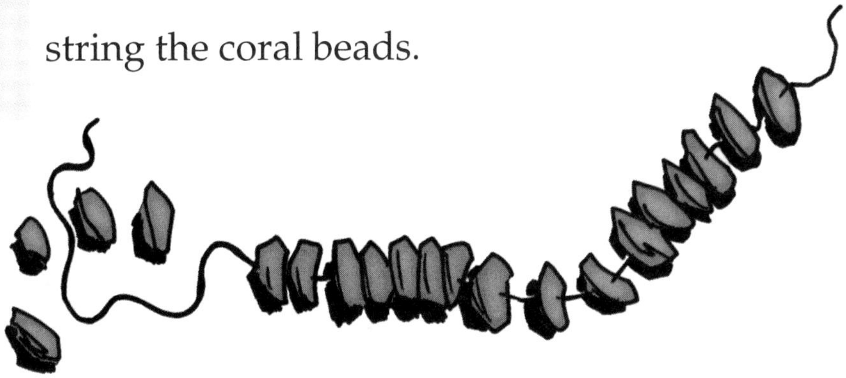

## Choose a Letter

Write the letter of each definition beside the correct word.

| | | |
|---|---|---|
| ______ | 1. misconduct | a. to open |
| ______ | 2. unhealthy | b. sick |
| ______ | 3. unlock | c. different |
| ______ | 4. ungrateful | d. bad actions |
| ______ | 5. untrue | e. without thanks |
| ______ | 6. unlike | f. false |

### Listen and Look

When is a vowel long?

We hear Miss Long if she is alone,

**no**

go

she

ta·ble

if she is followed by Marker *e*,

**note**

game

slide

choke

or if she is followed by Miss Silent.

**toad**

boat

seem

bead

Letter signals usually tell us when the vowel is long.

# ▸Paint It

Color the animals that Miss Long will take pictures of.

# *Why Does He Do That?*

## Working Together

Circle only the *or* words that make the /ûr/ sound.

| | | |
|---|---|---|
| born | work | stork |
| worm | worst | sport |
| world | thorn | cork |

Which *or* words make the /ûr/ sound? ______

What letter tells you that the *or* will say /ûr/? ______

Read the words.

| | | | |
|---|---|---|---|
| work | worse | worms | word |
| worst | worth | world | worship |

## Fill It In

Use the words from the box to complete the sentences.

1. “This is hard ______.”

2. “This is the ______ mistake I have ever made.”

3. The ______ could not help smiling.

4. “Don’t say a ______!” said Starfish.

5. “We didn’t mean to make you feel ______.”

6. “You were the funniest sight in the ______.”

When *w* is with *or*, *or* is pronounced /ûr/.

## ▸Find the Ones

Help the starfish get off the coral. Find sea worms with the same vowel sound as in *word* and draw a line from them to the starfish.

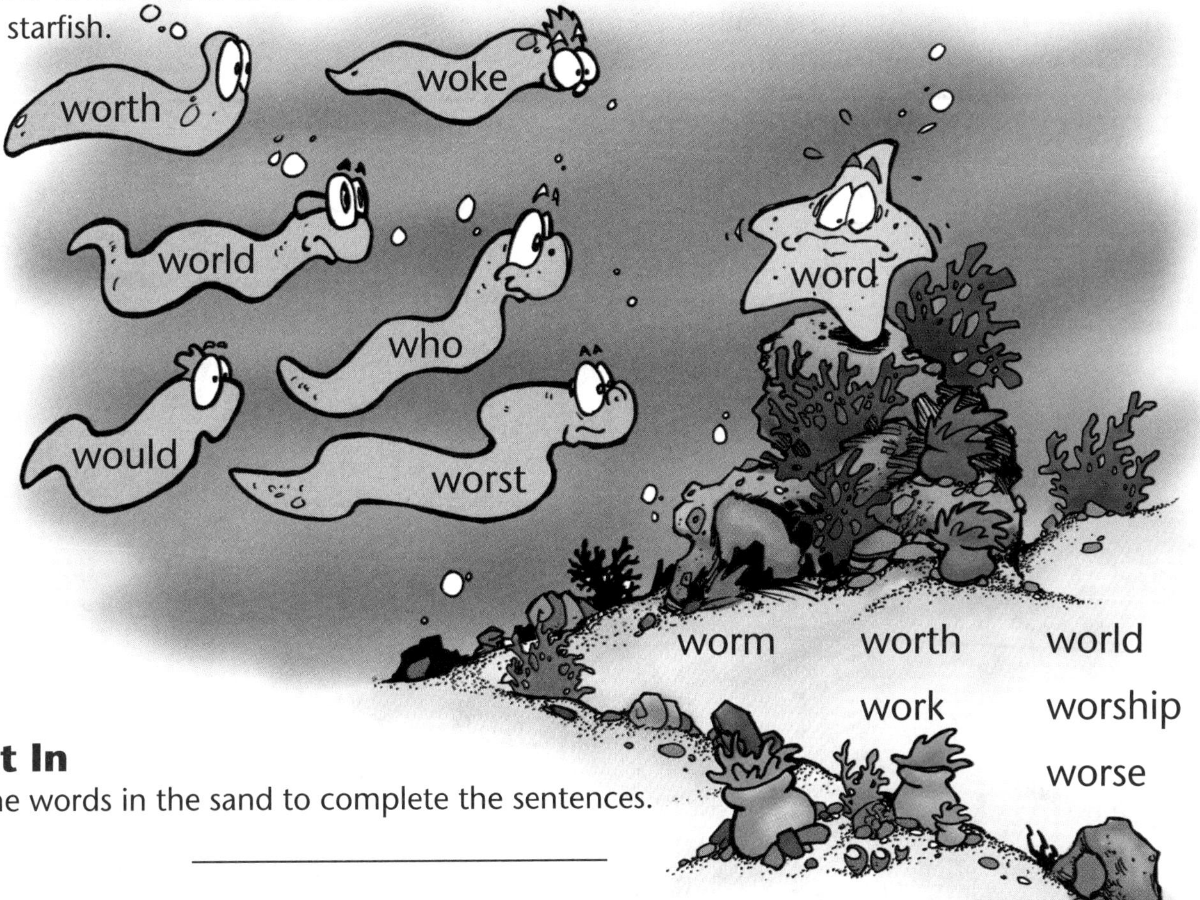

## ▸Fill It In

Use the words in the sand to complete the sentences.

1. Dave likes to ____________________ hard in school.

2. A good name is ____________________ more than riches.

3. Bob put a ____________________ on his fishhook.

4. God made the ____________________ in six days.

5. Sue feels ____________________ today than she did the other day.

6. We can ____________________ God at any time.

**Reading 2B: Skill Station Day,** Lesson 112
Phonics: using letter-sound association: vowels with *r*, /ûr/ after *w* as in *work*
Comprehension: developing sentence closure
333

# Is This Real?

## ▸Let's Talk About It

Look at the pictures. Mark the realistic picture with an *R*.
Mark the fanciful picture with an *F*.

Sometimes writers write about something that could happen.
These sentences are called *realistic*.

The children walked along the shore picking up seashells.

The children found a jellyfish in a pool of seawater.

Sometimes writers write about something that could not happen. These sentences are called *fanciful*.

At night, the fish come out of the water to walk along the shore.

The jellyfish sat on a beach towel and ate his picnic basket lunch.

Stories that could happen are called *realistic*.
Stories that could not happen are called *fanciful*.

## ▸ Read and Think

Read the story. Write two things that make it fanciful.

### Steaming Skyscrapers

"This city is too hot," griped Hancock Center. He was one of the tallest buildings in the city.

"You're right," agreed Sears Tower. "I have a plan."

That night Hancock, Sears, and their friends tiptoed to the lake. Their steel clanked as they splashed into the water. They played and laughed all night until the sun woke up.

"Look at the city," wailed Hancock. "It's lonely without us."

Splish, splosh—out of the lake they scrambled.

Back home Hancock sighed. "During the day we need to be here. But maybe we can cool off again another night."

# Fire! Fire!

**Reading Together**

Firefighters didn't always ride in big red trucks. Long ago, villagers lined up and passed along buckets of water to be thrown on a fire. This was called a bucket brigade.

In later years, many volunteers got together to pull carts with water tanks. Before long, fast horses took over the hard job of pulling bigger carts. Today, firefighters drive trucks to fires.

Some fire trucks are called pumpers. They quickly pump water through long, heavy hoses. If the truck needs more water, the firefighters hook the hoses to fire hydrants. With this supply of water, the firefighters don't need to leave to fill up their tanks again.

Other trucks are called ladder trucks. Motors raise the ladder so that firefighters can rescue people trapped in a fire.

*From buckets to trucks—firefighting has come a long way!*

Sometimes things work together. One thing affects another.

## ▸Pick One

Fill in the circle next to the correct sentence.

1. Why do people become firefighters?

○ They want to get hurt.
○ They want to help others.
○ They like getting hot.

2. Why do people find new ways to put out fires?

○ People don't care.
○ People want faster ways to put fires out.
○ People want to have more bright red trucks.

3. Why did people choose horses to pull the carts and not oxen?

○ Horses are faster than oxen.
○ Oxen are not strong enough to pull things.
○ Horses liked the fires.

4. Why aren't horses used for firefighting today?

○ Horses can't fit onto the trucks.
○ Oxen are now used to pull the carts.
○ Horses aren't needed anymore.

5. How do fire hydrants affect firefighting?

○ Fire hydrants make the streets pretty.
○ Fire hydrants are to be used only for firefighting.
○ Fire hydrants keep firefighters from running out of water.

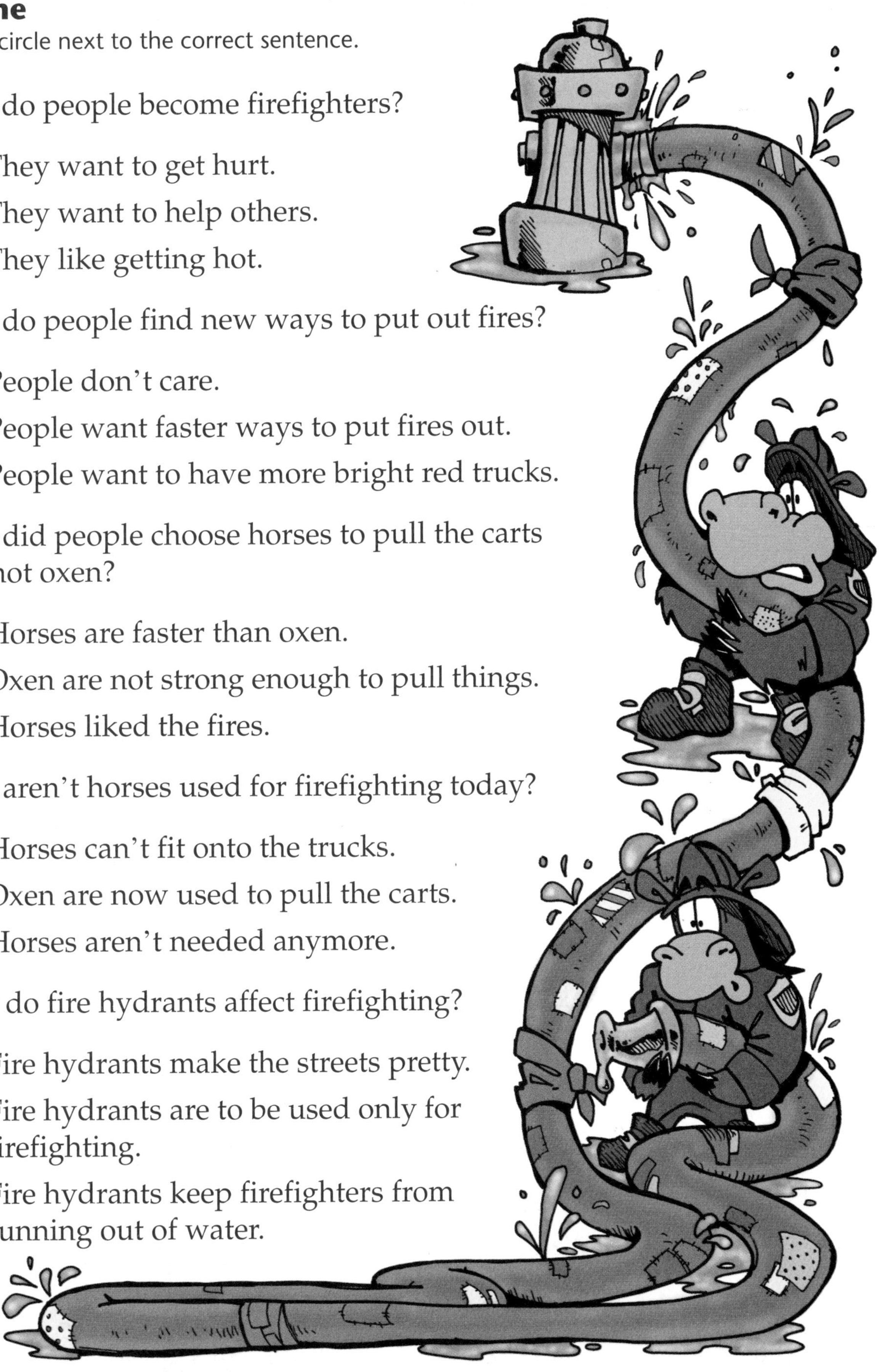

# Mark Your Calendar

## Let's Look

| March | | | | | | |
|---|---|---|---|---|---|---|
| Sunday | Monday | Tuesday | Wednesday | Thursday | Friday | Saturday |
| | | | 1 | 2 | 3 | 4 |
| 5 | 6  | 7 | 8  | 9 | 10 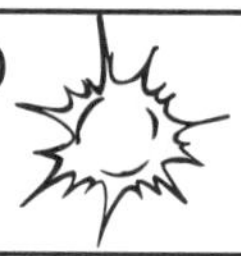 | 11 |
| 12 | 13  | 14 | 15  | 16 | 17  | 18 |
| 19 | 20 | 21 | 22 | 23 *Play* | 24 | 25 |
| 26 | 27 | 28 | 29 | 30 | 31 | |

Draw a line under the correct answer.

1. What day of the week is March 2?
   Wednesday Thursday Friday
2. What day of the week do the students who act as trees meet?
   Monday Wednesday Friday
3. What day of the week does the butterfly section meet?
   Monday Wednesday Friday
4. What day of the week do the students who act as stars meet?
   Monday Wednesday Friday
5. What day is the play?
   March 14 March 23 March 28

Calendars have lots of information to share.

## Mark It

Make this calendar look like this month's calendar. Think of pictures to use to mark birthdays, holidays, or weather.

| Sunday | Monday | Tuesday | Wednesday | Thursday | Friday | Saturday |
|---|---|---|---|---|---|---|
| | | | | | | |
| | | | | | | |
| | | | | | | |
| | | | | | | |
| | | | | | | |

## Tell About It

1. What picture did you use to show birthdays?

2. How many birthdays did you make? ______________

3. What picture did you use for today?

4. If there is a holiday, show the picture you used for it.

5. Show any other picture you used on the calendar.

6. What does it stand for? ________________________________

### Working Together

vacation
mention
salvation
definition

nation
action
devotions
directions

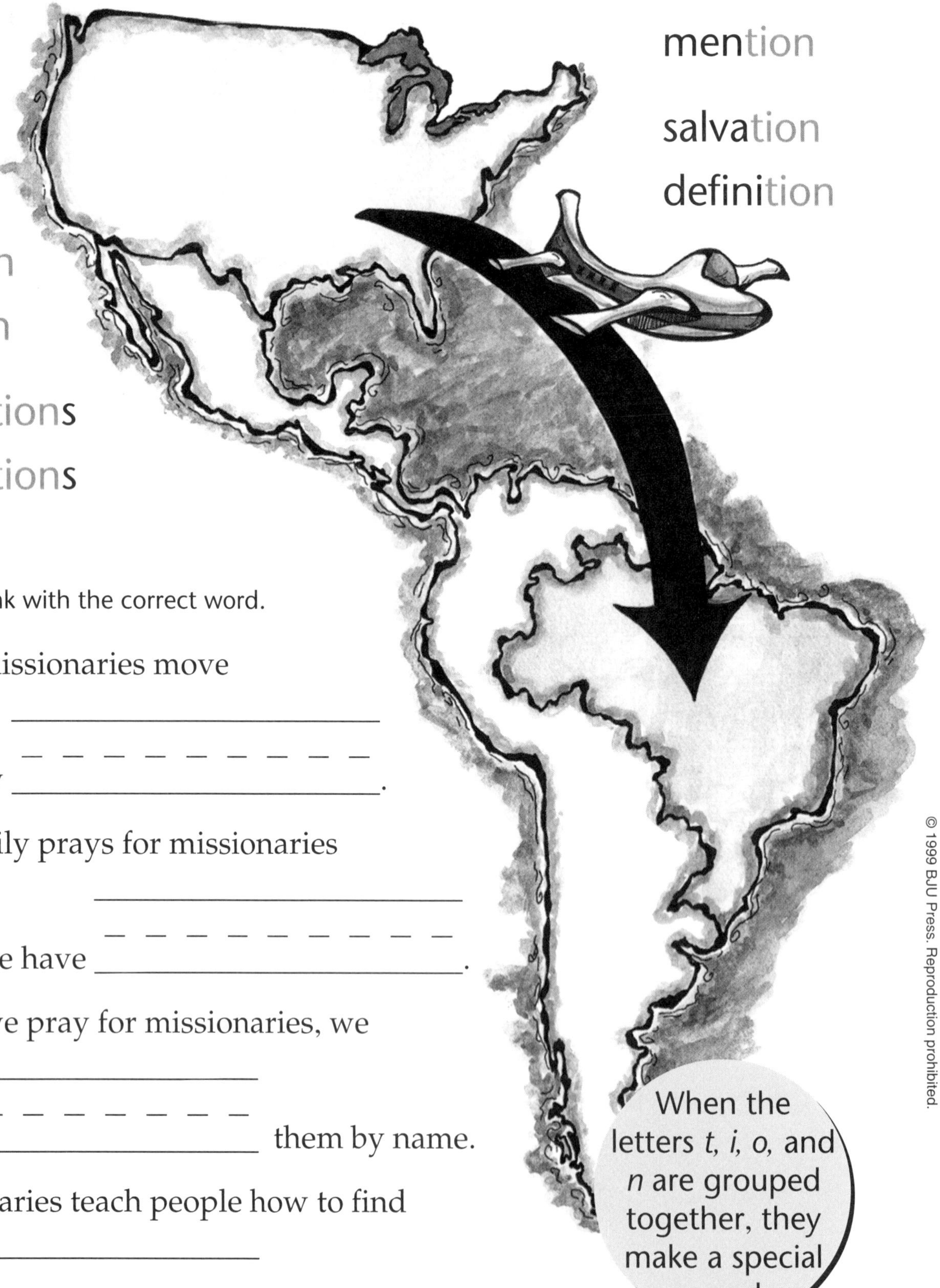

When the letters *t, i, o,* and *n* are grouped together, they make a special sound.

Fill in the blank with the correct word.

1. Many missionaries move ____________ to a new ____________.
2. My family prays for missionaries ____________ when we have ____________.
3. When we pray for missionaries, we ____________ ____________ them by name.
4. Missionaries teach people how to find ____________ ____________ in Jesus Christ.

John's family moved from England to Russia.

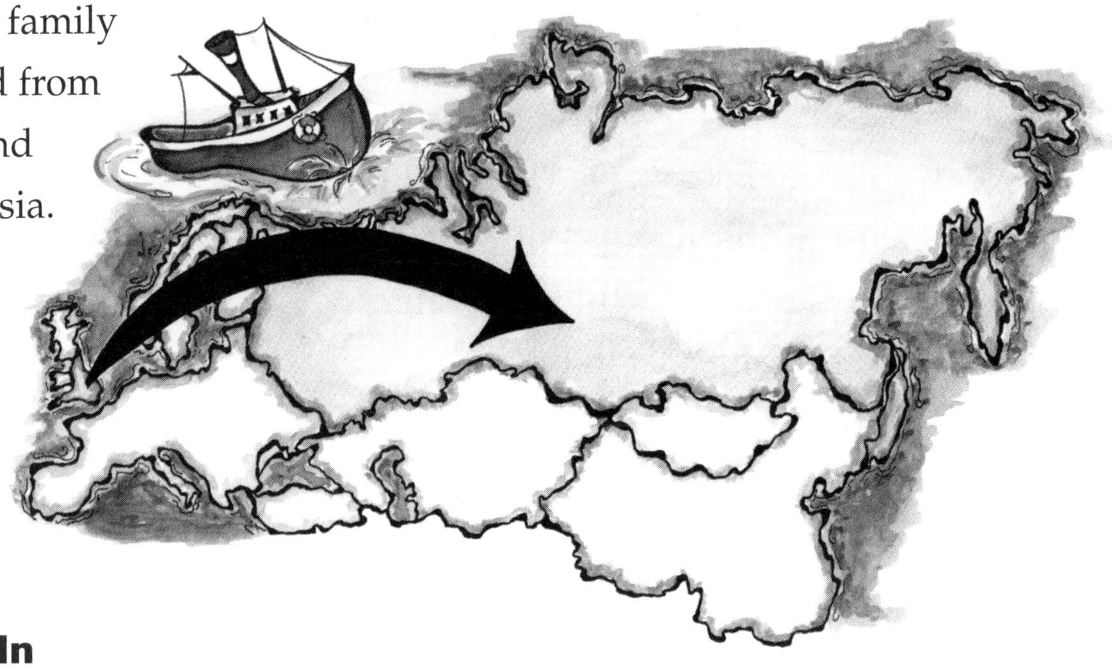

## ▸Fill It In

Put a word from the box in each blank.

| | | |
|---|---|---|
| action | nation | vacation |
| station | devotions | directions |

1. We are going to the seashore on our ____________.

2. Mother met Dad at the train ____________.

3. The president is the leader of our ____________.

4. Jim gave Kevin ____________ to get to his house.

5. Father read the Bible for family ____________.

6. The firefighter sprang into ____________.

# Family of Fishermen

## ▸Thinking Together

"Are we ready to go fishing, Dad?" asked Buck.

"Yes," Mr. Hensbee answered. "Will you get the fishing lines? I'll push the boat into the water."

Soon Buck and his father sat in the small boat. Each of them used a paddle to move it. Before long, they had enough fish for supper.

Which is their boat?

---

Mr. Hensbee works all night catching fish. He uses a boat for his job. This boat is moved by a motor.

Sometimes he and other men fish for a few days. They can eat and sleep on the boat. Then they bring back a load of fish to sell.

Where does Mr. Hensbee keep his boat?

The Hensbees are fishers of men too. Every week they have a Bible club in their home. Children come from all over the fishing town.

The Hensbees pray for the people in their town. They want their friends to ask the Lord for forgiveness from sin.

How do the Hensbees fish for men?

After careful thought, draw conclusions about what you read and hear.

## Read and Choose

Read this letter written to you from a missionary child in Scotland. Write your name in the blank and draw circles around the correct answers.

________________________

Dear ________________________,

I made up a game to tell you what we do in this land. I'll give you a clue, and you can pick the right answer.

1. Some people here have never heard how to get to heaven. We tell them _______.

   to be good    about God    to give us money

2. My friend was sick. I told Mom I was going out to _______.

   see another friend    go for a walk    visit my sick friend

3. When Bible club is over, I tell the other children to _______.

   go home    come back again    have fun

4. Tomorrow is my friend's birthday. I want him to learn more about God. I will give him _______.

   candy    a game    a Bible

5. I sent a blank sheet of paper and a stamp in this letter. Now you can _______.

   write me a letter    draw your family    do your homework

Your friend,
Rob

# *Blend the Words*

## Painting Together

Use some of this paint to add words to the word families.

| | | |
|---|---|---|
| cab | cove | bake |
| lab | dove | cake |
| tab | wove | lake |
| ___ab | ___ove | ___ake |

Consonant blends are clusters of two or three consonants.

Their sounds are blended together.

## Make a Word

Use the blends to make new words.

| bag | hand | meat |
| --- | --- | --- |
| | | |
| | | |
| | | |

## Find the One

Mark the correct sentences to match the pictures.

○ Marker *e* smells the fresh paint.

○ Marker *e* puts his paws over his eyes.

○ Uncle Short puts stripes into the paint.

○ Uncle Short blends a new color.

# Is That a Fact?

**Talking It Over**

Read the story.

"What's this?" Kevin asked. He pointed at a red and silver object on Granddad's table.

"It's a harmonica," Granddad said. Granddad blew into the harmonica. "What do you think this sounds like?"

"I think it sounds like a train chugging down an old track," Kevin said.

"I think it sounds like a sad old owl," said Rob, Kevin's brother.

"Do you two want to learn to play the harmonica?" Granddad asked as he wiped the instrument on a napkin.

"We'll try," said Kevin and Rob.

"At first it may not sound right," Granddad said. "But if you practice, you will be able to make nice melodies."

Read each sentence. Draw a circle around *fact* or *opinion*.

1. Kevin pointed at the harmonica.

   fact opinion

2. Granddad played the harmonica.

   fact opinion

3. Harmonicas sound like trains.

   fact opinion

4. Kevin and Rob wanted to play the harmonica.

   fact opinion

5. Harmonicas sound like sad old owls.

   fact opinion

An opinion is what someone thinks or believes. | A fact is true.

## Read and Decide

Read the story.



Plink, plink, plank, plunk, plunk—Gwen plucked the five strings on her banjo. One end of her banjo was shaped like a hollow drum. Gwen rested that part on her lap and held the long, thin neck with her other hand. Then she plucked the five strings quickly. She thought the sound was like a mouse running across a tin plate. She played slowly and thought it sounded like raindrops hitting a window.

Now she was ready for another time of practice. Dad had told Gwen she must keep practicing in order to play well. She played songs about birthdays and cowboys and happy times.

At last she was finished for the day. "Practicing is fun for me!"

Read each sentence. Draw a line around *fact* or *opinion*.

1. One end of a banjo is shaped like a hollow drum.

   fact opinion

2. A banjo sounds like a mouse running across a tin plate.

   fact opinion

3. A banjo has a long, thin neck.

   fact opinion

4. A banjo sounds like raindrops hitting a window.

   fact opinion

5. Practicing is fun.

   fact opinion

6. Gwen plucked the five strings.

   fact opinion

# What Were the Clues?

## Listen and Think

Listen to the story your teacher reads.

Write a check mark beside the clues.

| | |
|---|---|
| ______ a bluebird<br>______ Skunk's footprints | ______ a mitten at the fishing hole<br>______ a fishing pole |
| ______ acorns<br>______ a white scarf | ______ the snowy tree stump<br>______ an otter's footprints at the lake |

Some details are more important than others.

## Find the Two

Read the story. Put a check mark beside the correct answer. There are two correct answers for each story.

Bill was going to pick apples on Saturday. He wanted apples to make candy apple treats for his class at school.

Bill called his friend Carl and invited him to go apple picking too. Then Bill bought some candy coating to cover the apples and some wooden sticks to put in them. After apple picking on Saturday, Bill and his mother made the candy apples. On Monday, Bill took the treats to school.

What helped to make treats for the class?

____ buying candy coating
____ giving an apple to Dad
____ picking apples

Sue took an old coin to school to show her teacher. Her father had gotten the coin when he was on a trip. It was very special to Sue.

When she got home, the coin was missing from her pocket. Sue put her books down on her desk and went outside. She looked on the ground around the car. She thought the coin might have rolled under the car, but it was not there.

Then Sue looked inside the car. She found the coin on the back seat. It had fallen out of her pocket.

What helped to find the coin?

____ mending her pocket
____ looking inside the car
____ looking on the ground

# Old Friends

## Let's Talk It Over

Who are Mr. and Mrs. Short? Who is Uncle Short?
Find them and circle them in these lists.

fit

fill

| | | | | |
|---|---|---|---|---|
| shape | glum | bead | pond | shy |
| sort | grew | shed | some | stick |
| scram | glue | Dean | toast | slide |

Who is Miss Long?
Use Miss Long to add to the word family.

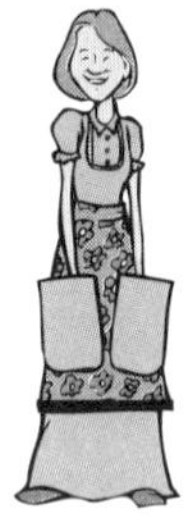

my

my

Do you remember Marker *e* and Miss Silent?

slide

coast

| | | | |
|---|---|---|---|
| rob | mad | got | ran |
| rob______ | mad______ | go______t | ra______n |

When we look at the vowels in their patterns, we know how to say them.

## Where Are They?

Circle the word that contains the vowel characters pictured.

wish
boast
tarp

spun
troop
main

feed
fort
fed

his
he
him

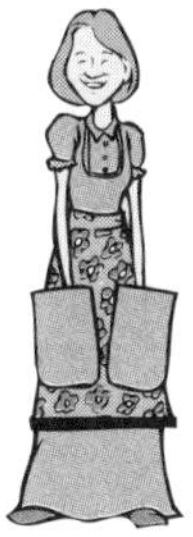

goal
greed
vine

cream
sand
try

short
stone
stood

hope
grain
grave

## Round Them Up

Draw ropes to Bossy *R*'s horses.

# Reading the Musical Way

## Finding Out Together

Songs in the hymnal usually have two parts.
Name the two parts.

____________________ and ____________________

This is called a system.

The words of each stanza are written with one line in each system.

The last part of the song is the chorus.

To sing the first stanza, sing the top line of words in each system.

To sing the second stanza, sing the second line of words in each system.

The chorus is repeated at the end of each stanza.

A stanza of music is written with one line of words in each system.

The chorus is sung after each stanza.

## Answer It

Write an answer.

1. What is the name of this song?

2. How many stanzas does it have?

3. What is your favorite sacred song?

Shade all of stanza one blue.

Shade all of stanza two yellow.

Shade all of stanza three green.

Shade the chorus red.

# Add a Suffix

## Do It Together

Add the suffixes to each group. Cross off Marker *e* before adding the suffix.

straight________

weak________

cheap________

trade________

shake________

mine________

paint________

wait________

claim________

place________

replace________

invade________

Even though Marker *e* has jumped out, the vowel is still long.

## Add One

Add suffixes to the base words to complete the sentences.

1. Frederick and his sisters like __________ up verses.
   make

2. Mother says that Frederick is the biggest __________ in the family.
   eat

hope

3. Frederick __________ that everyone would like the new hymn.

write

4. Frederick grew up to be a __________ of songs.

5. Frederick also became a __________.
   preach

dream

6. I'm sure that Frederick never __________ that some day he would write so many songs.

bleed

7. The hymn tells of Jesus' __________ on the cross for us.

# Paul's Shipwreck

## Talking It Over

Think about the stormy sea and the sinking ship.
What did the men—

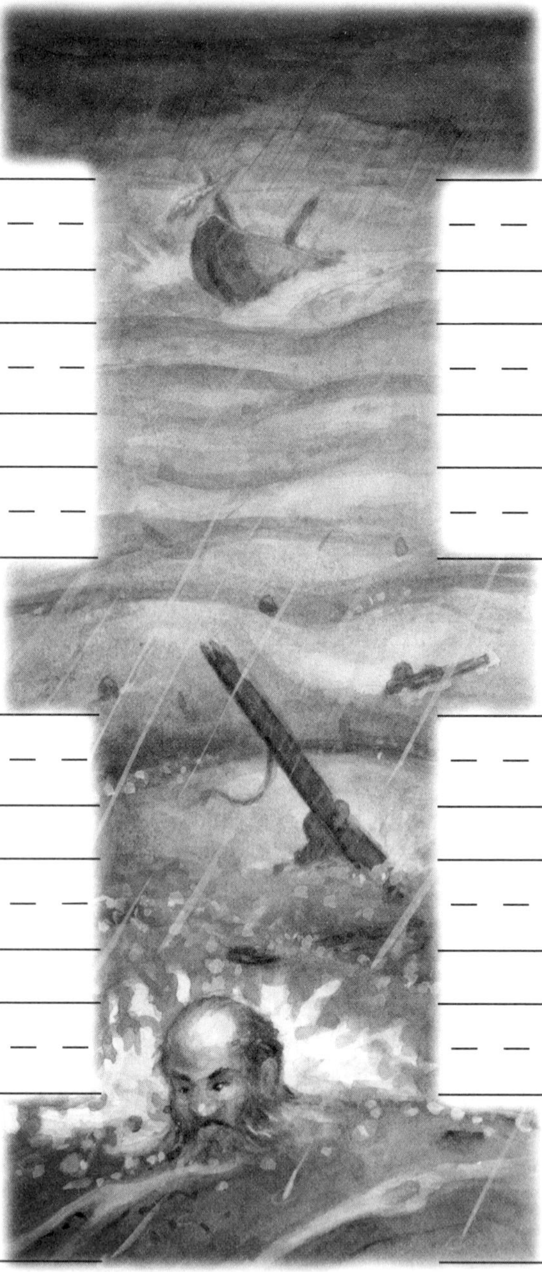

hear

smell

see

taste

feel

think

When we use our senses to choose words, others have a clearer picture of the event.

## What's It Like?

Think about the astronaut.
What did he—

hear

smell

see

taste

feel

think

## Decide Together

Put an ***X*** beside the definition that describes the word from the story.

"I don't know how much more this ship can ***bear***."

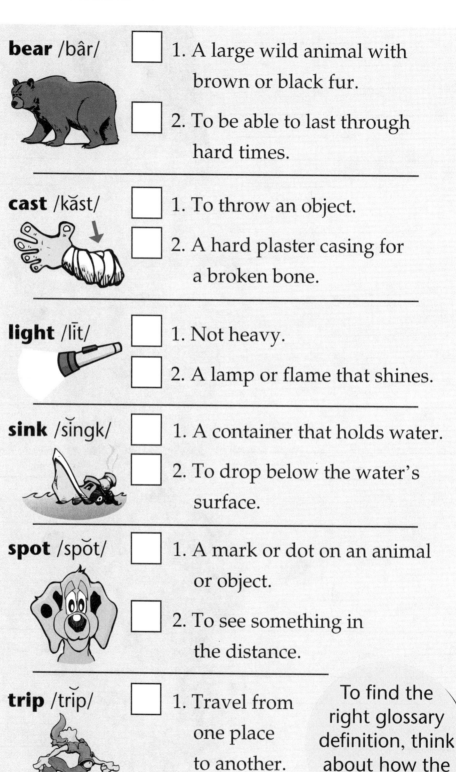

**bear** /bâr/

☐ 1. A large wild animal with brown or black fur.

☐ 2. To be able to last through hard times.

---

"Let's ***cast*** some things overboard."

**cast** /kăst/

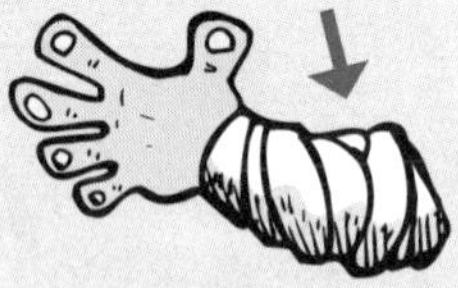

☐ 1. To throw an object.

☐ 2. A hard plaster casing for a broken bone.

---

"That will make the ship ***lighter***."

**light** /līt/

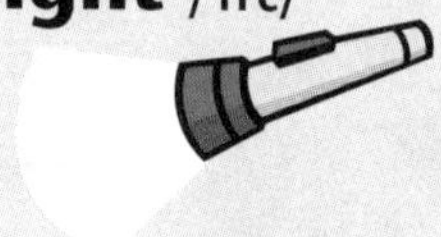

☐ 1. Not heavy.

☐ 2. A lamp or flame that shines.

---

The men were afraid it was going to ***sink***.

**sink** /sĭngk/

☐ 1. A container that holds water.

☐ 2. To drop below the water's surface.

---

"I've ***spotted*** land!"

**spot** /spŏt/

☐ 1. A mark or dot on an animal or object.

☐ 2. To see something in the distance.

---

The ***trip*** had been hard, but every man's life was spared.

**trip** /trĭp/

☐ 1. Travel from one place to another.

☐ 2. To stumble.

To find the right glossary definition, think about how the word is used.

## You Decide

Read the sentences. Put an ***X*** beside the definition that describes the word in the sentence.

Crude boats can be made of ***bark***.

**bark** /bärk/

☐ 1. The short, gruff sound made by a dog.

☐ 2. The outer covering of the trunks, branches, and roots of trees.

---

The lion ***glared*** at the wild dogs.

**glare** /glâr/

☐ 1. To stare in anger.

☐ 2. To shine brightly.

---

The goat's ***horns*** were tangled in the bushes.

**horn** /hôrn/

☐ 1. One of the hard, pointed growths on the heads of some animals.

☐ 2. A musical instrument played by blowing into one end.

---

The old toys were found in a ***chest*** in Grandma's attic.

**chest** /chĕst/

☐ 1. The upper front part of the body.

☐ 2. A strong box with a lid, used for holding things.

---

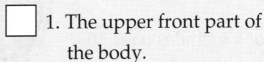

She ***jammed*** all her dresses into one suitcase.

**jam** /jăm/

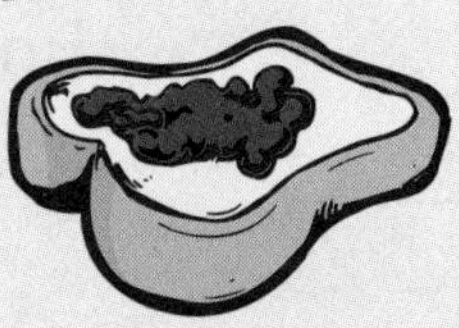

☐ 1. To squeeze or become squeezed into a tight space.

☐ 2. A thick, sweet food.

# Singing in the Word

**Let's Talk About It**

**EXODUS 15:1**

*Then sang Moses and the children of Israel this song unto the Lord, and spake, saying, I will sing unto the Lord, for he hath triumphed gloriously.*

Exodus begins on page ________.

What book includes page 29? ________________

Genesis begins on page ________.

Genesis ends on page ________.

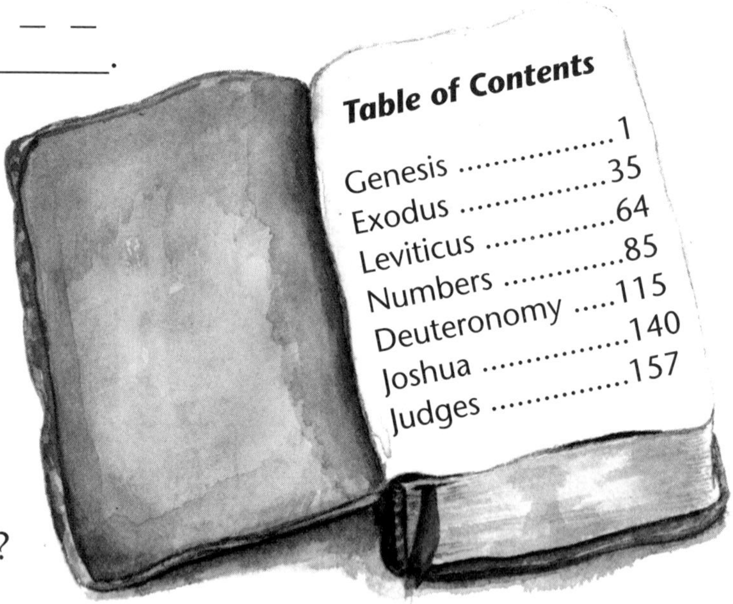


**NUMBERS 21:17**

*Then Israel sang this song.*

Which book includes page 100?

________________

How do you know?

The table of contents tells which pages the books of the Bible are found on.

This book begins on page ________.

It ends on page ________________.

## ▸ Look It Up

Use the table of contents in your Bible to look up these verses.
Read the verses to answer these questions.

### *Down*

1. **Deuteronomy 31:22**

   Who wrote a song?

   __________________

3. **Mark 14:26**

   What kind of song was sung?

   a __________________

5. **Isaiah 65:25**

   What animal sings with a howl?

   a __________________

### *Across*

2. **Psalm 96:11**

   How does the sea sing?

   with a __________________

3. **Luke 2:13**

   Who praised God?

   a heavenly __________________

4. **Psalm 33:3**

   What kind of song should we sing to the Lord?

   a __________________ song

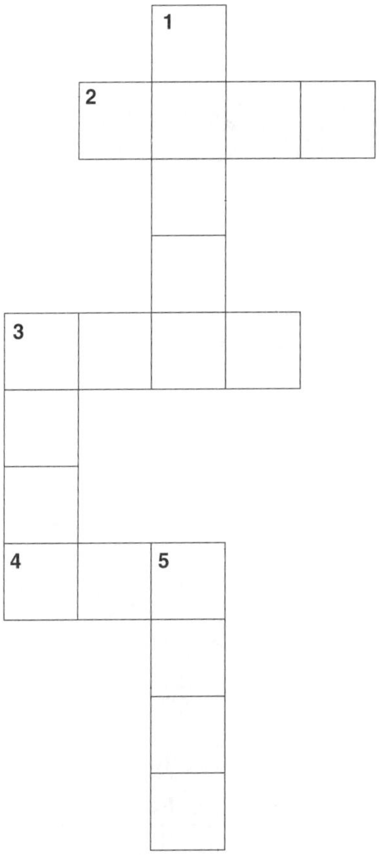

## Use What You Know

### Divide Together

What are these words? Use the lessons that you have learned to divide the syllables and to say the words.

| | | |
|---|---|---|
| s n a f f l e | p r a t t l e | f e r r e t |
| s c a f f o l d | h a g g l e | m u z z l e |
| t r e l l i s | c a d d y | w r i g g l e |

Now try to divide the syllables of these words. Say the words too.

| | | |
|---|---|---|
| t r u m p e t | h u s b a n d | l u m b e r |
| f i l t e r | h e m l o c k | s n o r k e l |
| c o n t e s t | v e s p e r | c a c t u s |

Divide words into syllables between like consonants or between two consonants in the middle of the word.

The first vowel will be short.

## Divide Again

1. Divide the words into syllables. Place dots between the correct letters.
2. Circle the best word.

1. Farmers gather this.

traffic   harvest

2. Something which is quick

sudden   funny

3. A preacher's speech

market   sermon

4. Use this at dinner.

napkin   scamper

5. Put two things together.

silly   connect

6. This is found on a bed.

pillow   coffee

7. Open this to get air.

window   enjoy

8. A kind of fastener

pencil   zipper

9. A kind of money

dollar   rabbit

10. A sore

comment   blister

11. An animal

horrid   squirrel

12. A family member

daddy   gospel

# A Summer Reading List

**Bond, Michael.** *A Bear Called Paddington.* 1958. In this fanciful tale a charming bear from "Darkest Peru" arrives in London as a stowaway.

**Dalgliesh, Alice.** *The Bears on Hemlock Mountain.* Illus. Helen Sewell. 1952. Jonathan safely crosses Hemlock Mountain to get a big iron kettle, but his trip back home is delayed, forcing him to walk in the dark.

———. *The Courage of Sarah Noble.* 1954. An eight-year-old girl, Sarah Noble, demonstrates courage and strength as she endures the difficult trek she and her family must make to move out west.

**Davis, Tim.** *Mice of the Herringbone.* BJU Press, 1992. Charles and Oliver, fanciful mice created by Tim Davis, rescue the queen's treasure.

———. *Mice of the Seven Seas.* BJU Press, 1994. Charles and Oliver join an expedition to the Great Continent.

———. *Mice of the Nine Lives.* BJU Press, 1994. Charles and Oliver search for the queen's ship.

———. *Mice of the Westing Wind, Book One.* BJU Press, 1998. A new adventure begins just when Charles and Oliver thought the pirate sea dogs were safely in prison.

———. *Mice of the Westing Wind, Book Two.* BJU Press, 1998. Two fierce rats are determined to destroy Charles and Oliver, no matter what.

**Duvoisin, Roger.** *Petunia.* 1989. Petunia, a fanciful goose, proudly pretends to "read" the book she's found.

**Hoban, Russell.** *Charlie Meadow.* 1984. Charlie, a fanciful beaver, takes the reader on an adventure.

**Howard, Milly.** *The Treasure of Pelican Cove.* BJU Press, 1988. Jimmy's dog disappears when everyone is scrambling for hidden treasure.

———. *The Mystery of Pelican Cove.* BJU Press, 1993. Jimmy and Blackie see a strange, dark shadow in the water.

**Kellogg, Steven.** *Johnny Appleseed.* 1988. The travels of John Chapman later become the legend of Johnny Appleseed.

**Lobel, Arnold.** *Frog and Toad.* 1988. This humorous story focuses on the friendship of a fanciful frog and toad.

**McCloskey, Robert.** *Blueberries for Sal.* 1988. Sal goes out with her mother to pick blueberries. They encounter a mother bear and her cub on the same errand.

———. *Make Way for Ducklings.* 1976. Mr. and Mrs. Mallard (ducks) search for a site to raise a family.

———. *One Morning in Maine.* 1988. Sal loses her first tooth and learns many interesting things about this exciting event.

———. *Time of Wonder.* 1989. The coming of a hurricane to a family's summer home on a Maine island provides anticipation and excitement.

**Milne, A. A.** *Winnie-the-Pooh.* Illus. Ernest H. Shepard. 1988. Milne's classic collection of episodic tales are brought to life through Shepard's pen-and-ink sketches of Pooh, Eeyore, Piglet, Kanga, Baby Roo, Owl, and the boy Christopher Robin.

**O'Neill, Mary.** *Hailstone and Halibut Bones.* Twelve children's poems make color come alive through the senses of sound, taste, smell, touch, and sight.

**Repp, Gloria.** *A Question of Yams.* BJU Press, 1992. Kuri's father dares to serve God, defying the traditions of the Head Men, and Kuri watches to see what will happen.

**Waber, Bernard.** *Ira Sleeps Over.* 1987. Ira's anticipated overnight stay with his friend becomes a special kind of struggle when his sister brings up the subject of his favorite sleep-time toy.

**Ward, Lynd.** *The Biggest Bear.* 1973. Johnny Orchard sets out to bring back the biggest bear in the forest.

**Watkins, Dawn.** *The Cranky Blue Crab.* Illus. Tim Davis. BJU Press, 1990. Crusty the Crab, bored and unhappy, sets out to find adventure in Sea Meadow.

———. *A King for Brass Cobweb.* Illus. Holly Hannon. BJU Press, 1990. Chipmunk leaves the comforts of home to seek a king who is wise and brave and true.

———. *Pocket Change.* Illus. Tim Davis. BJU Press, 1992. Five illustrated fables tell of alligators, monkeys, cheetahs, and many other animals that do and say remarkable things.

———. *Pulling Together.* BJU Press, 1992. What can a boy do to help his family keep its horses? Matthew takes a risk and makes a sacrifice so that Ben and Dolly can compete at the county fair.

———. *The Spelling Window.* Illus. John Roberts. BJU Press, 1993. Shelly has no time for the spelling window or for her deaf neighbor, Seth, who signs to her sister through it. Why should she?

———. *Very like a Star.* Illus. Dana Thompson. BJU Press, 1990. Rigel of Buzzle Hive has to discover whether she is like the star for which she is named.

**Yates, Elizabeth.** *Carolina's Courage.* BJU Press, 1989. Carolina Putnam is a little girl, but she finds out what it means to have the true spirit of a pioneer.

# A Message to Parents

## Ways You Can Help

Many parents ask the question, "How can I help my child become a good reader?" Reading outside the instructional setting is an essential ingredient for his success. You can make a difference.

- *Read to your child.* Children of all ages benefit as they listen to an adult read. When a child hears material that is *above his own reading level,* his vocabulary is stretched and enriched, and he hears the more interesting syntax patterns that he will encounter in his own reading in the future. When a child hears material *at his present reading level,* he is given a model for the fluency that he needs to attain. When a child hears material that is *easy for him to read,* he is invited to take up that very book and read it for himself.
- *Visit the library with your child.* Help him to select easy, interesting books for his independent reading and more difficult, appealing books for read-aloud time.
- *Read the newspaper with your child.* Study the weather map and compare the map to the forecast given. Look at the sports page. If a sports article is particularly interesting to a child he will read it eagerly. If any articles or editorials have content a child can reflect on, read them to him and discuss the facts and opinions given.
- *Ask your child to read to other family members.* Any homework that turns into family time has double benefits. A child's oral reading fluency will improve as he entertains a younger child or elderly relative by reading easy material to them.
- *Encourage meaningful writing.* Writing builds reading. Help your child to keep a journal of family trips. Enhanced with photographs or original art, it can become a record of his childhood that he will value all his life. Encourage him to write long letters to grandparents or aunts and uncles who live in other cities.
- *Show interest in your child's school papers.* Look with interest at the worktext pages that he has completed. Give value to his pages by commenting on their content, rather than concentrating only on the incorrect answers. If he knows you are interested, he may become more diligent in his efforts.
- *Be enthusiastic about the stories in your child's reader.* After your child has completed the reading lessons for a story in his reader, he will benefit from some good follow-up.
    1. Encourage him to read all or part of the story again silently for himself.
    2. Select parts with ample dialogue and read just the conversation with him as a "play."
    3. Ask him to read the most exciting paragraphs aloud. Praise him specifically if he makes you hear the character's voice, if he communicates fear or other emotions, or if he changes the pace or pauses to show suspense.



## Things to Avoid

Sometimes well-meaning parents cause problems unintentionally. Avoid practices that may become obstacles.

- *Allowing your child to read ahead in his reader is not a good teaching technique.* This will harm the book's effectiveness as a tool for teaching reading comprehension.
- *Avoid making your questions sound like a quiz.*
- *Don't allow your child to read his whole story aloud in a meaningless drone or in a hurried manner.* Good oral reading always communicates the message of the author.
- *Use caution as you correct misread words.* As your child begins to read fluently, he may say slightly different words. For example, the sentence *Jessie put her many toys away* might be read *Jessie put all her toys away.* This happens when his eyes begin moving across the text faster than his speaking voice can interpret it. In his mind the author's words and his own thoughts have become one. This is the sign of a good reader. It is the way you read. If we insist on asking him to go back and get each specific word we are asking him to revert to being a word-by-word reader rather than a fluent phrase-by-phrase reader.
- *Your child needs a different kind of help when practicing words out of context, such as word family lists.* When he has difficulty with a given word, say, "What is the first sound? . . Now look at the rest of the syllable." This will cause him to use phonics generalizations as well as letter/sound phonics knowledge. (This is important because in English each vowel letter represents several different sounds.)

## Tools for the Job

*READING for Christian Schools* emphasizes comprehension and develops phonics systematically. These materials provide the tools not only to teach reading well but also to encourage growth in Christian character. A variety of selections—family stories, adventure stories, Christian realism, historical fiction, Bible accounts retold, biographies, information articles, folktales, poems, and plays—offer engaging reading that provides both pleasure and understanding.

We trust your child will enjoy the school year as he uses his second grade reading materials to become a confident, eager reader—one who will continue to read all his life.

Bob Jones University Press

Materials in this section supplement lessons in the Teacher's Editions of *READING 2 for Christian Schools.*

# *What Miss Long Saw*

Name ______________________________

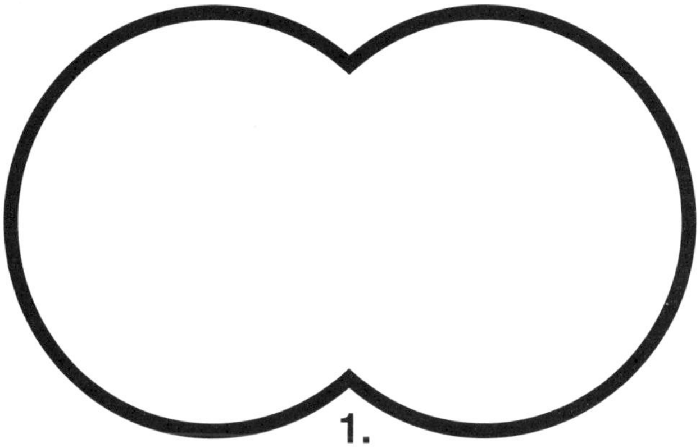

1.

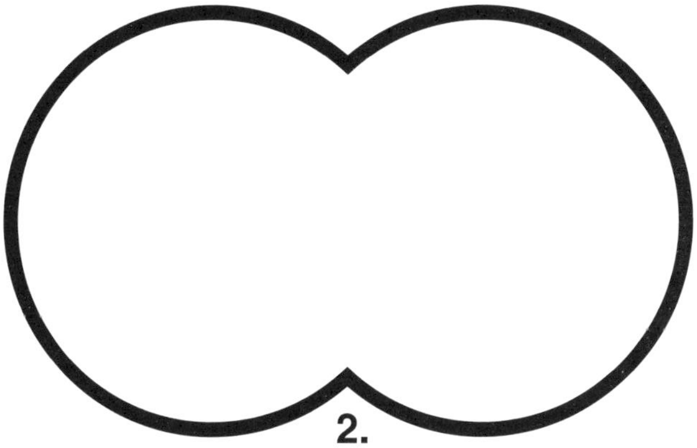

2.

3.

Name ______________________

raking
Thanksgiving
hot chocolate
burning wood
cool nights
school bells

# Fall

Weather ______________________

Activities ______________________

Sounds ______________________

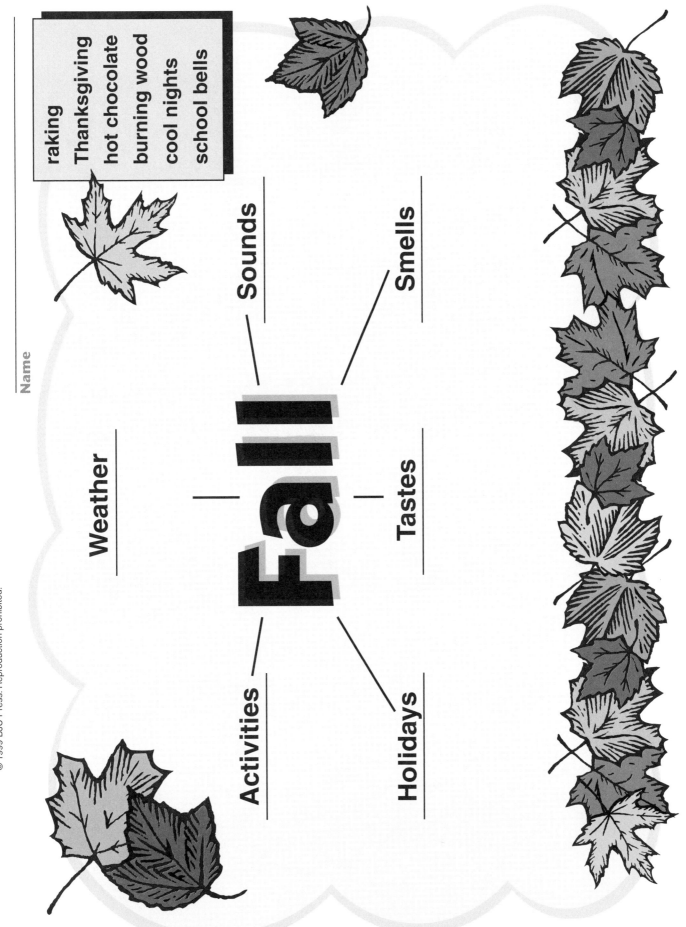

Holidays ______________________

Tastes ______________________

Smells ______________________

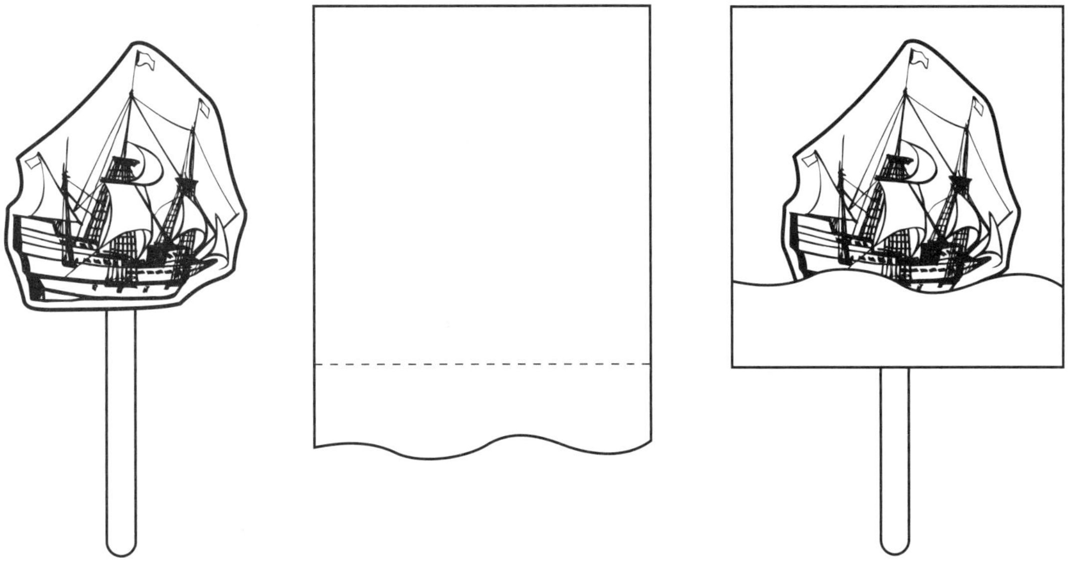

Name

Name ______________________________

| 1 | 2 | 3 | 4 | 5 | 6 | 7 | 8 | 9 | 10 | 11 | 12 | 13 |
|---|---|---|---|---|---|---|---|---|---|---|---|---|
| **A** | **B** | **C** | **D** | **E** | **F** | **G** | **H** | **I** | **J** | **K** | **L** | **M** |
| 14 | 15 | 16 | 17 | 18 | 19 | 20 | 21 | 22 | 23 | 24 | 25 | 26 |
| **N** | **O** | **P** | **Q** | **R** | **S** | **T** | **U** | **V** | **W** | **X** | **Y** | **Z** |

8 15 23    13 21 3 8    2 5 20 20 5 18

9 19    9 20    20 15    7 5 20

23 9 19 4 15 13    20 8 1 14

7 15 12 4 !    1 14 4    20 15    7 5 20

21 14 4 5 18 19 20 1 14 4 9 14 7

18 1 20 8 5 18    20 15    2 5

3 8 15 19 5 14    20 8 1 14

19 9 12 22 5 18 !

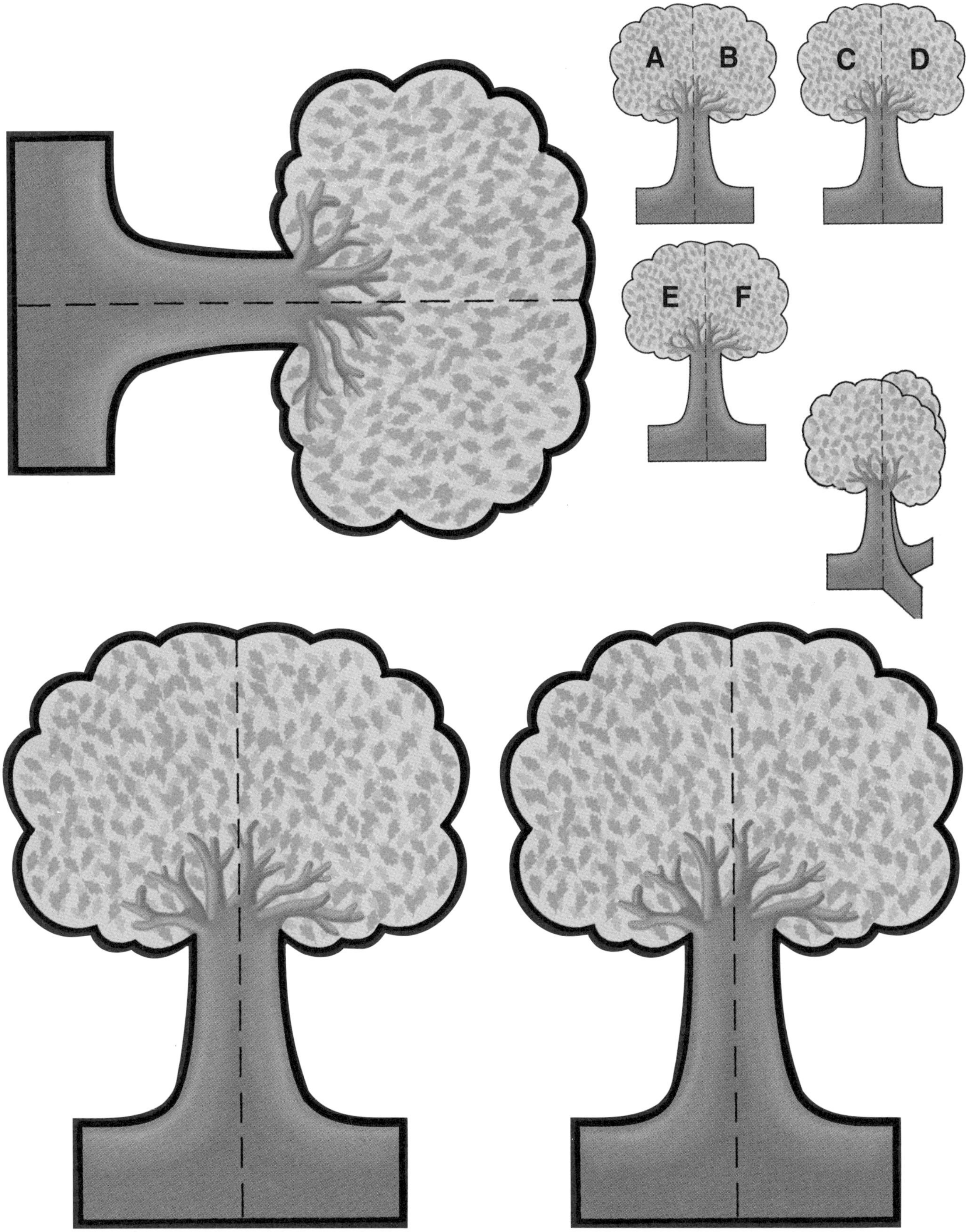
A
B
C
D
E
F

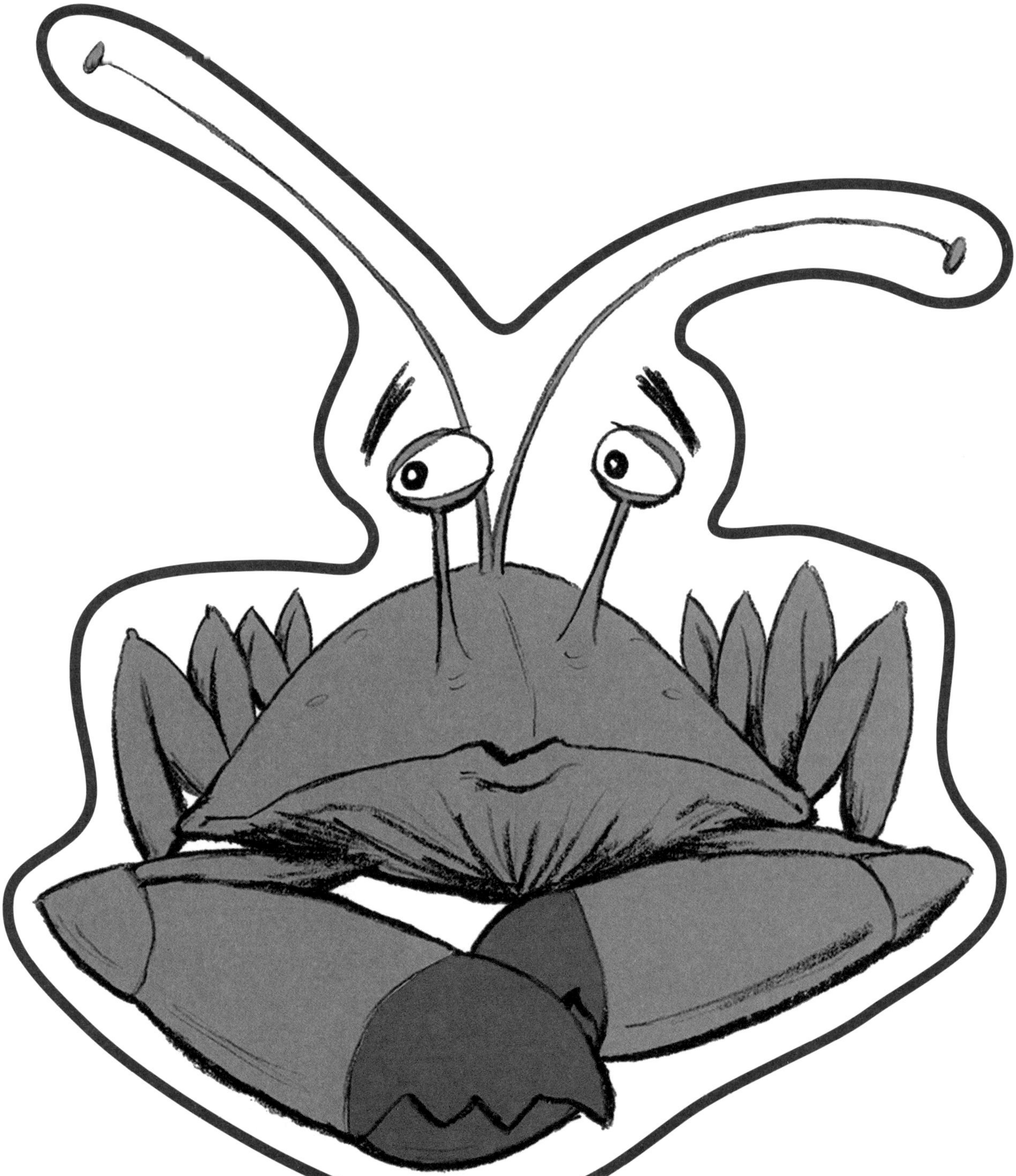

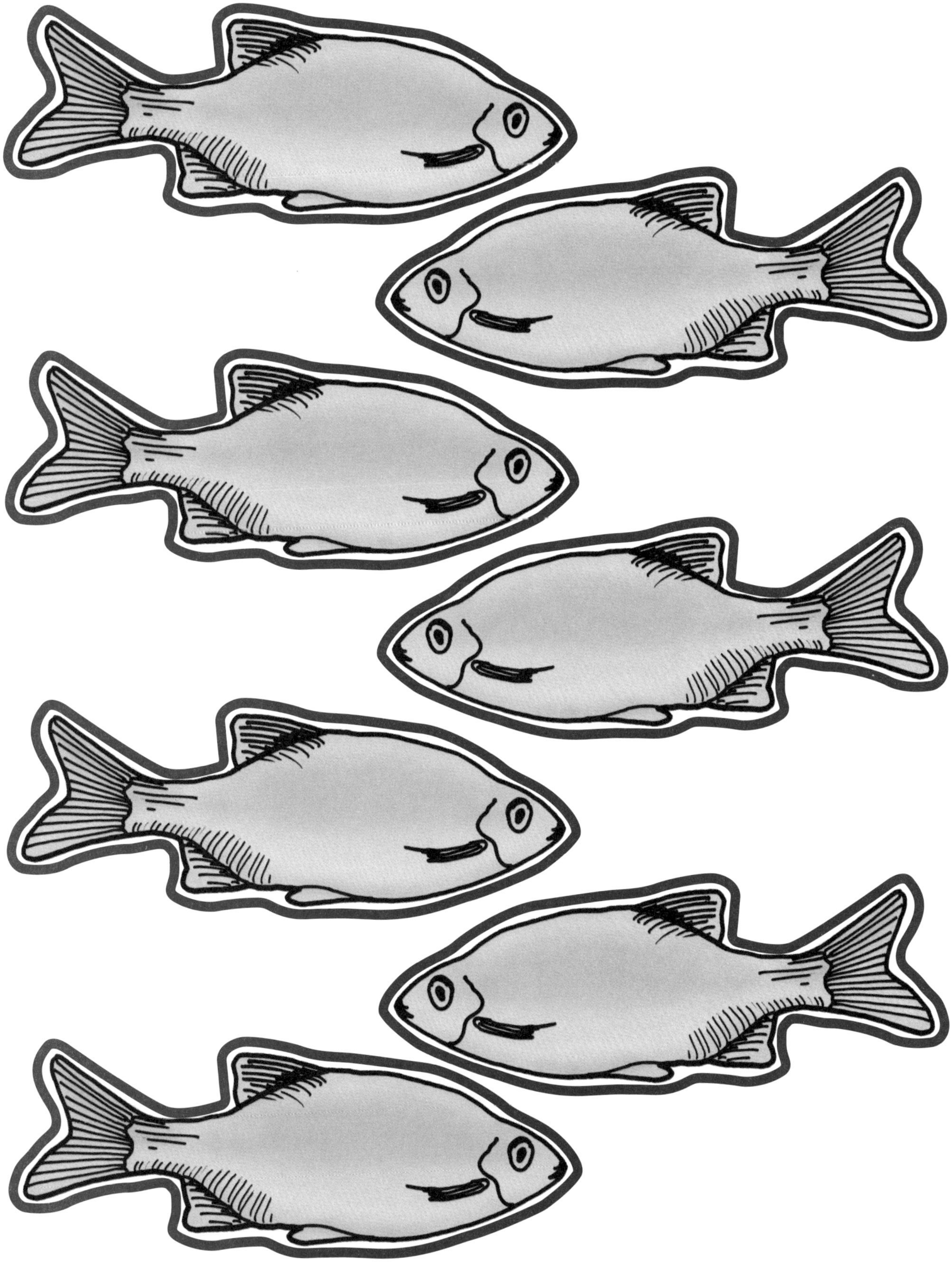

# Noodle Soup Recipe

Dear Parents,

Your child has finished reading "Noodle Soup" by Gloria Repp. This is a copy of the recipe for noodle soup that your child has read about in class. You may wish to prepare this soup together at home. A recipe for muffins is also being sent home that your child could prepare, with a little help from you when the time comes to place the muffins inside the oven and remove them. Children enjoy cooking, and this is a wonderful opportunity for your child to develop cooking skills.

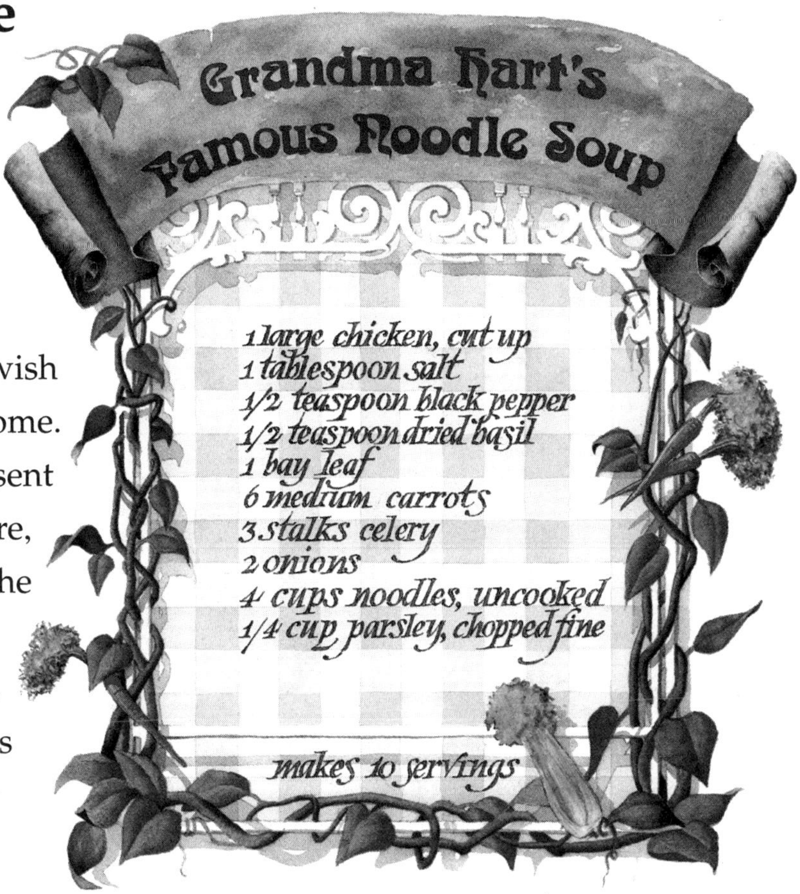
Grandma Hart's Famous Noodle Soup
1 large chicken, cut up
1 tablespoon salt
1/2 teaspoon black pepper
1/2 teaspoon dried basil
1 bay leaf
6 medium carrots
3 stalks celery
2 onions
4 cups noodles, uncooked
1/4 cup parsley, chopped fine
makes 10 servings

## Instructions

1. Wash chicken. Place in a large pot and cover with 12 cups water. Add salt, pepper, basil, and bay leaf.
2. Simmer, covered, for 1½ hours or until chicken is just tender.
3. While chicken is cooking, prepare vegetables. Scrub carrots; cut in ½" chunks. Wash celery; cut in ½" chunks. Peel onions; chop.
4. When chicken is done, remove it, along with bay leaf, from the chicken broth. Skim off as much fat as possible from the broth.
5. Bring broth back to boiling. Add carrots, celery, and onions. Simmer 45 minutes.
6. While vegetables are cooking, remove skin and bones from chicken. Cut chicken into bite-size pieces.
7. Ten minutes before vegetables are done, add noodles and chicken pieces to soup. Cook for remaining 10 minutes.
8. Sprinkle with parsley.

# *One Doesn't Belong*

**Name** ________________________________

Cross out the word that does not belong.

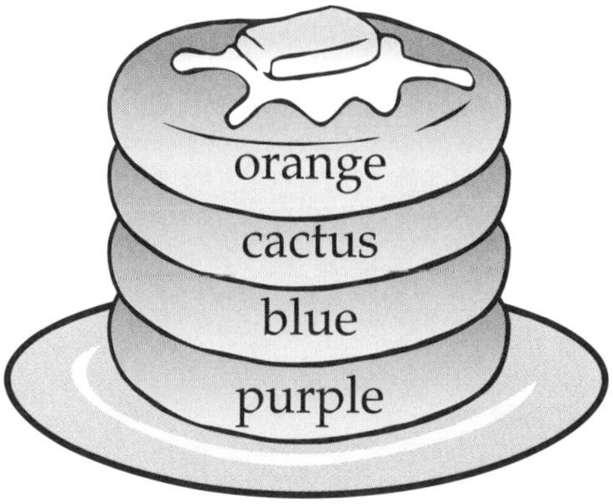


Cross out the sentence that does not belong.

The boys skated on the griddle.
My uncle took us to the circus.
Paul Bunyan carried Johnny in his pocket.
Babe drank all the water from the river.

# Index